ROUTLEDGE LIBRARY EDITIONS
BROADCASTING

Volume 10

BROADCAST VOICE PERFORMANCE

BROADCAST VOICE PERFORMANCE

MICHAEL C. KEITH

LONDON AND NEW YORK

First published in 1989 by Focal Press

This edition first published in 2024
by Routledge
4 Park Square, Milton Park, Abingdon, Oxon OX14 4RN

and by Routledge
605 Third Avenue, New York, NY 10158

Routledge is an imprint of the Taylor & Francis Group, an informa business

© 1989 Michael C. Keith

All rights reserved. No part of this book may be reprinted or reproduced or utilised in any form or by any electronic, mechanical, or other means, now known or hereafter invented, including photocopying and recording, or in any information storage or retrieval system, without permission in writing from the publishers.

Trademark notice: Product or corporate names may be trademarks or registered trademarks, and are used only for identification and explanation without intent to infringe.

British Library Cataloguing in Publication Data
A catalogue record for this book is available from the British Library

ISBN: 978-1-032-59391-3 (Set)
ISBN: 978-1-032-62598-0 (Volume 10) (hbk)
ISBN: 978-1-032-62610-9 (Volume 10) (pbk)
ISBN: 978-1-032-62602-4 (Volume 10) (ebk)

DOI: 10.4324/9781032626024

Publisher's Note
The publisher has gone to great lengths to ensure the quality of this reprint but points out that some imperfections in the original copies may be apparent.

Disclaimer
The publisher has made every effort to trace copyright holders and would welcome correspondence from those they have been unable to trace.

BROADCAST VOICE PERFORMANCE

Michael C. Keith

Focal Press
Boston London

Focal Press is an imprint of Butterworth Publishers.

Copyright © 1989 by Michael C. Keith.
All rights reserved.

No part of this publication may be reproduced, stored in a retrieval system, or transmitted, in any form or by any means, electronic, mechanical, photocopying, recording, or otherwise, without the prior written permission of the publisher.

Library of Congress Cataloging-in-Publication Data
Keith, Michael C.
  Broadcast voice performance / Michael C. Keith.
    p. cm.
  Includes bibliographies and index.
  ISBN 0-240-80003-6
  1. Radio announcing.   2. Television announcing.
3. Voice culture.   4. Broadcasting—Vocational
guidance.   I. Title.
PN1991.8.A6K45   1989   88-18866
791.44′.3—dc19   CIP

British Library Cataloguing in Publication Data
Keith, Michael C.
  Broadcast Voice Performance.
1. Radio Programmes. Announcing.   2. Television
Programmes. Announcing.
I. Title
791.44′3
  ISBN 0-240-80003-6

Butterworth Publishers
80 Montvale Avenue
Stoneham, MA 02180

10 9 8 7 6 5 4 3

Printed in the United States of America

To Susanne, and Lou, John, Lindy, Roger, Marion.

*Who among us has not enjoyed
The company of these voices from the
void.*

Marion Wrye

CONTENTS

FOREWORD by
  Cousin Bruce Morrow   xi
PREFACE   xiii

1 THE BROADCAST VOICE PERFORMER   1

Voices Heard Around the World   1
Broadcast Voices   2
The Duties of the Broadcast Voice Performer   4
Entering the Profession: First On-Mic Job   11
Where to Look: Job Sources   14
The Audition   14
Remuneration: Getting Paid   15
Future Prospects   15
Broadcast Voice Performer and New Wave Technology   15
Suggested Further Reading   18

2 BROADCASTING'S GOLDEN VOICES   21

Dots and Dashes in the Air   21
The Radio Music Box   22
Buying Time   22
Compensation   24
Too Many Voices at Once   25
The Networks Are News and Commentary   25
Good Fortune During Bad Times   27
Voices of War   28
Enter "Radio With Pictures"   29
Voice Styles Then and Now   30
Suggested Further Reading   31

3 THE NEW AGE ANNOUNCER   33

A Change in the Air   33
The Early Eye   34
Radio Reacts   34
LPs and 45s   35
Specialized Programming   35
The Top 40 Deejay   36
New Formulas   36
FM Evolves   37
The Separation   38
Voices in the Vortex   38
Into the 1970s   40
Shifting Bands   41
Suggested Further Reading   41

4 ANNOUNCING IN FORMAT RADIO   43

Fitting the Format   43
Degrees of Announcer Prominence   43
Adult Contemporary   44
Contemporary Hit Radio   49
Country   54
Easy Listening   57
Album-Oriented Rock   59
Classical   64
Vintage   66
Announcing in Other Formats   70
Suggested Further Reading   71

5 THE BROADCAST NEWS VOICE   73

Radio in the News   73
Radio Goes to Press   73
The War Is News   74
Television News   75
Formatting the News   76
Local News   77
News Broadcasts Today   78
The Electronic Newsroom   78
Newscaster Criteria   81
Interviewing   84
Prepping for the Newscast   85
Newscasting Pros and Cons   89
Radio Versus Television Newscasting   91

	News Copy	92	Sports Voice Do's and Don't's	122
	Copy Format	95	Suggested Further Reading	124
	Suggested Further Reading	97		
	Appendix: *UPI Wire Service News Copy*	97	**8 THE BROADCAST VOICE WORKSHOP**	**125**

6 THE ON-CAMERA AND BOOTH VOICE — 101

Television Voice Performance	101
Appearance	101
Addressing the Camera	103
Microphone Use	104
Hand Signals	106
On-Camera Voice Criteria	106
Prepping for On-Camera	110
Booth Criteria	111
Weathercasting	113
Suggested Further Reading	114

7 THE BROADCAST SPORTS VOICE — 115

Sports Announcing	115
Sports Voice Duties	115
Television Sports Voice Responsibilities	117
Sports Voice Criteria	118
Preparing for a Sports Voice Job	120

Voice Quality	125
Articulation	126
Inflection	126
Mic Fright	127
Accents	127
Pronunciation	129
Phonetics	129
Ad-Libbing	130
Interpretation	131
Suggested Further Reading	132

9 BROADCAST STUDIOS AND EQUIPMENT — 133

Tools of the Trade	133
The Radio Studio	133
The Television Studio	141
Edit Suite	148
Suggested Further Reading	151

INDEX — **153**

FOREWORD

by Cousin Bruce Morrow

Bruce Morrow began his career at WINS and soon moved to WABC, where he reigned from 1961 to 1974. He then moved to WNBC as deejay and entertainment reporter. He currently hosts "Dance Party" and "Cousin Brucie's Countdown" on WCBS-FM radio in New York, as well as "Crusin' America," a nationally syndicated radio show on CBS RADIORADIO. His autobiography, Cousin Brucie, *was published by Beech Tree Books in 1987. Morrow is the first "radio personality" to be inducted into the Emerson Radio Hall of Fame. He lives in New York City.*

I believe I first realized the power of communications, especially broadcast communications, when I was about eight years old. I just finished school for the day and was merrily walking home. When I reached my block (New Yorkese for "street") I noticed that my mother and several of our neighbors were standing on our porch listening to a little brown box, and they were all weeping.

My mom and all of those other strong Brooklyn women belonged in the kitchen preparing the evening repast for their families. What could have kept these loyal domestic stalwarts from their usual chores, I wondered. The little brown box was the table model Philco radio. This magical cube was telling these ladies that President Roosevelt had died and that the nation was in a state of mourning. I realized at that moment that anything so small that could cause such a big emotional reaction had to be magic, and I have always loved magic.

Well, here I am a few years later, utilizing that magic box, broadcasting information and entertainment. However, one thing has changed. I now realize that it is not entirely magic. This little box is an emotion grabber and certainly disseminates information and entertainment magically, but this is accomplished through the skill and dedication of broadcast professionals.

There are two tools when used properly that are more powerful than any other communication tools—the human voice and body.

Body language is one of our most overlooked and perhaps underdeveloped communication devices. By using body posture—head, arms, shoulders, hands—a person conveys emotion and attitude to others. But the voice, that little set of strings coupled with breath, producing strange vibrations, can cause armies to march, or more importantly, can prevent armies from marching.

By learning to control and use your voice properly, language barriers can be crossed. The most direct avenue to success in our daily human experience, and certainly to success in business, must begin with learning to use your voice effectively.

Oh, yes, there are lots of tricks to be mastered. How do you attain drama with your voice to assure an emotional reaction? How do you communicate so you will influence others? Do you sound sincere and credible? Questions, questions, questions . . . and now finally the answers.

Michael Keith has carefully researched and collected the insights and strategies for reaching these goals. Will it be easy? I doubt it. Read on and then practice what Michael preaches.

Communication is not easy, but when you discover the way to use it properly, you will be on your way.

PREFACE

When I decided to write this book, it was not my intention to create another announcing "text." There are a number of fine announcing primers on the market already, and in my opinion the world is not begging for another. So how is *Broadcast Voice Performance* different from all the rest? As the author of several other books on the broadcast media, it has never been my goal to produce a conventional text, and therein, I hope, lies the difference. The term *textbook* has always conjured in me an image of something flat, static, contrived, and pedantic—prose showcased (or encased) in a lackluster package. As far as I can see, many textbooks have done more to "turn off" students to a subject than inspire them.

Therefore, *Broadcast Voice Performance* follows the approach I have used in *The Radio Station* and *Radio Programming: Consultancy and Formatics*, which involves communicating the industry's perspective on the subject to the reader in as candid, accessible, timely, and illustrative fashion as possible.

To be precise, *Broadcast Voice Performance* is a "real-world" examination of the topics and issues relevant to the field. How is this accomplished? To begin with I rely heavily on the opinions and insights of the folks in the "trenches," those men and women who earn their living performing in front of the microphone. Who better to serve as educators than those already occupying positions in the profession?

I have solicited and received input from hundreds of broadcast voice performers, and this forms the spine—the backbone—of the book. Unlike other texts that address the subject of broadcast announcing, this text does not devote copious space to foreign pronunciation. There are several excellent handbooks that deal with this area more effectively and comprehensively than could be accomplished here. (In Chapter 8 the reader is directed to these sources and advised as to their use.)

This is not a speech text, either. Therefore the rudiments of verbal exposition are dealt with in a more circumspect manner, that is, within the specific context of on-microphone performance.

Chapters 1 through 3 examine the evolution of the field of broadcast voice performance: its tentative beginning in the 1920s, its growth in the 1930s, and its transitions and changes in the 1940s and 1950s.

Chapter 4 discusses the announcer's role in today's highly formulated radio industry, and in subsequent chapters the broadcast voice performer is scrutinized within the context of news, sports, and on-camera presentation.

Chapter 8 addresses some fundamentals of voice use, and the final chapter (Chapter 9) surveys the equipment with which broadcast voice performers come into contact.

I owe a debt of gratitude to every broadcast professional who contributed to the making of this book. In particular, I wish to express my most sincere appreciation to Ed Bliss, Norman Corwin, Bob Skedgell, Gaylord Avery, Ed McMahon, Dick Clark, and Cousin Bruce Morrow, who took time from their demanding schedules to generously contribute to this project.

It is to these individuals, and to all those whose names appear within these covers, that I also dedicate this book.

BROADCAST VOICE PERFORMANCE

1

THE BROADCAST VOICE PERFORMER

VOICES HEARD AROUND THE WORLD

Today over one hundred thousand men and women are paid to speak into the microphones of approximately twenty thousand radio, television, and cable stations in the United States. It would be safe to say that in excess of a quarter million individuals worldwide spend time communicating to audiences over the radiowave portion of the electromagnetic spectrum. These voices moving through the ether cover every square inch of the planet's surface—land and sea. There is rarely a moment of the day or night when a broadcast voice performer cannot be heard or seen plying his or her craft from one of the hundreds of channels scattered across the domestic AM, FM, VHF, and UHF bands.

The broadcast voice performer is a byproduct of turn of the century technological ingenuity and vision. Guglielmo Marconi, who conceived the means for transmitting sound from one point to another without benefit of wires, initially did not envision sending voices but rather code through the air. Later innovators would mount human utterings onto radio waves to create the first electronic mass medium and subsequently the "announcing" profession.

The announcer, as he came to be known, is a unique outcropping of a dynamically innovative era that brought about a dramatic transformation in communication modes. In the twentieth century the printing press has taken a back seat to radio and television as the primary form of mass communications. Today, most of us are informed about nearly every aspect of daily concern by broadcast voice performers, whose words move through the vast expanses of global space at the speed of light.

Actually, until the advent of the printing press in the fifteenth century, the individual voice served as the primary instrument for communicating information, both factual and fictional. Academicians, storytellers, orators, troubadors, and town criers were voice performers in their own right and era. In ancient times, Plato, Cicero, and Quintilian practiced the art of verbal exposition, and the latter taught public speaking in Rome.

A text on voice communication was formulated twenty-five hundred years ago in Greece. Through the ages, voice performers

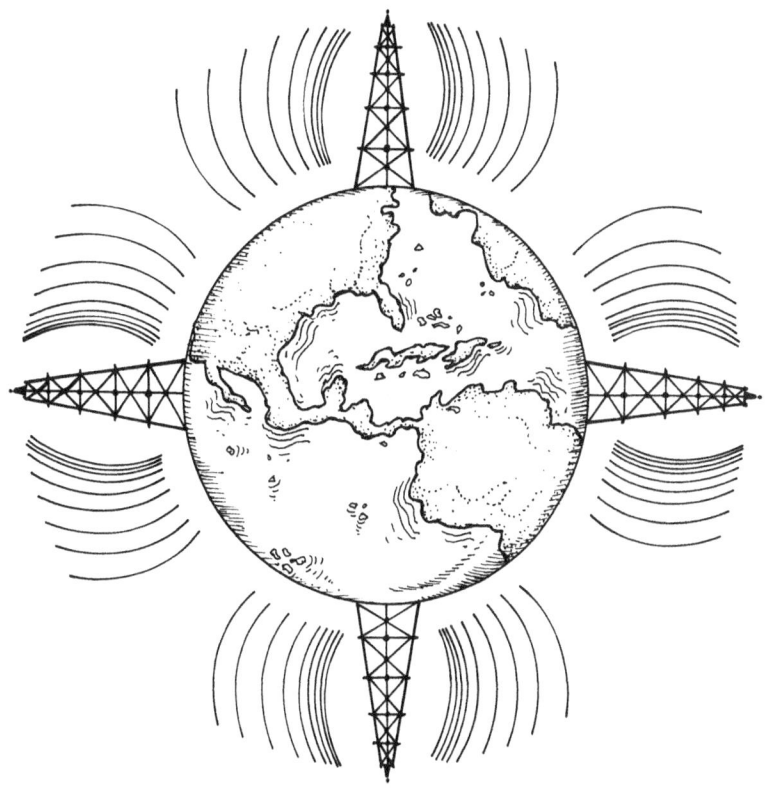

FIGURE 1.1
Voices are transmitted via the electromagnetic spectrum to every corner of the earth.

FIGURE 1.2
The "father of radio," Guglielmo Marconi. Courtesy RCA.

FIGURE 1.3
An ancient world voice performer.

have shared a desire to be both intelligible and interesting to the listener. The ancient Greek orator standing before a crowd in an amphitheatre possessed no less a desire to communicate in an articulate fashion than the contemporary television newscaster on the six o'clock report. In both instances, the speaker's first and foremost goal is to be understood by the public. Granted, the challenges of vocal communication in these two examples are unique to their particular settings and venues—the ancient orator speaking without the aid of electronic amplification and the newscaster speaking with it—but their objectives are similar. Both voice performers wish to convey some sort of data to an audience.

It certainly is not the author's intent to present evidence linking the ancient orator with the broadcast announcer but rather to impress upon the reader the fact that the essential aim of voice performers throughout the millennia has been to communicate effectively. It is in this mutually shared goal that the broadcast announcer may claim a tie with those voice performers of the preelectronic world.

BROADCAST VOICES

There are many kinds of broadcast voice performers. The term *announcer* is used primarily to describe anyone who conveys information via the electronic media. Using *announcer* as a kind of umbrella term, several categories may be established, such as deejay, newscaster, emcee, sportscaster, host, narrator, commentator, and so forth. Each of these categories constitutes a unique type of broadcast voice performance requiring specific skills and talents. Subsequent chapters of this text will examine these announcing specialties.

The announcing profession is made up of both men and women. This has been true since the inception of the electronic media. What is also true is that broadcast announcing has, until recent years, been a male-dominated profession. Women were all but excluded from the staff announcer ranks at the major networks during radio's "golden age." This was not a field that welcomed the female speaking voice in roles other than acting or characterization.

The "Man" Behind the Mic

It was the prevailing sentiment at the networks that the male voice was simply better suited for air work—more authoritative and commanding of attention; thus women found little real opportunity behind the microphone as broadcast voice performers until well after the auspicious arrival of the television set.

When any reference is made to the great voices of radio's heyday, invariably it is to conjure up the names of H.V. Kaltenborn, Orson Welles, Gabriel Heatter, and other male announcers. Women's names are noticeably absent from such rosters and reminiscences.

World War II temporarily jarred open the studio door to women as radio stations sought to fill announcer vacancies left by men who were drafted or enlisted in the armed services. Having a female behind the mic was a first for many radio stations. This phenomenon would last the duration of the war, until men returned to reclaim their positions. Once again, most female would-be announcers found themselves on the outside looking in—good enough to be members of the audience but not good enough to be members of the fraternity of working broadcast voice performers.

Television's debut did little initially to enhance job prospects for women announcers, although it did expand on the actual number of available broadcast voice performance slots. In the early 1950s, the male announcer was still the norm. Women were called upon by television to sell domestic goods, but more often than not, those hired were chosen because they possessed name value to the viewing public and brought "instant" credibility with them. Betty Furness is a noteworthy example of the "homemaker's" advocate who pitched household products on television.

The practice of permitting women to sell domestic items grew during television's early years, but hiring women for more mainstream announcing duties remained limited.

Evidence of the discrimination against women announcers and the bias toward the male speaking voice is apparent in a statement in a widely used announcing text of the 1950s (*The Announcer's Handbook*, Rinehart Press). The book's authors, Ben Graf Henneke and Edward S. Dumit, merely reflect the prevailing attitudes of the period when they state "Women's delivery, that in general is lacking in the authority needed for a convincing newscast, is frequently just right for commercials demonstrating household items and fashion trends."

During this period, and into the 1960s, radio stations employing soft music formats often hired women with sultry, if not sensual, voices for evening airshifts. Although this practice served to get more women on the air, it tended to strengthen the stereotype of women as unsuitable for traditional or conventional announcing positions. Even-

FIGURE 1.4
Newsman and commentator Gabriel Heatter was one of radio's early luminaries. Courtesy MBS.

FIGURE 1.5
Betty Furness was one of television's early voice performers. Courtesy NBC.

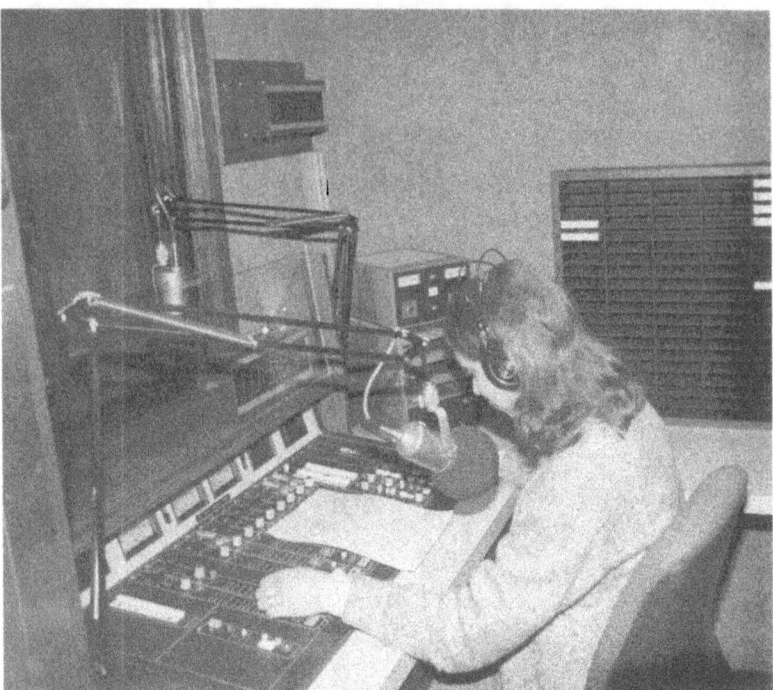

FIGURE 1.6
Since the 1970s, women have become a more integral part of the broadcast voice performance profession.

tually, however, station managers and program directors became more aware of the fact that the female voice possessed other qualities that were complimentary to the airwaves.

As the radio medium became more specialized in its programming approach in the 1960s, women found the climate more favorable for landing on-air positions, especially on FM, which became the home of the progressive rock format—later known variously as underground, acid, and psychedelic radio.

The age of the female deejay had arrived in earnest, if not in full force. The less formulated album cut format strived to contrast with the super mainstream sound of Top 40. The supertight, "big-daddy" jock of Top 40 was virtually antithetical to the conversational, laid-back communicator residing at these new-order outlets. The female voice served as perfect counterpoint to the all-male pop rockers that dominated the AM band.

The women's movement of the 1970s provided essential impetus to the campaign seeking to reverse the male supremacy extant since the broadcast media's birth. This progress also was aided by the continued proliferation of electronic media. In the 1960s and 1970s, hundreds of new radio and television stations entered the airwaves.

As FM gained in audience popularity due to its efforts to offer listeners a greater variety of mainstream formats, women found stations more receptive to their applications. In different parts of the country, stations promoted the fact that their entire airstaff consisted of females, while other stations boasted of having a female newscaster or deejay.

Television, too, liberated itself somewhat of its propensity for the male broadcast voice performer. Women became more visible in news reporting, program hosting, and commercials.

The distribution of broadcast voice positions, although still far from equitable today, is significantly better than it once was for women, and if the current trend continues, the job prospects for women seeking on-mic opportunities will increase. There is every reason to suspect this will happen. However, there remains substantial ground to be traveled in the quest for true equality for both women and minorities in the area of broadcast voice performance.

THE DUTIES OF THE BROADCAST VOICE PERFORMER

The primary responsibility of the broadcast voice performer is to communicate in an intelligible way. This requires the development and refinement of a host of basic speaking skills, including articulation, enunciation, pronunciation, variety, intonation, and naturalness, to list a few. Subsequent chapters examine announcing skills within the context of their particular emphasis, and Chapter 8, "The Voice Workshop," focuses on specifics of verbal communication relative to broadcast performance.

The daily duties of a broadcast voice performer depend largely on the position (for example, deejay, newscaster, booth announcer) and often vary depending on station and market size. Since subsequent chapters deal extensively with the nature and responsibilities of the many types of broadcast voice performers, it is not the intent to do so here. However, it might benefit the reader to encounter what a typical day might be like for one of the field's major practitioners, the radio deejay. There are more deejays than any other type of broadcast voice performer.

For our purposes, the daily activities of an Adult Contemporary (see Chapter 4) formatted radio station deejay will be scrutinized. For the sake of contrast, the first sketch will examine the routine of a deejay at a small radio station and the second will focus on the activities of a major market deejay.

A Day in the Life of a Small Market Deejay

John Jones ("J.J.") arrives at WXXX-AM, a low-power outlet in southeastern Ohio, at 3:00 P.M. His airshift covers the hours between 4:00 P.M. and 11:00 P.M., which is sign-off (the hour at which the station goes off the air for the day). John works the same hours Monday through Saturday (including holidays that fall on those days) in what can be called an entry-level radio job.

John is expected to be at the station one hour prior to his airshift because he must perform several tasks. He first checks his production box (located in the station's production studio) to see if he has commercials to voice and mix (announce and produce). There are usually two or three pieces of copy that require his attention. This involves taping the commercial copy and then assembling the necessary production elements (bed music, sound effects, etc.). This accomplished, John then produces the commercials (spots) onto cartridges (carts) for use on the air.

Next, John must prepare for his airshift. This involves gathering the music for broadcast during his program. At small stations, the album library is often in the on-air studio. Based on a music playlist prepared by the station's program director, John pulls the records necessary to get him into his first hour. This achieved, John then retreats to the newsroom to break down and assemble wire service (United Press International, Associated Press) copy suitable for broadcast during the 4 P.M. news, which he is responsible for delivering. He has fifteen minutes in which to prepare the newscast.

At the top of the hour, John relieves the midday deejay and takes over the operation of the broadcast studio by signing the station logs. Manning the controls, he delivers the news that he has prepared. At 4:05, John launches into the music segment of his shift, greeting his audience with "Welcome to Lite 1560's *J.J. Show*."

Once the record is spinning, John returns the news copy to the newsroom, placing it onto hooks labeled "local," "regional," "national," "world," and "sports" for later use. He will return in three quarters of an hour to gather another top of the hour newscast. John will repeat this process throughout his airshift, and he will return to the newswire machine several times in between to gather feeds (for example, stock market closings, weather updates, news headlines, features) necessary for his program. Before broadcasting the wire copy, he will read it over a couple of times to gain familiarity with its contents and to correct any errors.

Just before the five o'clock news and every two hours thereafter, John takes meter readings that have to do with the station's technical operations. The readings are entered

FIGURE 1.7
Small radio stations dot the American landscape.

FIGURE 1.8
A voice performer at work in a small station production studio.

into an operating log kept in the vicinity of the meters.

Throughout his airshift, John will deliver live commercial copy. In order to do an effective interpretation, he reads the copy aloud a few times before going on mic. (He knows from experience that it is tempting disaster to read copy *cold*, so he takes the time to go over it.)

John is at his busiest between 4:30 P.M. and 6:30 P.M. because this period constitutes afternoon drive-time, a period of the day that the station regards as prime time because commuter listening expands the audience

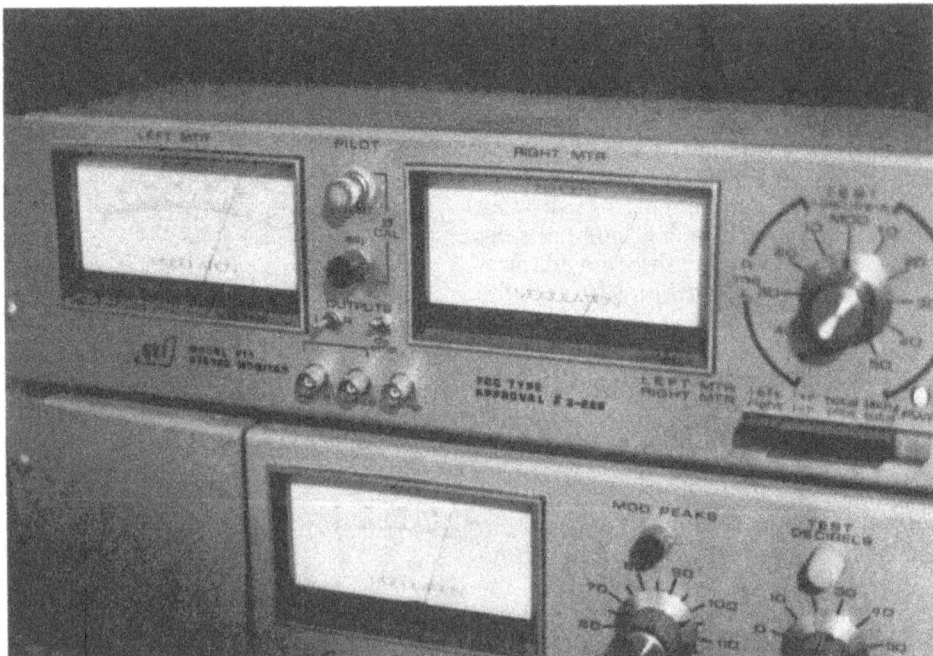

FIGURE 1.9
Station meters reflect technical operating parameters.

size. This means more advertisers, which translates to more live copy. At the same time, responding to the shift in listening patterns, the station increases its service effort, which means more information such as sports, activity updates, weather forecasts, stock market reports, traffic conditions, and so forth. John is now in the thick of things.

The pace slows somewhat as the evening progresses. At eight o'clock the station shifts its music emphasis to oldies, so John must adapt. The station expects the host of the oldies show to be upbeat and knowledgeable about the era from which the music is derived. For John, age twenty-two, this requires some homework, since the music is drawn from the 1950s and early 1960s. Before he comes to work most days he pores through

FIGURE 1.10
A morning drive-time program log reflects the increased spot load during this period of the broadcast day.

PAGE 4   DAY Tuesday   DATE March 26, 1991
Announcer or Operator: Gunter Rusdae   Time On 6 A.M.   Time Off _____
(Full Name)   Time On _____   Time Off _____

STATION IDENT.	PROGRAM TIME ON	PROGRAM TIME OFF	PROGRAM TITLE–SPONSOR	MECH.	COMM'L. MAT'R. DURATION	COMM'L. MAT'R. TYPE	✓	PROGRAM SOURCE	PROGRAM TYPE	ANNC INIT
			STATION ID							
	:00	:04	LOCAL NEWS					L	N	
1	:04	:05	Benton's		60	L				
	:05	:06	SPORTS					L	S	
			WEATHER					L	N	
			WGNG MUSIC					R	E	
6	:10	:12	Star Floral		30	R				
			Baker Shoes		60	R				
			WEATHER					L	N	
			PSA/ Project Hope		10	PSA				
3	:20	:22	Connor Mills		60	L				
			McZ Ltd.		30	R				
7	:25	:26	House Lumber		60	L				
	:30	:32	ABC/NEWS					ABC	N	
	:32	:34	LOCAL/NEWS					L	N	
2	:34	:35	Child's Farms		60	R				
	:35	:37	SPORTS					L	S	
			WEATHER					L	N	
			PSA/ American Cancer		10	PSA				
5	:40	:42	Leo's Emprium		30	L				
			Peggy's Cheeses		60	R				
			WEATHER					L	N	
			PSA/ AARP		10	PSA				
4	:50	:52	Millside Tire		30	L				
			Big Burgers		60	R				
8	:55	:56	Super Save		30	L				

trivia books, old newspapers, and magazines in order to derive a sense of the period and information useful during the program.

At 8:30 P.M., John must make technical adjustments to the station's transmitter to keep WXXX operating according to Federal Communications Commission (FCC) rules and regulations. The station is required to go "directional" (shift the path of its signal) to prevent interfering with other stations on the same frequency. It is up to John to make and log this change according to instructions established by the station's engineer.

Although this task sounds complicated, it is relatively simple, and once the procedure is learned it is accomplished in a matter of moments. However, failure to make the necessary signal alterations can create serious problems for the station and the assigned operator, who in this case is John.

Following the eleven o'clock newscast, John broadcasts the station's sign-off and terminates the signal by turning off the transmitter. He then reshelves his albums and clears the teletype machine one last time.

Before departing from the station, he turns off all the lights (except for one in the station's lobby) and secures all the doors.

It is the end of another broadcast day for deejay John "J.J." Jones.

A Day in the Life of a Major Market Deejay

Sue Thomas, a nine-year broadcast veteran, is employed by a large metropolitan station (WYYY-FM) located in the Northeast. She arrives at noon each day, one hour before her 1:00 P.M. to 4:00 P.M. airshift. During her first hour at the station, Sue voices spots for the production director, who then mixes the commercials onto carts for later airing.

In what time remains, Sue pulls the music (compact discs, albums, carted music) for her show as outlined by the playlist. She is assisted in this effort by a member of the music department. The music library is separate from the station's on-air studio and consists of thousands of titles. The station's entire music inventory is committed to computer file and is accessible by the press of a button.

At 1:00 P.M., Sue goes on the air, noting her arrival on the station's log. Unlike her deejay counterparts at WXXX-AM, she does not broadcast the hourly news. The station employs a full complement of newscasters

FIGURE 1.11
A station's playlist is called up on a video display terminal.

for this purpose. The newscaster on duty during Sue's shift is required to provide her with those items from the wire service pertinent to her time on the air: weather updates, special features, sports scores, news, and information tidbits and teasers.

On-air personnel at WYYY-FM do not log meter readings because the station employs a round-the-clock technical staff to monitor operating parameters.

Like WXXX's John Jones, Sue has devoted time earlier in the day to catching up on topics that can be incorporated into her program. Regardless of station size, air personnel should be able to relate to the interests of those tuned. Listener sensitivity has contributed to Sue's success and will be a factor in John's as well.

Although major market airshifts generally are considerably shorter than those at smaller stations, the preparation time is often more extensive. Being at a top station means being a top-notch communicator, and this requires a significant investment of time, each and every day.

Interestingly, there are frequently more live commercials on the logs of small stations than there are at larger stations. A number of reasons account for this. For one thing, a major market station emphasizing music is likely to work at keeping the spot load down (fewer commercials). These stations offset the lower spot content by charging more per ad. The small market station often must run more commercials to make the money it must have to operate. This is not to say that small stations clutter the air with commercials, while big stations run fewer. There can be as much commercial log-jamming on major stations as there is on small stations.

For the sake of illustration, however, let us assume a low spot count at WYYY-FM, and that, as often is the case, most commercials are taped (carted) in advance. Thus Sue reads less live copy than does John, and this is all right. John is learning the craft of broadcast voice delivery, and he needs all the practice and experience he can get.

At the conclusion of her shift (4:00 P.M.), Sue returns to the production studio to see if her voice is needed on more commercials. By 5:15 P.M. she is on the road home. It is Friday, and she has the weekend off.

The contrast between these two chronicles is sharp. A further comparison of the daily routines is revealing. To begin with, it would be hard to portray John's day as a glamorous experience. Work at a small market station seldom is. The hours are long, and the duties are manifold. However, a few months or a year at a small station is rarely without its tangible rewards. It is the best possible proving ground. Not everyone survives the rigors of small station employment, but for those who do, bigger things are usually in store.

It would be wrong to assume that extended service at a small station is something to be avoided. Working at a small broadcast outlet is just right for many people, and, in most cases, the longer an individual spends at a station, the better the benefits. The fact is many broadcasters have spent their entire careers at small-town radio stations and have been very fulfilled by the experience. Small-market radio can be rewarding.

As an introduction into the field of announcing, the small station is unsurpassed. Sure, John's day is strenuous and demanding, but what he gains is bankable. Recall what was expected of him from the start of his workday to its conclusion: commercial voice tracking (taping) and mixing, newscasting throughout his seven-hour airshift, music deejaying, delivery of live copy—such as commercials, public service announcements (p.s.a.s), promos, weather and stock reports, sports scores—and so on. Indeed, no one would argue that the life of the beginning announcer is an easy one. The announcer pays his or her dues and receives a baptism under fire, so to speak. But this is how a broadcast voice performer acquires and sharpens his or her skills, and skills are what the larger stations are looking for.

Without argument, Sue's day is more alluring, but do not forget that she has spent nearly a decade behind the microphone to get where she is. Yes, her hours are shorter and her paycheck significantly larger, but she has earned these perks, and she will readily tell aspiring announcers that it was not without formidable challenges that she got to where she is.

It also must be pointed out that although Sue's position may appear less laborious and grueling than John's, the pressure of ratings inherent in large-market radio is a factor not to be ignored. John works hard and for doing so has considerable security at his small station. Hard work does not always guarantee job security at metro stations, which largely depend on their rankings in the ratings to generate income and profits. Working diligently is the best way to prevent ratings slippage, but serendipity must be included in the equation. Most broadcasters or deejays can recall or cite at least one example of hard work being nullified by a sudden shift in the winds of ratings.

Summing Up

Both levels of experience (large and small market) present their own challenges and rewards. Dan Collier, Operations Manager, WJCC-AM, Norfolk, Massachusetts (a small community twenty-five miles south of Boston) assesses the broadcast voice performer's experience at his station. "This is a great place for an inexperienced announcer to collect his bruises and master his craft. To be on the air here is to do it all—news, jocking, remotes, play-by-play—you name it, the air people do it, and they do it for long hours and small paychecks. But the value of the experience is priceless. This is the place to test your mettle, to learn the basics. Not everybody goes on to shine brightly in the broadcasting firmament. Some would-be broadcasters are cured of their urge really fast and go elsewhere, but even more come to grips with the reality of the profession and embrace the attitude necessary to survive and

FIGURE 1.12
Many big market deejays live or die according to the ratings.
Courtesy Birch Radio.

Target Demographics
WOMEN 25-64

AVERAGE QUARTER HOUR AND CUME ESTIMATES

	MON - SUN 6:00AM-12:00 MID				MON - FRI 6:00AM-10:00AM				MON - FRI 10:00AM-3:00PM				MON - FRI 3:00PM-7:00PM				MON - FRI 7:00PM-12:00 MID			
	AQH PRS (00)	AQH PRS RTG	AQH PRS SHR	CUME PRS (00)	AQH PRS (00)	AQH PRS RTG	AQH PRS SHR	CUME PRS (00)	AQH PRS (00)	AQH PRS RTG	AQH PRS SHR	CUME PRS (00)	AQH PRS (00)	AQH PRS RTG	AQH PRS SHR	CUME PRS (00)	AQH PRS (00)	AQH PRS RTG	AQH PRS SHR	CUME PRS (00)
WAGO-FM	11	.1	.3	90	8		.1	59	33	.2	.8	59	16	.1	.4	59				
WAIT	41	.2	1.1	629	55	.3	1.0	406	75	.4	1.8	184	37	.2	1.0	234	13	.1	.6	119
WALR-FM	5		.1	97									8		.2	41				
WBBM	145	.7	4.0	2513	289	1.4	5.2	1678	106	.5	2.5	610	53	.3	1.4	412	64	.3	3.1	389
WBBM-FM	119	.6	3.3	1343	127	.6	2.3	646	175	.9	4.1	595	224	1.1	5.8	764	105	.5	5.0	582
WBMX-FM	88	.4	2.4	1351	115	.6	2.1	663	137	.7	3.2	594	29	.1	.7	340	92	.5	4.4	490
WCFL	28	.1	.8	527	64	.3	1.2	200	51	.3	1.2	159	8		.2	60	8		.4	51
WCLR-FM	164	.8	4.5	2153	201	1.0	3.6	1405	239	1.2	5.6	701	199	1.0	5.1	841	146	.7	7.0	751
WFMT-FM	54	.3	1.5	753	96	.5	1.7	430	54	.3	1.3	169	44	.2	1.1	239	59	.3	2.8	156
WFYR-FM	146	.7	4.0	1787	210	1.0	3.8	983	203	1.0	4.8	517	159	.8	4.1	871	68	.3	3.3	416
WGCI	116	.6	3.2	937	153	.8	2.8	491	136	.7	3.2	334	144	.7	3.7	470	105	.5	5.0	217
WGCI-FM	199	1.0	5.5	2482	244	1.2	4.4	1367	174	.9	4.1	758	165	.8	4.2	705	169	.8	8.1	914
WGN	381	1.9	10.6	3978	789	3.9	14.3	2917	387	1.9	9.1	1564	408	2.0	10.5	1526	112	.6	5.4	660
WIND	138	.7	3.8	1404	265	1.3	4.8	931	72	.4	1.7	363	95	.5	2.4	392	93	.5	4.5	410
WJEZ-FM	87	.4	2.4	1315	135	.7	2.5	674	137	.7	3.2	526	94	.5	2.4	698	28	.1	1.3	231
WJJD	102	.5	2.8	1214	92	.5	1.7	470	139	.7	3.3	535	115	.6	3.0	412	63	.3	3.0	245
WJOB	18	.1	.5	379	42	.2	.8	157					8		.2	38	21	.1	1.0	109
WJOL	9		.2	243	28	.1	.5	158	11	.1	.3	85	4		.1	42	11	.1	.5	43
WJPC	29	.1	.8	440	16	.1	.3	100	19	.1	.4	150	31	.2	.8	150	45	.2	2.2	100
WKQX-FM	175	.9	4.8	2064	317	1.6	5.8	1463	224	1.1	5.3	651	128	.6	3.3	627	69	.3	3.3	399
WLAK-FM	150	.7	4.2	2050	153	.8	2.8	839	222	1.1	5.2	750	75	.4	1.9	405	145	.7	7.0	737
WLOO-FM	131	.7	3.6	1384	130	.6	2.4	788	176	.9	4.1	543	194	1.0	5.0	920	54	.3	2.6	245
WLS	229	1.1	6.3	3491	453	2.3	8.2	2596	364	1.8	8.5	1269	226	1.1	5.8	1403	42	.2	2.0	350
WLS-FM	163	.8	4.5	2996	274	1.4	5.0	1763	165	.8	3.9	785	228	1.1	5.9	1284	109	.5	5.2	624
WLUP-FM	38	.2	1.1	751	44	.2	.8	358	51	.3	1.2	237	31	.2	.8	296	51	.3	2.5	178
WMAQ	130	.6	3.6	2641	197	1.0	3.6	1264	108	.5	2.5	854	201	1.0	5.2	1474	96	.5	4.6	485
WMET-FM	37	.2	1.0	811	37	.2	.7	236	70	.3	1.6	355	47	.2	1.2	292	17	.1	.8	127
WNIB-FM	18	.1	.5	345	8		.1	41	15	.1	.4	47	73	.4	1.9	265				
WOJO-FM	40	.2	1.1	298	33	.2	.6	99	56	.3	1.3	148	44	.2	1.1	106	13	.1	.6	42
WUSN-FM	118	.6	3.3	1138	151	.8	2.7	584	160	.8	3.8	445	152	.8	3.9	558	52	.3	2.5	329
WXRT-FM	111	.6	3.1	992	162	.8	2.9	801	74	.4	1.7	219	160	.8	4.1	506	74	.4	3.6	464
WYEN-FM	16	.1	.4	232	4		.1	59					20	.1	.5	119				
PERSONS USING RADIO	3610	18.0		19336	5508	27.4		16746	4260	21.2		12530	3885	19.4		13767	2080	10.4		9293

* ESTIMATES ADJUSTED FOR ACTUAL BROADCAST SCHEDULE

BIRCH RADIO
COPYRIGHT 1984 BIRCH RADIO INCORPORATED

prosper. Keep in mind that nearly every major market announcer began his or her career at a small station."

Joe Cortese, announcer, WROR-FM, Boston (one of the nation's top ten broadcast markets) gives his perspective on working at a large radio station. "I always dreamed of jocking at a big city station, and I guess I was luckier than most because I realized my dream quickly. Before coming to WROR, I worked in radio three years at both small and medium market outlets. Most of my fellow deejays are several years older than I am, so that adds to my sense of accomplishment.

"Being on the air has always been a pleasure rather than a task for me. From the moment I first went on mic at my college's station, I knew that deejaying was the career for me. It felt right—natural. It wasn't work in the true sense of the term. I'm told that I possess natural talent for airwork, meaning that I was a step ahead of many others entering the field. I don't know. All I do know is that performing on mic felt right from the very start.

"Working here is great. The hours are excellent and the financial benefits are exceptional. Working conditions are super, too. The station has the best in state-of-the-art studios and equipment. You can't rest on your laurels, though. This is a ratings-intensive market, so you have to strive to be the best on the air. There is always someone out there who wants your job. The trick is to keep your perspective and objectivity. You can never stop working at being good."

ENTERING THE PROFESSION: FIRST ON-MIC JOB

Academic Credentials

Education has become an increasingly important factor in hiring broadcast voice performers. This was not always true. In the early days of radio, a person with a college education was a rarity. Today it is more common for individuals entering the field to possess formal training beyond the high school level.

At the network level in the 1950s, a college background was already a requisite for employment, as this excerpt from the National Broadcasting Company Department of Information pamphlet, "Announcer's Qualifications," testifies. "An announcer is expected to have a college education in cultural subjects; he must possess a general background of music and dramatics. He should be familiar with the pronunciation of foreign names and titles constantly recurring in programs of music and news. A knowledge of news values plus a wide variety of interests is essential to enable him to describe sports and other special events with authority."

In the thirty some years that have passed since the publication of this statement, most broadcast stations, large and small, have assumed this position. Simply put, an education is essential in today's highly competitive marketplace. Granted, the degree or diploma does not win the candidate the job, but the individual who possesses a good education is out in front of one who does not. "It's a very sophisticated audience out there. The on-air person must bring credibility to the airwaves to succeed. You can't fake knowledge, nor should you. Education gives you many things that you can apply to on-air communications. For one thing, education gives you understanding and perspective. This helps you relate to the audience more intrinsically and in less general terms. Of course, education should not end with graduation. The effective broadcast communicator is a student in perpetuity," says Gary Reynolds, Program Director, KGTO-AM, Tulsa, Oklahoma.

As the NBC pamphlet made clear, courses in "cultural subjects" are of special use to the on-mic person. An aspiring broadcast voice performer will benefit from a curriculum that focuses on liberal arts subjects, while providing a communication arts core. Students majoring in broadcasting on the college or university level are typically expected to enroll in courses in literature, business, mathematics, and science, as well as fine arts, social sciences, and languages.

While a strong case can be made for a formal education, it must be restated that an education alone does not guarantee employment. To be sure, it enhances prospects, but in actuality radio looks for sound first and credentials second. A case in point: Two individuals apply for the same announcing position at WZZZ-FM. One candidate has a degree in broadcast communications from a major university and two years of experience at the school's radio station. The other can-

FIGURE 1.13
A two-year college curriculum in Communication Arts.

FIRST YEAR
First Semester	Credits
Composition	3
Introduction to Broadcasting	3
Introduction to Mass Media	3
Fundamentals of Speech	3
Foreign Language* or Social Science Elective	4-3
Physical Education	1
	17-16

Second Semester	Credits
Composition and Literature	3
Radio Production	3
Introduction to Journalism	3
Voice Performance or Free Elective	3
Foreign Language* or Social Science Elective	4-3
Media Practicum	1
Physical Education	1
	18-17

SECOND YEAR
First Semester	Credits
Communication Elective	3
Literature Elective	3
Foreign Language* or Free Elective	4-3
Video Production or Free Elective**	3
Free Elective	3
Media Practicum	1
	17-16

Second Semester	Credits
Communication Elective	3
Literature Elective	3
Foreign Language* or Free Elective	4-3
Video Production or Free Elective**	3
Free Elective	3
	16-15

Internship
Internship may be substituted for 3 or 6 credits of free electives during the second semester of the senior year. Internship placements provide job-oriented experience for students who do not intend to transfer.

*Students intending to transfer upon graduation are strongly advised to take at least 8 credits of language beyond the introductory level. Bachelor programs in Communications generally require 16 credits of language beyond the introductory level.

**Students are required to take Video Production, but they may select either semester to fulfill the requirement.

Communications Electives
Introduction to Public Relations, Media Writing, Broadcast Sales and Advertising, Journalistic Style and Technique, Voice Performance, Cable Television and Small Format Video Production.

Suggested Free Electives
Typewriting I, Keyboarding, Introduction to Computer Science, Photography I, Business Organization and Management, Principles of Marketing, Small Business Management I and II, Report Writing, Cinema: Films from Literature, Creative Writing, Dramatic Literature, Introduction to Music, International Relations, Introduction to Theatre, Acting/Improvisation, Acting/Scene Study, Technical Production I and II.

---

didate is a high school graduate with a year of part-time work at a local commercial radio station under his belt. On paper, candidate number one looks very impressive, but on audition tape, candidate number two comes across better. His voice is more resonant and his delivery is more polished. The program director chooses the latter candidate, since he is most concerned with the bottom line—sound.

Whether or not the program director's decision proves the most fruitful over the long haul remains to be seen, but like the majority of programmers, he is concerned with satisfying the station's immediate and pressing needs in the most efficient and effective manner. Candidate number two meets this criteria from his perspective. He will fit into the "feel" of the station better than candidate number one. "If you have a guy with a PhD in radio, a mediocre voice, and fair delivery and a guy with a high school diploma but a better voice and delivery, the one with the better pipes and presentation wins nine out of ten times," observes Dave Richards, Program Director, WRX-FM, Westerly, Rhode Island.

Subsequent chapters discuss the role of education in the various areas of broadcast voice performance in greater detail. For the moment, it suffices to say that a good education is an excellent, if not necessary, starting point for anyone planning to pursue a career behind the broadcast microphone.

Experience

A job applicant with experience is also more attractive to a prospective employer. The key question is how does a person gain on-air experience before getting his or her first professional job. Experience comes in all shapes and forms. Of course, regardless of how modest, a background in the field in which a person seeks permanent, full-time employment is an asset. However, any legitimate work experience reveals character. A job applicant who has worked for two years at a fast food restaurant looks better to an employer than a person who has never worked.

Without a doubt, the person who can cite some relevant job experience has the advantage over one who cannot, and there are numerous ways to acquire experience within the field. Most colleges with broadcast programs have campus stations that are staffed by students. College stations provide students a perfect place to gain on-air experience. Enough cannot be said about the value of this kind of exposure, and it surely impresses potential employers.

A case in point: Before WXXX's John Jones landed his full-time radio job he served as program director for two years at his college's station. During that period, John spent an average of ten hours each week on the air doing a music show. On weekends he did live, play-by-play sportscasts of the school's football and basketball games. He also taped the station's promotionals and identifications and a myriad of other materials, such as feature intros and p.s.a.s. When John applied for the job at WXXX, the program director weighed his background against those of other applicants, and he came out ahead.

College stations provide students limitless opportunities to learn while adding credibility to their employment applications. There are hundreds of noncommercial, educational college stations on the air. Some of the nation's foremost broadcast voice performers began their careers on the college station level.

In addition to the opportunities available to aspiring broadcasters on the noncommercial end of the FM band (88.1 to 91.9 MHz), many small commercial stations have part-time and fill-in entry level openings for individuals who exhibit an aptitude and desire for on-air work. These stations generally provide limited training for those they hire. For the most part, it is a "learn by doing" kind of experience.

Part-time work can lead to full-time work (when shifts become available) for the person who has demonstrated to the station programmer that she or he has developed the necessary skills. "Foot-in-the-door" positions frequently lead to bigger and better things.

Cable television operations frequently offer opportunities to those interested in gaining video voice performance experience. Community groups involved in taping features, as well as presenting live programs over access channels, often need narrators and emcees. This is an excellent place to get valuable experience.

Local television stations seldom use inexperienced announcers, but volunteering or interning provides an insider's view and establishes contacts that can be very beneficial. Of course, there are exceptions to every rule.

FIGURE 1.14
Voice performer on-mic in a small video studio.

On more than one occasion a person with exceptional skills has landed an on-air television job directly out of college.

To be certain, getting that first broadcast voice performance job is a challenge. Education, experience, and, yes, luck, all play a role. The latter has more to do with timing than anything else. In radio, especially, on-air openings typically need to be filled with great speed. Approaching a station when it is "under the gun," so to speak, to fill an on-air vacancy greatly enhances a program director's receptivity to a job seeker. This is not to suggest that a programmer will hire just anybody when she is under pressure to fill a slot, but she is sometimes more tolerant of shortcomings and is more prepared to invest time and energy in the grooming of a person who is within hand's reach.

WHERE TO LOOK: JOB SOURCES

Radio and television positions are listed in several industry trade journals such as *Radio and Records*, *Broadcasting*, *Electronic Media*, *Television and Radio Age*, and *Billboard*. However, entry level jobs are less likely to be advertised in national publications; if advertised at all, they are more apt to be found in local newspapers. There are a number of broadcast job services (advertised in the classified sections of trade journals) that provide listings of openings. In most cases, a fee is charged.

Perhaps the most effective way to locate an opening is by calling area stations and querying program directors. Many industry people swear by the "law of average" method that involves actual "in person" visits to stations. "Get out there and hit the stations. The turnover in this business is greater than in most, especially at certain times of the year. Spring and summer are job jumping periods in deejaying, and stations try to fill gaps as quickly as they form, which can be pretty fast. The person walking in off the street at the right moment has the job, if he's any good," says Chris Nelson, Program Director, WFAL-FM, Falmouth, Massachusetts.

Sending unsolicited tapes and resumes to stations is not a good idea and can prove to be expensive. Stations not in the market for air personnel seldom take the time to examine materials they have not requested. Some stations file resumes and tapes in the event of future openings. After a few months, however, material is often discarded.

THE AUDITION

The audition for the first on-air job, or subsequent jobs for that matter, can be both an exhilarating and nerve-racking experience. Preparation is essential, but the question is how does one prepare for an audition. Usually a job candidate has no idea what kind of copy will be included as part of the audition. For a radio announcing position, delivery is usually tested by commercial copy; a mood piece for an elegant restaurant or a high-intensity commercial for a discount store are examples. News copy from a wire service is invariably a part of the audition, and station promo (liner) copy and IDs are usually included.

Television auditions contrast to the degree that the audition is generally before a camera, and the job candidate must be practiced in reading teleprompter copy, cue cards, and hand-held material.

Poise Plays Best

Both situations call for composure, presence of mind, and, of course, communication skills. Assuming an applicant has been sufficiently schooled in the latter, let us briefly discuss composure and presence of mind. Overcoming nervousness and anxiety is not easy, but with some concentration these feelings can be channeled in a constructive manner. In other words, you can get the juices to flow in a positive rather than a negative direction.

Prior to the audition, establish a good attitude about the impending experience. Avoid dwelling on the possible problems that might occur and construct a mental scenario that portrays the success that will come from hard work. The fact is, a poor or defeatist attitude has undone the good preparation of many an aspiring voice performer.

Maintaining perspective, that is, staying tuned to self and surroundings, goes a long way toward retaining control of the situation. "Stay focused and do not allow your mind to wander off the path that leads to your objective. Before the audition, tune in the station as much as possible. What you hear or see provides the model to emulate. The deejay on the station is there because he or she is what management wants, so listening gives you a good idea of what to get across. With good preparation comes confidence, and confidence is a perfect antidote for the jitters," offers Donna Halper, President, Halper and Associates, Radio Programming Consultancy.

Look the Part

Personal appearance and grooming elicit a response that can count for or against the job seeker. What a person wears reveals almost as much about character as words and actions. It may sound trite, but the first impression is often the most important. An individual who arrives at a station for an interview and/or audition in jeans and a sport shirt has two strikes against him before he opens his mouth. Dress to suit the occasion. As the title of a popular 1980s how-to book suggests, *Dress For Success*.

REMUNERATION: GETTING PAID

Broadcast voice performer salaries vary dramatically. Station and market size have a direct bearing on the industry's pay scale. The general rule is the bigger the station, the bigger the financial rewards. Perhaps no other profession can claim such a salary range. Whereas many entry level radio positions pay near minimum wage, six-figure salaries are common in major markets, and there are a few radio luminaries who have reached and even exceeded the coveted seven-figure mark.

Six- and seven-figure salaries are commonplace for television voice performers, and starting salaries in the video medium, in general, are higher than in radio.

Despite all the impressive figures, the average salary for middle-size market announcers falls somewhere between a modest twenty and thirty-five thousand dollars annually. But, again, keep in mind that there are exceptions. The salaries of top deejays in many medium markets hover around the six-figure range.

On the whole, the profession is well rewarded for its unique services.

FUTURE PROSPECTS

In the past twenty-five years, the number of broadcast outlets has doubled, and cablecasting has virtually evolved from a seedling state into a booming industry. This rapidly accelerated growth is likely to slow somewhat in the next decade. However, more stations are an inevitability as the result of several FCC actions.

During the first half of the 1980s, Docket 80-90 made room for the creation of hundreds of new FM frequencies, while the FCC petitioned the World Administrative Radio Conference (WARC) for an extension of the beleaguered AM band. The request was approved, and the AM band now has slots for stations to 1700 KHz. This allows for the construction of hundreds of new AM stations as well. Due to the decline in AM listening over the past decade and a half, it remains to be seen if the extension of the band will arouse significant interest. Meanwhile, the new FM allocations are being scooped up quickly.

On the video side, many UHF signals have entered the airways since the 1960s, and more are on the way. A bill for the establishment of low-power television (LPTV) stations was approved in the early 1980s. By the mid-1990s, it is hoped that this newest medium will be serving millions.

In 1989, nearly seven thousand cable systems offered tens of millions of subscribers a variety of program options, while significantly cutting into network viewership.

What all this means is jobs. Opportunities for the broadcast voice performer will be enhanced by the continued proliferation of electronic media. At the same time, more colleges and universities offer communication arts curricula than ever before, and it looks as if more will be doing so as the broadcast industry expands. Therefore, competition for on-mic positions will increase as well. But jobs will always exist for the most qualified.

THE BROADCAST VOICE PERFORMER AND NEW WAVE TECHNOLOGY

Since the advent of automation systems in the 1960s, there has been a looming fear that the number of on-air positions would decline. To date, this has not been the case.

A

B

FIGURE 1.15A–C NAB career booklets and a classified page from *Radio and Records.* **Courtesy** *Radio and Records* **and National Association of Broadcasters.**

OPPORTUNITIES

OPENINGS

NATIONAL

10,000 RADIO and TV JOBS!
The most complete list of job openings ever published by anyone! Up to the minute, computer printed, and mailed to the privacy of your home. As many as 300 weekly. All formats, all market sizes, all positions! Many jobs for beginners and minorities.

One week $7.00 —
Yearly $120.00
SPECIAL SIX WEEKS $15.95 ... SAVE $20.00
MONEY BACK GUARANTEE

American Radio
JOB MARKET
1553 N. Eastern, Las Vegas, NV 89108

Seriously Seeking Placement? National Leads All Others!

NATIONAL, the Nation's oldest exclusive Radio Personnel Placement Service, and acknowledged leader in radio placement, is now in its sixth year of successful radio placement. Over 3,000 radio stations have placed job orders with NATIONAL. NATIONAL receives a constant flow of job orders from radio stations coast to coast, in all size markets, for all on-air and radio sales positions. If you are **seriously** seeking a move up, contact NATIONAL now. For complete confidential details including brochure and registration form, enclose $1.00 P&H to:

NATIONAL BROADCAST TALENT COORDINATORS
Dept. R., P.O. Box 20551 • Birmingham, AL 35216 • (205) 822-9144

ACT NOW!

JOB HUNTING?

If you need a job, you need MediaLine. We give you job listings in news, weather, sports, production, programming, promotion, engineering and sales. For $30 you get a daily report of job listings for 6 weeks. Learn more: 312-855-6779. MediaLine. P.O. Box 10167, Columbia, MO 65205-4002.

THE BEST JOBS ARE ON THE LINE

R.M. LOWRY & CO.

Creative, progressive, Easy Listening Ops Manager needed. Must have vision of where format can go. Cassette, resume & brief philosophy of format to: Lowry & Company, 5888 E. Onyx Ave., Scottsdale, AZ 85253. NO CALLS.

TALENT POOL NEEDED

AM Media Consultants creating a talent pool for the nation's best air personalities, newscasters, talk show hosts. Small to major markets. T&R: Steve LaBeau, AM Media Consultants, 22910 Styles St., Woodland Hills, CA 91367. EOE

EAST

WBAZ/Southold seeks production manager to effectively develop an inexperienced staff. Joe Sullivan & Associates, 340 West 57th Street, New York, NY 10019 EOE (11/28)

WRSC State college seeks AM PD/OD with good pipes for immediate opening. T&R: Sid Levine, WRSC, 160 Clearview, State College, PA 16803 EOE (11/28)

Community-minded New England AC has evening opening. Must have creative production skills. T&R: Bob Flint, WCFR, Box 800, Springfield, VT 05156 EOE (11/28)

OJ-103/Carthage/Watertown, NY is seeking AC afternoon & midday personalities. Nothern NY's fastest growing market. T&R: Joe Brosk, OJ-103, 199 Wealtha Avenue, Watertown, NY 13601 EOE (11/28)

WFIL/Philadelphia seeks news anchor who is conversational, sounds human & writes tightly. T&R: Wayne Cabot, WFIL, 440 Domino Lane, Philadelphia, PA 19128 EOE (11/28)

FM rocker seeks 3rd wheel on our morning circus to deliver news & sports in conversational style. T&R: Thom Robinson, OM, WAMX, Box 1150, Huntington, WV 25713 EOE (12/5)

Seek mature relatable announcer to co-host morning show at AC. Pros only. T&R: Thom Robinson, OM, Box 1150, Huntington, WV 25713 EOE (12/5)

Staff announcer/MD needed 1st of '87. T&R: Thom Robinson, Box 1150, Huntington, WV 25713 EOE (12/5)

WYYD/Roanoke seeking applications for ND. T&R: Kenny Shelton, WYYD, Box 522, Amherst, VA 24521 EOE (12/5)

Mid-Atlantic AC seeks announcer with production skills. T&R: Pete Low, WGLL, Box 92, Mercersburg, PA 17236 EOE (12/5)

WLAN accepting T&Rs for immediate openings in News. Experience & creativity a must. T&R: Ellen Wascou, ND, 252 N. Queen St., Lancaster, PA 17603 EOE (12/5)

Are you ready for Boston? Immediate openings for warm, sincere, witty AC personalities. T&R: Mark Edwards, Box 9250, Haverhill, MA 01831 EOE (12/5)

Central Virginia AM/FM seeks experienced announcers. AC/Country/Oldies. Females especially. T&R: Joe Beail, WPED/WJLT, Box 8011, Charlottesville, VA 22906 EOE (12/5)

WOBM/Toms River NJ updating files for possible full/parttime airshifts. T&R: Rick St. James, Box 927, Toms River, NJ 08754 EOE (12/5)

PD/MD small market CHR. Some experience, good with people. Also seeking fulltime announcer with good voice & production. T&R: Y94FM, Box 251, Oak Hill, WV 25901 EOE (12/5)

WBAZ/Southold seeks Production Manager to effectively develop an inexperienced staff. Contact: Joe Sullivan & Associates, 340 W. 57th St., New York, NY 10019 EOE (12/5)

Shadow traffic NY seeks experienced traffic reporter. Must have personality & strong knowledge of NY area roads. T&R: Susan Berkley, Shadow Traffic, 1600 Route 22, Union, NJ 07083 EOE (12/5)

MORNING TEAM/PERSONALITY

AOR on the North Jersey Shore in the shadow of New York is beginning its search for an adult, topical, humorous, communicator/team. We're #1 and want someone to win with us. T&R to John Ford, Y-107, 156 Broadway, Long Branch, NJ 07740. EOE

LET'S HEAR FROM YOU!!!
Major NYC full service AM is looking for a bright, talented programmer to join one of America's premier outlets in the newly created position of assistant program director.
If you are . . .
* An organized self-starter
* Able to work as a team member
* A creative contributor with show-biz instincts
* An idea person with follow-through skills
* Strong in the area of on-air production
* Anxious to be "Hands-On" involved with key promotional activities
* A "Pro" able to relate to and motivate seasoned air personalities
Let's hear from you. Please send a resume and any other materials that help to tell your story to Radio & Records, 1930 Century Park West, #545, Los Angeles, CA 90067. EOE

. . . ANCHOR/REPORTERS . . .
. . . PRODUCERS/WRITERS . . .

Southern New England's finest broadcast group needs Anchor/Reporters and Producers/Writers for positions about to become available. Strong writing, editing, and delivery are essential. Only team players need apply. Send T&R and at least four references to Radio & Records, 1930 Century Park West, #539, Los Angeles, CA 90067. EOE

ANCHOR/REPORTER
NORTHERN NEW ENGLAND SMALL MARKET station with major-market news philosophy seeks anchor/reporter to be #2 morning-drive plus street reporter. Hard, hard worker needed — experienced required. Job opens in early '87. Send T&R to Radio & Records, 1930 Century Park West, Box #551, Los Angeles, CA 90067. EOE/AA

#1 MORNING NEWSBLOCK
Southern New England's number one morning newsblock needs personable Host/Anchor/Reporter with strong delivery, astute news sense, excellent writing and reporting skills, along with a good attitude. If you want to join one of the finest broadcast groups in the country send T&R and at least 4 references to Radio & Records, 1930 Century Park West, #538, Los Angeles, CA 90067. EOE

FULL SERVICE LEADER
Southern New England's full service leader is looking for an Afternoon Drive entertainer. Should have great one-on-one communications skills, able to work the phones, and interact with full service elements. Strong people and production skills are necessary. If you want to join one of the finest broadcast groups in the country send T&R to Radio & Records, 1930 Century Park West, #540, Los Angeles, CA 90067. EOE

TOP 10 TRAILBLAZER
WANTED: Warm, creative, reliable ADULT communicator with America's most solid knowledge of music for grownups . . . from oldies to new era, bring your talent, imagination and enthusiasm to our top 10 market trailblazer. Rush your T&R to Radio & Records, 1930 Century Park West, #546, Los Angeles, CA 90046. EOE

TITLE	AVE. # FULLTIME EMP.	AVE. ANNUAL COMP.	MEDIAN ANNUAL COMP.	AVE. STARTING COMP.
On-Air Personality	5	17,445	14,000	15,048
News Announcer	2	17,910	15,000	15,946
Sports Reporter	1	19,598	15,000	16,356

Source: BFM/NAB 1987 Radio Employee Compensation and Fringe Benefits Report.

FIGURE 1.16
Radio compensation table. Courtesy National Association of Broadcasters.

Computer technology has raised a similar concern.

As of this writing, voice synthesizer technology is being marketed by Digital Equipment Corporation (DEC). Their device called DECtalk is capable of simulating a variety of different voices that can be programmed to deliver copy, like news and commercials. In fact, the DECtalk voice can be adjusted to read quickly or at a more leisurely pace.

Proponents of such new technology claim that the human voice will eventually be replicated for widespread application over the airwaves. Combined with the computer-driven automation systems, this synthetic voice technology would doubtlessly have some impact on the announcing profession. How much of an effect it will have is a subject for speculation. Most top industry figures take the position that technology exists to serve human beings and not to replace them.

SUGGESTED FURTHER READING

Bittner, John R. *Broadcasting and Telecommunications*, 2nd ed. Englewood Cliffs, N.J.: Prentice-Hall, 1985.

Blythin, Evan, and Samovar, Larry A. *Communicating Effectively on Television*. Belmont, Calif.: Wadsworth Publishing, 1985.

Broadcasting Yearbook. Washington, D.C.: Broadcasting Publishing, 1935 to date, annual.

Bryant, Donald C., and Wallace, Karl R. *Oral Communication*. New York: Appleton, 1962.

Edmond, I.G. *Broadcasting For Beginners*. New York: Holt, Rinehart and Winston, 1980.

Foster, Eugene S. *Understanding Broadcasting*, 2nd ed. Reading, Mass.: Addison-Wesley Publishing, 1982.

FIGURE 1.17
A community cable access television (CATV) system. Thousands of cable systems provide home viewers extended services.

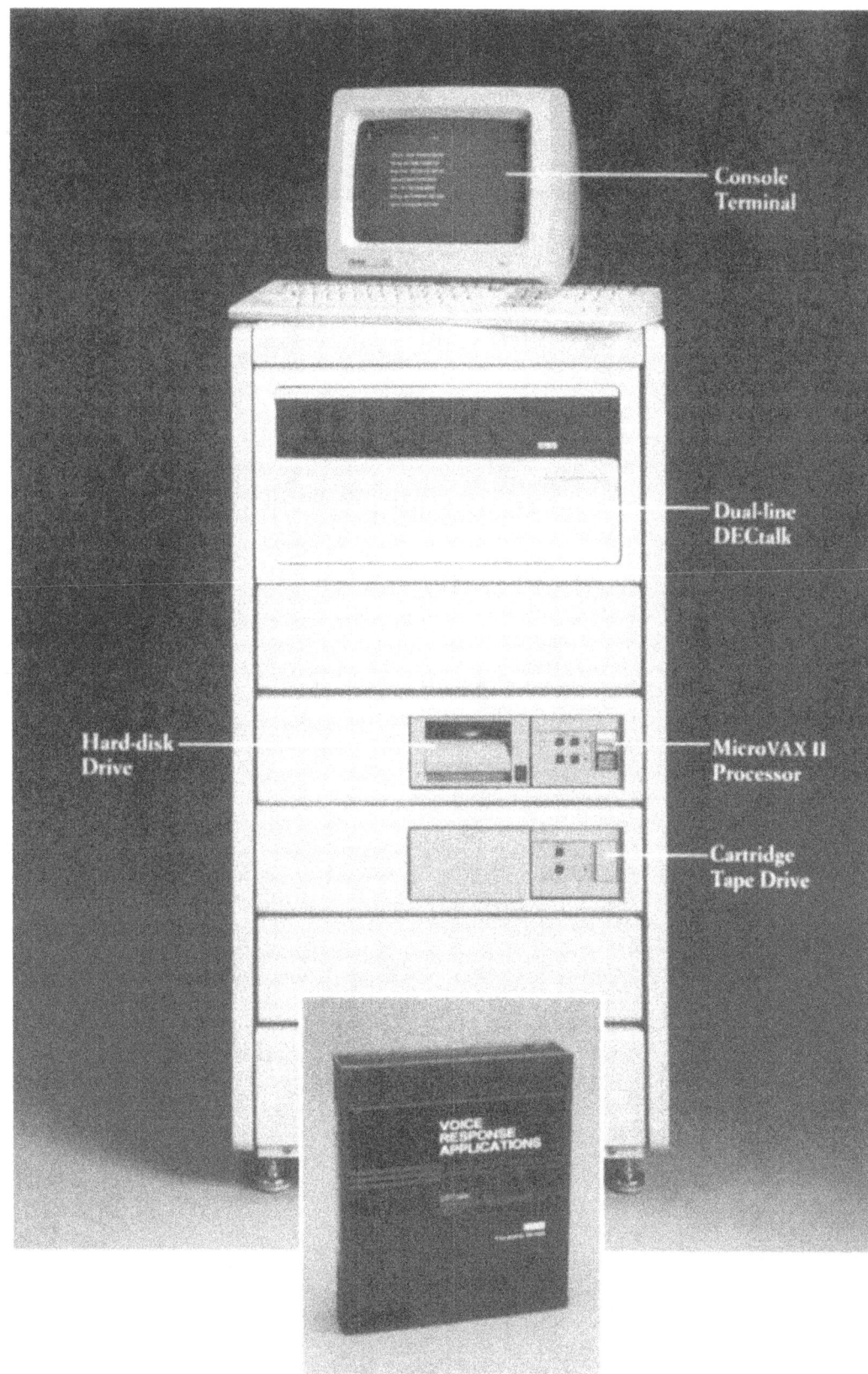

FIGURE 1.18 Computer voice response systems like this one have led to broadcast applications. Courtesy DEC.

Hawes, William. *The Performer in Mass Media.* New York: Hastings House Publishing, 1978.

Head, Sidney W., and Sterling, C.H. *Broadcasting in America: A Survey of Television, Radio, and the New Technologies,* 4th ed. Boston: Houghton Mifflin, 1982.

Hilliard, Robert, ed. *Radio Broadcasting: An Introduction to the Sound Medium,* 3rd ed. New York: Longman, 1985.

Hyde, Stuart W. *Television and Radio Announcing,* 5th ed. Boston: Houghton Mifflin, 1987.

Keith, Michael C., and Krause, Joseph M. *The Radio Station.* Stoneham, Mass.: Focal Press, 1986.

Sterling, Christopher H. *Electronic Media.* New York: Praeger, 1984.

2   BROADCASTING'S GOLDEN VOICES

DOTS AND DASHES IN THE AIR

At its inception, radio was not a voice medium. Dots and dashes, known as Morse Code, emanated from the crude wireless telegraph invented by the young and brilliant Italian, Marconi. In the 1890s, Marconi began transmitting his first airborne, wireless messages. This was a fitting conclusion to the century that witnessed the start of the industrial revolution. Barely into his twenties, Marconi had little idea of the magnitude of his creation. The idea of sending voice transmissions, not to mention music and other forms of sound, to home receivers would be proposed nearly two decades later, and not by Marconi. However, the pioneer innovator would be a prime player in the development of his device as it evolved into the world's first electronic mass medium, thus changing the world forever.

Reginald Fessenden, an engineering professor at the University of Pittsburgh, was one of the first to actually speak over the air. On Christmas Eve in 1906, Fessenden transmitted a wireless message that included his voice and a phonograph recording of a carol. It is doubtful that the young scientist realized that his experiment would both mark the start of a new era in communications and anticipate one of the most prominent conventions of modern radio—the deejay.

Fessenden was not the only scientist to expand on Marconi's wireless contraption. The refinement of transmission and receiving apparatus fell into the hands of several noteworthy Marconi disciples, among them Lee De Forest, inventor of the audio tube; Ambrose Fleming, developer of the two-element vacuum tube; and Edwin Armstrong, creator of the regenerative circuit and later Frequency Modulation (FM). Legions of other technical innovators contributed to the further development of Marconi's wireless telegraphy.

However, radio remained primarily an experimental device during the first decade of this century. The first to benefit from the wireless were ships at sea, which had hitherto floated the high seas incommunicado. The wireless telegraphy provided a bridge of communications for the maritime services. Seamen were very thankful for the voiceless clacking of keys that connected them with the rest of the world.

By 1910, many countries required that ships carrying fifty or more passengers have a wireless on board. This proved prophetic two years later when the supposedly invincible *Titanic* struck an iceberg and sank in the north Atlantic on her maiden voyage. Were it not for distress signals sent by the ship's wireless operator and picked up by, among others, a young radio operator in New York named David Sarnoff, the survivors in life rafts would likely have perished from exposure.

The general public's awareness of radio communication was heightened by the tragic event. Manning a wireless station in Wannamaker's department store, Sarnoff worked day and night before an anxious audience (including public officials and members of the press), receiving and relaying messages relevant to the disaster.

As radio's stock rose, so did the indefatigable wireless operator's. Sarnoff would be heard from, time and time again, as one of the medium's staunchest advocates and brilliant innovators.

The public's use of radio was curtailed when the government took it over for mili-

FIGURE 2.1
David Sarnoff, one of broadcasting's foremost pioneers. Courtesy RCA.

tary purposes during World War I. In fact, private wireless experimentation was regarded as treasonous until the war's end. Despite the nation's preoccupation with the global conflict, David Sarnoff's thoughts were of the future.

THE RADIO MUSIC BOX

In 1915, Sarnoff composed a memorandum that proposed the manufacture and sale of home radio receivers. In effect, his "radio music box memo" introduced the idea of an electronic mass medium—broadcasting. Sarnoff's proposal went largely ignored for five years, but eventually the Radio Corporation of America (which employed Sarnoff and which later would be run by him) gambled on the idea. Sarnoff's bold prediction of a substantial consumer market was amply realized as sales for RCA receivers soared. In 1921, Sarnoff became RCA general manager, and the radio medium flexed its infant limbs for the remarkable race that was about to begin.

Radio was actually launched in earnest in 1920 on KDKA. The station, which was the brainchild of Dr. Frank Conrad, was the first to offer regularly scheduled daily broadcasts. Until then it was catch-as-catch-can, since stations broadcasted at random or transmitted local events as they unfolded.

KDKA's broadcast studio amounted to a canvas tarpaulin stretched across a section of rooftop belonging to the Westinghouse Electric plant in East Pittsburgh, Pennsylvania. Under these less than favorable conditions, KDKA's only full-time announcer, Harold W. Arlin, broadcasted.

Arlin, one of the industry's first professional broadcast voice performers, arrayed himself in a tuxedo to mitigate the effects of the makeshift surroundings and to convey a sense of seriousness to those persons appearing on and visiting the station. Arlin served as both the voice and guest coordinator of KDKA.

Tales abound as to the incidents inspired by the temporary facilities. Singers were either choked mid-aria by flying insects or were covered from head to toe by clouds of black soot spewed forth by passing locomotives. All in all, a less auspicious introduction into the medium for both announcer and guests would be hard to imagine.

However, Arlin, who became known as the "Voice of America," remained undeterred by these early mishaps, remaining in front of the microphone for many years, broadcasting, among other things, play-by-play sports.

BUYING TIME

While KDKA serves to mark the birth of broadcasting, New York radio station WEAF represents the beginning of commercialism within the industry. The AT&T-owned station began an experiment in "tollcasting" on August 28, 1922. The very first commercial to penetrate the airwaves was introduced by the station's announcer, Vischer Randall, in the following manner: "This afternoon the radio audience is to be addressed by Mr. Blackwell of the Queensboro Corporation, who through arrangements made by the Griffin Radio Service, Incorporated, will say a few words concerning Nathanial Hawthorne and the desirability of fostering the helpful community spirit and the healthful, unconfined homelife that were Hawthorne's ideals. Ladies and gentlemen, Mr. Blackwell."

Blackwell then proceeded to deliver the commercial, which is excerpted here:

"It is fifty-eight years since Nathanial

Hawthorne, the greatest of American fictionists, passed away. To honor his memory, the Queensboro Corporation, creator and operator of the tenant-owned system of apartment homes at Jackson Heights, New York City, has named its latest group of high-grade dwellings 'Hawthorne Court.'

"I wish to thank those within sound of my voice for the broadcasting opportunity afforded me to urge the vast radio audience to seek the recreation and the daily comfort of the home removed from the congested part of the city, right at the boundaries of God's great outdoors, and within a few minutes by subway from the business section of Manhattan. This sort of residential environment strongly influenced Hawthorne, America's great writer of fiction. He analyzed with charming keenness the social spirit of those who had thus happily selected homes, and he painted the people inhabiting those homes with good-natured relish.

"There should be more Hawthorne sermons preached about the utter inadequacy and the general hopelessness of the congested city home. The cry of the heart is for more living room, more chance to unfold, more opportunity to get near the Mother Earth, to play, to romp, to plant and dig.

"Let me enjoin upon you as you value your health and your hopes and your home happiness, get away from the solid masses of brick, where the meagre opening admitting a slant of sunlight is mockingly called a light shaft, and where children grow up starved for a run over a patch of grass and the sight of a tree.

"Apartments in congested parts of the city have proven failures. The word neighbor is an expression of peculiar irony—a daily joke. . ."

For fifty dollars, WEAF allowed the Queensboro executive to wax philosophically about the virtues of country living. The announcement resulted in the sale of two apartment units and signaled to other companies the effectiveness of radio advertising. Thus the American broadcasting medium as we know it today was born. What began as an experiment in free enterprise that netted WEAF less than six hundred dollars in 1922 would grow into a multibillion-dollar industry.

The style and form of commercial announcements changed little until later in the 1920s. The minilecture approach, exces-

FIGURE 2.2
H.W. Arlin was one of the country's first full-time radio announcers. Courtesy Westinghouse.

sively pedantic in many instances and delivered in a somewhat formal and lackluster manner, remained the norm until the industry had settled in and made itself more comfortable.

Meanwhile, the government, namely Department of Commerce chief Herbert Hoover, disapproved of commercialism, fearing that the medium with so extraordinary a potential for public good would be "drowned in advertising chatter." To placate the chagrined Commerce Secretary, stations took to program "sponsorships," wherein an announcer would introduce a program underwritten or supported by an advertiser, e.g., "Good evening ladies and gentlemen and welcome to the *Milestone Hardware Music Variety Hour*." Upon a program's conclusion, an announcer would read a closing that would again identify the program's benefactor.

RADIO DIGEST—*Illustrated*

King, Charles, Tenor, KNX.
King, Gerald, Manager, KFWB.
King, Mildred, Pianist, WSM.
King, Dr. O. H., Baritone, KTHS.
King, Mrs. William, Organist, WOC.
Kingins, Mrs. M. J., Soprano, WLAC.
Kings of Rhythm, WWJ.
Kinkaid, Mildred, Contralto, KWK.
Kinman's Melody Boys, KGA.
Kirby, Corley W., Director-Announcer, WGHP. He has the distinction of having worked in all the Detroit stations. He was with WWJ three years, WJR 1½ years and WGHP 2 years. Famous for his saying that announcers have bankers' hours in the morning and burglars' hours at night. After serving in the Army during the World War, he spent some time in Europe. This experience is invaluable in announcing musical selections.
Kirtley, Lucille, Soprano, KGW.
Kitts, Evelyn, Studio Hostess of KOIL. Gives Aunty Sammy's Chats, serves as accompanist and occasionally offers programs of popular songs.
Klemm, Gustav, Program Supervisor, WBAL.
Klier, Bob, Zither-player. "Bob" is a monument in the cafe life of San Francisco, a tradition for 21 years. "Bob," incidentally, is also an artist at Hungarian goulash, which, unfortunately, he can't cook over the air, KFRC.
Kline, Ted, Tenor, WCCO.
Klotz, Heinie, Tenor, WDAF.
Kma String Trio, Bernice Currier, Birdie Baldwin, Doc Bellamy, KMA.
Kneisel, Jack and His Gypsy Barons Orchestra, WWJ.
Kneiss, Professor Henry, Violinist, Director of Lincoln Salon Orchestra and KFAB Symphony, KFAB.
Knickerbocker Quartet, WEEI.
Knowles, Lillian, Contralto, WENR-WBCN.
Knox, Wm. Morgan, Staff Violinist; Instructor of WSAI Radio Violin Lessons; Assistant Director of Orchestras, WLW Director.
Knutson, Erling, Violinist, WDAF.
KNX Concert Orchestra, KNX.
KOA Mixed Quartet, Bernice W. Doughty, Soprano; Lucille Fowler, Contralto; Ralph Freese, Tenor; Everett E. Foster, Baritone; Freeman H. Talbot, Director, KOA.
KOA Orchestra, KOA.
Koehne, Freida, Violinist, KYW.
KOIN Male Quartet, Emil Brahms, bass; Bud Abbot, Baritone; Denton Denman, Tenor; Lloyd Warren, Tenor.
KOIN Radio Players, KOIN.
Konecky, Eugene, Grand Champion Staller, WOW. He is well remembered for his Blah Club which ceased to operate because Dizzy Izzy, none other than our hero, was too busy to blah. Mr. Konecky has been with the Omaha station since it began as WOAW. Among his other duties he sends out all the station's publicity. In his spare time Mr. Konecky writes poetry, some of which has been published.

Kopec, Mike, Pianist, Piano-Accordianist, KFAB.
Kooker, Ethel, Book Reviews, WFI.
Kornstein, Egon, Violaist, Columbia Broadcasting System Symphony Orhcestra.
Kraft, Vincent, I., President, KJR.
Kramer, L. J., Guitarist, KVOO.
Kresge, S. S., Quartet, WJR.
Krueger, Florence, Soprano, WOC.
Kuhn, Eddie, Kansas City Athletic Club Orchestra, WDAF.
Kuhn, Vincent, Baritone, WSM.
KWK String Trio, Dorothy Davidson, Pianist; Marie Golub, Violinist; Louise Evers, Cellist, KWK.
Kyle, Muriel Magerl, Soprano, WJR.
Kynett. Mrs. Xenophen, Contralto, KOIL.

LADY BALTIMORE, WBAL Sandman Circle.
Lamb, Christine, Contralto, WLAC.
La Ferrara, Vincent, Violinist. Director of "The Trocadrans," Pacific Coast Network, National Broadcasting Company.
LaGue, Charles J., Transmission Engineer, KOA.
Laidley, Isobel, Cellist, WIBO.
Lambert, John, Violin and Saxophone Player, National Battery Symphony Orchestra, KSTP.
Lamborn, Betty, Woman's Hour, WGHP.
La Mother, Gertrude, "Mrs." of Universal Radio Features, WEEI.
LaMotte, George, Bass, KVOO.
Lampe, J. B., Director, WMBB-WOK.
Lancey, Loraine, Accompanist, WJR.
Lang, Harry, Orhcestra Leader of Arcadians, KMOX.
Lange, Verne, Tenor, KFAB.
Lantrip, Rev. W. M., Baritone, WLAC.
Lantry, C. C., Announcer, KHQ.
Largent, Mrs. D. W., Soprano, KFDM.

FIGURE 2.3
An excerpt from an announcer's directory published in the October 1928 *Radio Digest* magazine.

This subtle way of generating revenue accomplished its goal of keeping Hoover's dissatisfaction from flaring to a dangerous level, which many broadcasters feared would end over-the-air advertising. Shortly, however, broadcasters would throw caution to the wind and air advertising messages in a far more overt style. Indirect advertising, or program sponsorships, would remain a popular method of selling airtime, but direct pitches for goods and services became the prevailing modus operandi.

As the result of the growing commercialism and the entering of more stations to the airwaves, programming became more diversified. This created a greater demand for broadcast voice performers. Following Harold Arlin's example, other pioneer broadcasters entered the airwaves in the 1920s. Counted among them were Graham McNamee, who joined Vischer Randall at WEAF, and Thomas H. Cowan, a former extra with the Metropolitan Opera, as well as Ted Husing. Cowan and Husing were both hired by Newark, New Jersey, station WJZ. Cowan departed WJZ in 1924 to assume chief announcer duties at WNYC, New York City.

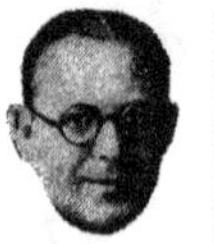

The same year, WEAF's Graham McNamee was joined by Phillip Carlin and Norman Brokenshire for the purpose of reporting on the Democratic convention. While McNamee and his cohorts continued to fulfill the various announcing needs of the station, their involvement in news and public affairs programming deepened. Eventually their duties rested exclusively in the area of broadcast journalism.

Versatility was a requisite for station announcers during radio's infancy. To possess good speaking skills and a dignified delivery were not enough. Station announcers were frequently called upon to fill airtime between guests, or to speak at length in the absence of one. Musical talents (the ability to play an instrument or sing) and storytelling or recitational skills were common among voice performers of the period.

COMPENSATION

Despite the demands and expectations heaped on early broadcast voice performers, the wages were modest. However, as the profession grew in stature, money for outside personal appearances became significant. Up

75

Lane, Frank, Announcer-Director of WDOD. One of the younger announcers who began his Radio work at KFRU, Bristow, and stayed with the station until the call letters were changed to KVOO. Last June he went to Chattanooga. As Frank is only twenty-two years old, he is getting along rather rapidly, and, as his is one of the favorite voices of the South, he will, no doubt, be heard from in the future. However, he is interested in a fruit and poultry farm in Oklahoma and may leave his announcing for a farmer's life.

LaRowe, Phillip, Central High School Organist, KVOO.
Larsen, Dorothy, Pianist, WSM.
Larson, Bennett, Uncle Ben in charge of children, Announcer, KDYL.
Lasky, Philip G., Announcer-Director, KDYL.
Latner, Mrs. Morris, Soprano, WLAC.
Laughton Family Orchestra, KVOO.
Laurier, Ludwig, Musical Director, National Broadcasting Company.
Laux, J. Francis, Assistant Announcer, Sports, KVOO.
Lawrence, May F., Organist and Composer, WLAC.
Lawrence, Mrs. May F., Pianist, WSM.
Lawrie, Justin, Tenor, National Broadcasting Company.
Leaska, Mme. Leah, Operatic and Concert Soprano, KGW.
Le Barre, Stuart, Violinist, presents the early morning test program over WMAQ and WQJ. A violinist of promise himself, Le Barre gives preference to the classics in picking his records each morning at 6 and 7 o'clock.
LeBow, Dan, Violinist, Conductor of Orchestra, KTHS.
Lederer, John, Conductor of Marylanders, WBAL.
Lee, Virginia, Soprano, WOC.
Leek, Helen, Soprano, WLAC.
Lem and Lafe, Black-Face Team, KPO.
LeMon, Mel, Announcer, KFWB.
Lennox, Elizabeth, Contralto, Columbia Broadcasting System.
Leon, Frank, Orchestra Pianist, KOMO.
Leonhardt, P. A., comes over from the central YMCA early in the mornings to give WMAQ and WQJ fans their setting up exercises.
Leotta, Mme., Reader, KOIN.
Levienne, Kola, Cellist, KJR.
Levienne, Mischa, Violinist, KJR.
Levine, Shepard, Tenor, WJAZ.
Levine, Walter, Baritone, WJAZ.
Lewis, John, Baritone and pupil of Signor Guaetona S. De Luca of Nashville Conservatory of Music. Mr. Lewis is also a Member of the Announcing Staff of WLAC, and appears weekly as a soloist. WLAC.
Lewis, Marion, Accompanist, WLAC.
Lewis, Dorothy, Contralto, KGW.
Lewis, Ednyfed, Tenor, Director, WFI.
Lighthall, Mrs. Ray, Soprano, KFDM.
Lilligren, Alice, Soprano Soloist, KSTP.
Lincoln Salon Orchestra, KFAB.
Lind, George, Baritone, KFDM.
Lindstrom, Everett, KSTP Troubadour, came to the National Battery station from the University of Minnesota. He had formerly broadcast with WAMD and WCCO. His crooning voice and his 16-string Gibson-harp-guitar, provide entertainment for KSTP listeners.
Linden, Jack, Violinist, has been Director of Hotel LaSalle Orchestra, Capitol Theater Orchestra, Member of Chicago Grand Opera Company. Now directs WSBC Orchestra.
Lindhe, Vin, Pianist, Reader, WFAA.
Lindsay, Art, Announcer, KFOA.
Lindsay, Walter, Radio Engineer, WMAQ.
Lingeman, Caspar J., Minstrels, WJR.
Lingeman, Johann, European Cellist, WGN.
Linick, Art, The Famous "Mrs. Schlagenhauer," a "Dutch Treat," WBBM.
Link Bolines Cowboy Band, KVOO.
Lincoln, Waldo, Old Time Fiddler, WSUN.
Linn, Eddy, Announcer, Baritone, Little Clown of the Four K Safety Club of WSAI.
Linn, Martha, Directs "The Women's Exchange of Ideas," Features range from child study, parent education, styles, character analysis, travel talks to beauty culture, WHT.
Linthicum, Walter N., Baritone, Announcer, BAL.
Lion's Club Quartet, WDBO.
Litterer, Dr. Henry, Guitarist, WSM.
Little Brown Church Quartet, Lucille Magill, Soprano; Bernice Ozmun, Contralto; Eugene Leonardson, Baritone; William O'Connor, Tenor, WLS.
Little, Charles W., The Blind Violinist, WSUN.
Little, Jack, Traveling Artist.
Little, Mrs. Angeline H., Manager, KGA.
Livingston, Charles, Baritone, WHT.
Locke, Mrs. Iona Towne, Soprano; KFDM.
Loder, Kenneth, Cellist, KFAB.
Lombardo, Guy, Director of Guy Lombardo's Orchestra, WBBM.
Lombardis, Lela and Harry, Comedy and Musical Sketches, WLS.

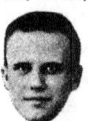

FIGURE 2.4
***Radio Digest* announcer directory.**

to one thousand dollars for an evening's work as an emcee or host (for a special community or show business function) was paid. The money garnered from this moonlighting was slow in coming, however, since stations prevented announcers from using their own names on the air. This situation existed until the mid-1920s and impeded the arrival of public recognition and fame and the accompanying financial benefits.

Announcers were known only by initials until the public's demand for identification of the voices (of which they had become enamored) pressured stations into changing their policies. The unwillingness on the part of stations to permit announcers to use their names was, at least in part, born out of a fear that on-air people would demand greater financial rewards as they gained public recognition. This fear was justified as many announcers went on to become celebrities and public figures. The public's adulation bore even greater fruit as some announcers went on lucrative tours and others wrote books. For example, WJZ's Ted Husing enjoyed sizable profits from his autobiography, *Ten Years Behind The Mike*, and other radio personalities followed suit by publishing books of poetry, essays, and even novels. The listener's interest in the voices behind the mic grew as radio became more of an integral part of America's daily routine. The radio voice performer had arrived.

Broadcast historian Erik Barnouw states in his book, *A Tower of Babel* (Oxford University Press, 1966), that "the rise of personality coincided with the rise of commercialism." As stations made money, so did the individuals whose voices flowed from the home receivers. Quite simply, announcers were a factor in motivating audiences to tune in and had to be rewarded accordingly.

TOO MANY VOICES AT ONCE

The growth of the medium far exceeded all initial predictions. Between 1920 and 1925 over eight hundred stations went on the air, creating a log jam that threatened to choke the medium. Little legislation had been passed to prevent signal interference, and only two frequencies existed for broadcast purposes. Thus station signals overlapped and home reception was garbled. It was not uncommon for listeners to pick up two or more stations simultaneously, especially in metropolitan areas where many radio stations operated.

Stations were swamped with complaints by both listeners and advertisers. "You can't hear one announcer for the other," was the cry. Concerned broadcasters formed an organization to lobby for a remedy. Between 1922 and 1925 the National Association of Broadcasters (NAB) pressed for government intervention. After a series of national radio conferences, the government passed legislation aimed at resolving the predicament. The Radio Act of 1927 authored the creation of the Federal Radio Commission (FRC), which set about the task of improving signal reception.

In one year the FRC established an entire broadcast band (AM), assigned call letters, allocated frequencies, issued station licenses, and assigned specific operating parameters. It then scrutinized existing outlets, pulling the plug on nearly one quarter. To assure compliance with their standards, the FRC maintained the authority to inspect radio facilities and license operators. Since many announcers, especially at small stations, handled technical operations, they were required to possess a license.

Within a year of the FRC's remediation, the radio medium was back on track and healthier than ever.

Despite its problems during this period, the medium managed to maintain a forward movement. In 1926, at the very height of the interference problem, the first radio network was born.

THE NETWORKS ARE NEWS AND COMMENTARY

Combining stations it had purchased from AT&T with the ones it already owned, the Radio Corporation of America formed the National Broadcasting Company. A year and a half later, in 1928, William S. Paley, heir to a cigar company fortune, formed the nation's second broadcast network, the Columbia Broadcasting System. Remarkably, as of this writing, Paley remains active in the company, although he is well into his eighties.

The networks spurred the growth of broadcast journalism and significantly expanded the opportunities for radio voice performers.

FIGURE 2.5
An account of the announcer's life during radio's formative years. Courtesy WTIC-AM.

▲ *Veteran announcer Bernard "Bunny" Mullins had a rich baritone voice that gave "class" and dignity to dramas, musical shows, special events and commentaries. Mullins' high standards helped WTIC's younger announcers perfect their technique.*

◄ *This rather nervous looking young gentleman reflects the formal nature of radio announcing in the early years. In 1936, Bob Steele announced one of WTIC's most popular live music shows, "Hall's Hour of Cheer."*

◄ *A trio of WTIC announcers, circa 1950. From left to right: Ed Anderson, Bob Steele, Bruce Kern.*

The announcer's life.

Throughout the 30's and 40's, radio grew slightly less formal than it had been in its earliest days. After the war, fewer and fewer programs were entirely scripted. Still, jackets and ties were the order of the day for all men working at WTIC. If suspenders were worn, they were not to show. An attitude of formality and politeness reigned.

WTIC's salaries were slightly higher than those at competing area stations. There were no contracts for announcers and other professional staff members. Morency didn't believe in them. If an announcer wanted to move on, he should be free to do so. WTIC offered a level of pay and professionalism that was hard to match elsewhere in the area.

The Chief Announcer set the schedules for the rest of his staff. In addition to regular assignments, announcers earned extra pay for hosting special shows, for which they were selected, and for handling commercials. Management required that two announcers and two engineers be on duty at all times when the station was on the air. All news programs were handled by two staff announcers. One read the news, the other read commercials. While the station news staff wrote and edited the news, they were not allowed to read it over the air.

Even though they maintained a sense of formality in their duties, the announcing staff still found ways to have fun. A favorite trick was to touch a match to a fellow announcer's copy as he read his final item over the air. The poor victim had to blow out the flames without losing his cool or letting his huffs and puffs be heard over the microphone.

Sometimes the practical jokes got a bit out of hand. During the height of UFO fever, announcer Bob Tyrol nearly created panic in The Travelers building. He glued two 16" records to a spool of twine. Then, he dropped the assembly down the side of the building and made it travel up and down like a yo-yo. To the secretaries below, it looked like flying saucers were hovering over downtown Hartford.

By the mid-1920s the field of radio news was well on the way to establishing itself. The medium had from its inception attempted to provide listeners with information of a topical nature, such as convention coverage and presidential addresses. The advent of the major networks deepened radio's commitment to news and commentary.

FIGURE 2.6
Lowell Thomas's career as a broadcast commentator spanned several decades. Courtesy CBS.

Among the most heralded personages of radio's golden era were its network news commentators. In 1930, Lowell Thomas, Boake Carter, and H.V. Kaltenborn (the "dean of radio commentators") joined the networks. The previous year Floyd Gibbons was hired by NBC to host *The Headline Hunter*, a weekly half-hour program. Gibbons went on to become the network's first full-time newsman.

By the early 1930s, news and commentary were a mainstay for the networks and remained so throughout the following two decades. The radio audience was delighted with the words, opinions, and insights of Gabriel Heatter, Elmer Davis, Upton Close, Drew Pearson, Fulton Lewis, Dorothy Thompson, Raymond Carter, and Edward R. Murrow.

Commentator delivery styles ranged from the histrionic and floral to the unaffected and low-key or conversational. With few exceptions, network commentators possessed pleasant, cultivated voices and the unique ability to stir the emotions and sensibilities of their listeners.

In the opening chapter of *Those Radio Commentators* (Iowa University Press, 1977), author Irving Fang writes, "There was a time when radio news was more than headlines ripped from a wire machine and read by an announcer who couldn't care less whether Paris was in France or Kentucky. There was a time when lots of people looked forward each evening to hearing news and opinions from a favorite commentator, a span of 15 minutes that put an exclamation point on the day!" Fang goes on to lament, "Alas, that time exists no longer."

GOOD FORTUNE DURING BAD TIMES

The Depression, which spanned much of the 1930s, had an ironic impact on radio. The medium actually prospered, not so much financially, but rather in terms of audience growth and popularity, as the nation staggered from the worst economic blow in its history.

Perhaps contributing most significantly to radio's good fortune in the face of the consuming economic turmoil was its accessibility and affordability. Radio was free. Furthermore, the medium offered a means of escape from the bleak realities of a blighted economy through programming that attempted to ameliorate the gloom, and audiences and advertisers responded.

Just as the stock market took its fateful plunge, the most popular program in radio history, *Amos 'n' Andy*, began its three-decade run. Radio was alive with comedy, variety, and drama, and broadcast voice performers were among the lucky few whose profession enjoyed continued growth and prosperity.

Recognizing the immense potential of the radio medium, President Franklin D. Roosevelt went to the airwaves to convey his plans for economic recovery, which he hoped would elicit the backing of the American public. The effects of his "fireside chats" have become legendary. FDR possessed an almost uncanny ability to utilize the medium to its fullest. Despite his lack of formal broadcast training, he was right at home in front of the microphone, communicating warmth, sincerity, and conviction. "Hearing his voice, we sensed a gallant, generous-spirited human being, not a party hack or a synthetic product packaged by Madison avenue," noted Howard Koch, a prominent writer during radio's golden age, and author of *The Panic Broadcast*, which details the events surrounding the infamous broadcast of his radio script, *Invasion From Mars*.

The President's reliance on the medium enhanced its already formidable image as an instrument for public good. Indeed, the 1930s were the prime years of the medium's heyday. Against a backdrop of national crisis, radio reached its full stride.

Programming was at its apex with features such as CBS's *Mercury Theater of the Air*, under the unique direction of one of the medium's greatest voice performers, Orson Welles. In his book *The Panic Broadcast*, Koch observes about Welles that "his resonant, throbbing voice can invest a simple declarative sentence with a sense of excitement and importance."

Burgess Meredith and John Houseman also lent their considerable vocal skills and talents to the weekly program, which, among other noteworthy productions, offered the adaptation of H.G. Wells' classic tale, *War of the Worlds*, on Halloween eve 1938. In his role as actor and director, Orson Welles managed to strike fear in the heart of listeners across the country. No other program in the annals of radio history created such an uproar. Such were the formidable skills of the voice performers and production staff that a nation responded in panic, choking telephone switchboards at police stations with inquiries and pleas for help.

Radio certainly had served to distract the focus of millions of Americans away from the unpleasant hardships of the decade, yet the medium would serve an even greater role as the nation faced a more harrowing experience—World War II.

VOICES OF WAR

Radio's status as a news medium grew dramatically as the country dedicated itself to the war effort. No topic so preoccupied the mind of the American public. Nearly everyone knew of a person involved in some aspect of the global conflict, and news information was in fierce demand.

The networks expanded their news departments to meet this need. Under the direction of Paul White, CBS assembled a stellar crew of news broadcasters and correspondents, who reported from the war-torn cities of Europe and the steamy jungles of the South Pacific. The distinctive reporting of William Shirer, Eric Sevareid, Robert Trout, Howard K. Smith, Richard C. Hottelet, John Daley, and many others kept the public up to date as never before.

The scenes of war were vividly reported to the American living room from London by Edward R. Murrow. His original style and delivery captivated listeners. Ed Bliss, who served as Murrow's writer, editor, and occasional producer at CBS, makes this observation: "The central fact about Murrow's effectiveness as a deliverer of news and opinion is that he did not announce in the popular sense of the word but spoke. Though rarely informal, his manner was conversational. He possessed such a substantial voice—the opposite of former President Carter's reedy, almost querulous voice—that his sentences, with their strong nouns and verbs, demanded attention. He spoke with authority, as someone who knew what he was talking about, as indeed he did. I have wondered to what degree the Southern accent with which he spoke during the first

FIGURE 2.7 Welles with reporters following the panic broadcast. Courtesy CBS.

years of his life may have influenced his broadcast voice. It was, in any case, a trained voice, distinguished by its richness and his extraordinarily effective use of the pause."

Murrow became noted for his use of the pause in the opening to his war reports from England. Bliss explains, "The story has it that it was Murrow's former speech instructor, Ida Lou Anderson, at the State College of Washington (now Washington State) who suggested that he pause momentarily after the word *this* in 'this is London.' After the war, on his nightly radio program, 'This . . . is London' became 'This . . . is the news.' "

Commentator Walter Winchell is said to have brought the dramatic pause technique to radio in the 1930s. Contemporary commentator Paul Harvey uses the pause no less successfully today: "This is Paul Harvey . . . good day." Millions of radio listeners are familiar with his famous style and closing signature, which epitomizes the pause effect.

ENTER "RADIO WITH PICTURES"

The war's end paved the way for the implementation of an entirely new electronic medium. Within a couple of years, television began to make inroads into the living rooms of America. By 1948, television programs were cutting into radio audience figures and radio personalities were migrating in vast numbers to the visual medium.

Not everyone who attempted to make the transition from radio to television performing succeeded. Not everyone was suited for the new medium. A comparison can be made with the experiences of certain actors who attempted to make the change from the silent screen to the talkies; while perhaps visually appealing to the audience, they lost credibility when they spoke. For one reason or another their voices simply did not match their screen images.

Television brought with it its own unique criteria, and camera presence was one. Not all radio performers had the "look" that television wanted. Of course, not everyone was interested in making the leap to television, even though the older medium was losing fans to the new kid on the block.

As the 1940s came to a close, television receiver sales were brisk, while radio advertising revenues were softening in comparison to previous years. By the early 1950s, television was the number-one entertainment medium. Radio management was perplexed and frustrated as it made unsuccessful attempts to stem the tide. Tit-for-tat programming practices did little to reverse the effects of television. It became evident that if television and radio both offered a similar type program at similar times, the audience would opt for the visual presentation over the strictly audio.

While television was a boon to broadcast voice performers, it was a thorn in the side of radio executives, whose fortunes were on

FIGURE 2.8A and B Edward R. Murrow in war-time London and on the set of his 1953 television program *Person to Person*. Courtesy CBS.

A

FIGURE 2.8 Continued

FIGURE 2.9
Murrow's actual script showing how he marked for effect. His writer, Ed Bliss, notes that "Murrow's nightly broadcasts always ended with the 'word for today,' which tied in (complimented) his commentary. It came after the last commercial. The announcer, George Bryan or Bob Dixon, would say 'Now here is Mr. Murrow with his word for today.'" Courtesy Ed Bliss.

B

the wane. It became clear that radio had to leave behind its traditional approach to programming and embark on a whole new course in order to survive and prosper, and that is what it did (see Chapter 3).

```
Word for Today                          March 8, 1957



          Archibald MacLeish once said...with regard to

   radio broadcasting...that the freedom of speech of which

   this country is so proud, is also freedom to hear...that

   freedom to hear is indeed the whole foundation and reason

   of freedom to speak.  In chatting these few minutes with

   Louis Seltzer, it occurred to this reporter that freedom

   to see...though it be second-hand by means of a camera...is

   no less a part of freedom of the press.

          Goodnight and good luck!
```

VOICE STYLES THEN AND NOW

The broadcast announcing profession is about to enter its eighth decade. Thousands of voice performers have come and gone, leaving behind a rich legacy of styles. Over the years, the audience has been exposed to every imaginable type of delivery, but do voice performers sound significantly different today than they did years ago? Ed McMahon, *Tonight Show* cohost and one of the country's most familiar voice performers, does not think so. "I began as a radio announcer at WLLH in Lowell, Massachusetts. It was in the early forties before I became a Marine fighter pilot in World War II. Reflecting back I would have to say that the voice qualities most admired in those days are the ones pretty much admired today.

"Radio and television have always sought distinctive voices. My role model was Paul Douglas, who went on to become a great motion picture star after working in radio. His 'style,' which I admired, was super casual. In the midst of all the other announcers, who were extremely precise in their pronunciation, bordering on the unctuous, he would say *yer* for *you*, as in 'yer going to like the taste of Chesterfields,' and get away with it. Today we have all kinds of distinctive voices, and the effective ones are well modulated, solid, and never shrill.

"The types of successful deliveries are so varied as to include Mason Adams, who does countless commercials in a kind of 'super folksy' style, and Alistair Cooke, who could make reading the yellow pages seem like high drama. The voice box is an instrument. Properly played, it has endearing and enduring qualities."

Gaylord Avery, senior staff announcer for CBS, claims that the criteria for hiring voices at the networks have changed little over the years. "In the 1940s and 1950s, the midwestern, 'flat' sound, that is, without discernible accent, was preferred, along with the medium baritone. I'd say this still holds true."

Robert Skedgell, former Director of News for CBS Radio, says the same pretty much holds true for news voices today as it did during the medium's earlier era. "Radio news broadcasters on the network level have generally been hired on the basis of their reporting experience, not their diction. Of course, a clear voice is a timeless criterion. William Shirer, a mumbler, wouldn't be hired today, but in the 1940s he was immensely popular. I believe contemporary announcing styles are somewhat less 'breathy' today than earlier, that is, less emotional—less à la Boake Carter and Gabriel Heatter."

The golden age of radio's most prominent writer and producer, Norman Corwin, contends that there has been very little change in announcing styles over the years. "Frankly, I don't see much change, but I don't consider myself an expert in this area. I think the best voices of the heyday were Frank Gallup, Ben Grauer, Harry Marble, and Mel Allen (before he became a sportscaster). There were, of course, marvelous voices of actors who never did announcing as such, most notably Martin Gabel, Arnold Moss, House Jameson, and Eric Burroughs. The CBS stable of announcers was a very good one, and so I was well served in that area. I'm afraid as a radio writer/producer I considered announcers to be often little more than doormen, that is, not necessarily an integral part of production."

Ed Bliss notes that one of the most familiar voices of recent decades has a style rooted in the past. "Walter Cronkite's delivery is a unique combination of old and new. His warmth of personality was reflected in his voice. This, I'm sure, contributed to his success. But, I believe, it was his experience, earnestness, and enthusiasm—his seriousness about news—that, more than anything else, made him 'the most trusted man in America.' "

In conclusion, what were valued voice characteristics in the past remain so today. The basics remain the basics. Topping the list then and now are good tonal quality, clarity of speech, and general expressiveness. "These are qualities that transcend time and work in any era," concludes Ed McMahon.

SUGGESTED FURTHER READING

Aitkin, Hugh G.J. *Syntony and Spark*. New York: John Wiley and Sons, 1976.
Archer, G.L. *History of Radio to 1926*. New York: Arno Press, 1971.
Baker, W.J. *A History of the Marconi Company*. New York: St. Martin's Press, 1971.
Barnouw, Erik. *A Tower of Babel: A History of Broadcasting in the United States to*

FIGURE 2.10
Paul Harvey is modern radio's most successful commentator. Courtesy *Paul Harvey News*.

FIGURE 2.11
Ed McMahon has one of the country's most familiar faces and voices. Courtesy NBC.

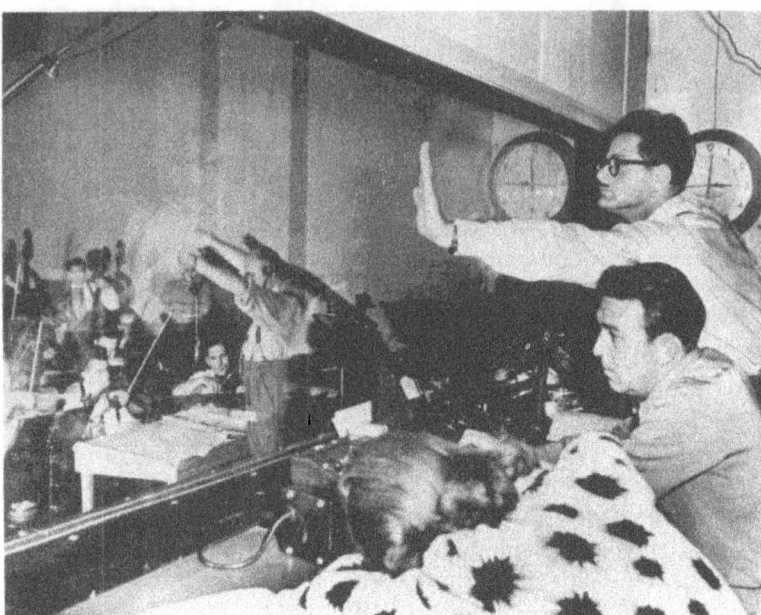

FIGURE 2.12
Producer and writer Norman Corwin cues his performers during a 1940s radio program. Courtesy Norman Corwin.

Campbell, Robert. *The Golden Years of Broadcasting.* New York: Charles Scribner's Sons, 1976.

Cantril, Hadley. *The Invasion from Mars.* New York: Harper & Row, 1966.

Delong, Thomas A. *The Mighty Music Box.* Los Angeles: Amber Crest Books, 1980.

Dreher, Carl. *Sarnoff: An American Success.* New York: Quadrangle, 1977.

Dunning, John. *Tune In Yesterday.* Englewood Cliffs, N.J.: Prentice-Hall, 1976.

Fang, Irving E. *Those Radio Commentators.* Ames, Iowa: Iowa University Press, 1977.

Lazarsfeld, Paul F., and Kendall, P.L. *Radio Listening In America.* Englewood Cliffs, N.J.: Prentice-Hall, 1948.

Levinson, Richard. *Stay Tuned.* New York: St. Martin's Press, 1982.

Lewis, Peter, ed. *Radio Drama.* New York: Longman, 1981.

MacDonald, J. Fred. *Don't Touch That Dial: Radio Programming in American Life, 1920-1960.* Chicago: Nelson-Hall, 1979.

1933, vol. 1. New York: Oxford University Press, 1966.

———. *The Golden Web: A History of Broadcasting in the United States 1933 to 1953,* vol. 2. New York: Oxford University Press, 1968.

Bittner, John R. *Broadcasting and Telecommunications,* 2nd. ed. Englewood Cliffs, N.J.: Prentice-Hall, 1985.

Paley, William S. *As It Happened: A Memoir.* Garden City, N.J.: Doubleday, 1979.

Seidle, Ronald J. *Air Time.* Boston: Holbrook Press, 1977.

Wertheim, Arthur F. *Radio Comedy.* New York: Oxford University Press, 1979.

FIGURE 2.13
Walter Cronkite—"the most trusted man in America." Courtesy CBS.

3 THE NEW AGE ANNOUNCER

A CHANGE IN THE AIR

The start of the 1950s did not bode well for the radio medium, nor for those who worked within the industry. Meanwhile, television, referred to by some chagrined radio executives as the "enfant terrible," was in a healthy skyward trajectory. The heavens beckoned.

At the beginning of the decade, barely three years after its auspicious debut, television claimed to be the primary source of home entertainment during the evening hours, and surveys corroborated this claim. This was a climactic turnabout for radio, which had served as the undisputed monarch of home entertainment for a quarter of a century.

The first full postwar decade provided the perfect climate for the ascent of the new medium. Economic prosperity, coupled with a sense of well being and optimism about the future, spurred television receiver sales. The public wanted something new and exciting, and television filled the bill. Many radio performers shared this sentiment. Television was perceived as a new frontier, the wave of the future, by an overwhelming majority of entertainers, who ultimately abandoned the aural medium for the visual. Within three years, radio had been dethroned and all but stripped of its talent by the "picture box," which in the 1950s reigned as the centerpiece of the American living room.

Was radio dead or close to it? It looked that way to some media observers. Radio's imminent demise was forecast by some of its strongest proponents. At the very least, many conceded a sharply declining audience in the face of television's explosive popularity.

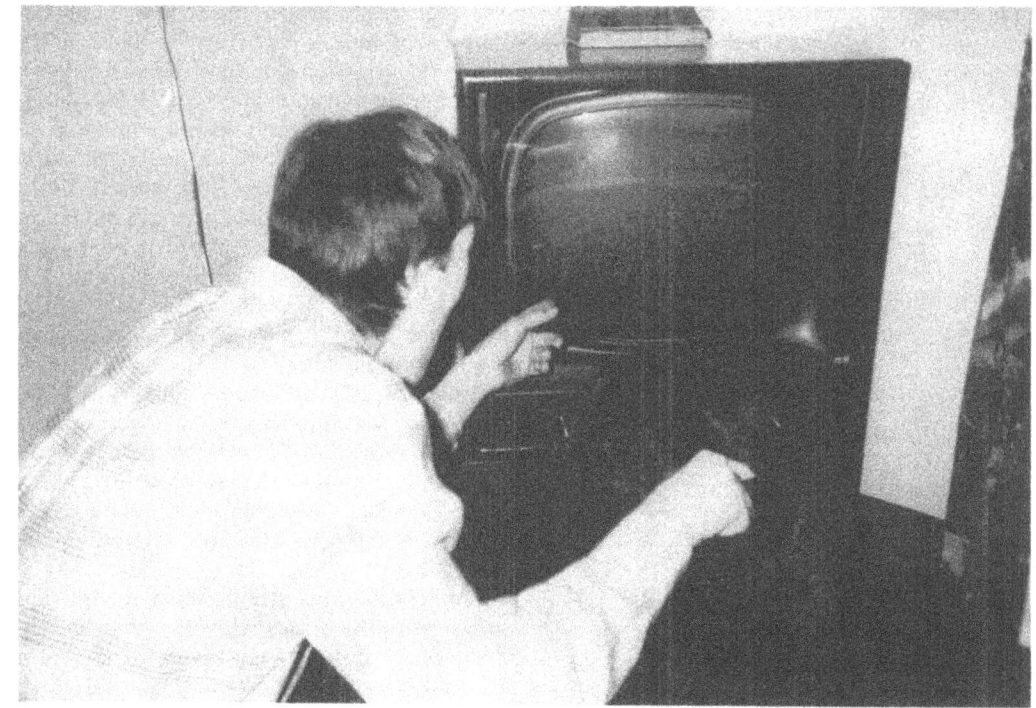

FIGURE 3.1
Television became the focal point of the living room in the 1950s. Courtesy Chris Dionisio.

33

According to broadcast historian J. Fred MacDonald, one media authority projected a decline in listenership to less than 15 percent.

Meanwhile, television was a boomtown, and wagonloads of talent arrived daily. Milton Berle, Sid Caesar, Kate Smith, Eddie Cantor, Jack Benny, Ed Wynne, Bob Hope, and Ed Sullivan were drawing legions of fans away from the medium that once had served as a stage for their considerable talents. Programs that once were the heart blood of network radio's evening lineup surfaced on television, often replete with the same actors, producers, writers, and announcers.

THE EARLY EYE

Early television production values were, if anything, crude. No lavishly produced visuals sprang from the small black and white screens encased in jukebox-sized cabinets. To the contrary, visuals were limited to the sets, scenery, and props of the variety found in the dusty storage lockers of community theater companies. In fact, 1950s television was little more than a proscenium arch with an electronic eye.

Adding to the sense of theater was the fact that broadcasts were invariably live. Sets collapsed, actors missed cues, and, on more than one occasion, products simply refused to work as millions watched on their home screens. One infamous on-camera calamity involved Betty Furness with a jammed refrigerator door which refused to open despite her persistent and embarrassed coaxing.

Commercials during the maiden days of television consisted primarily of announcers with hand-held scripts. Cue cards were used as well, and announcers often memorized copy so as to maintain eye contact with the camera.

In the early 1950s, commercials became more sophisticated. Announcers became somewhat less visible as the "voice-over" technique became more prevalent. Announcer voice-overs were delivered live as well as prerecorded onto film; videotape would not surface until the 1960s.

Voice-overs removed the announcer from the camera's eye, placing him into the "booth" or recording studio. Graphics and/or production footage supplanted the on-camera announcer when the voice-over approach was employed.

Meanwhile, on-camera announcers were expected to cultivate a certain look to satisfy the expectations of advertisers, who desired sleeker presentations. Television announcers became more cognizant of the importance of wardrobe, makeup, and movement.

RADIO REACTS

Technology gave radio a much needed boost in the early 1950s. An invention by Bell Laboratory scientists, called the "transistor," gave the medium a crucial shot in the arm. Transistors allowed for the miniaturization of radio receivers, which fostered greater mobility. Radio, unlike its bulky visual cousin, could be taken anywhere: the beach, the picnic, or the mountains. Radio was the all-occasion companion, and the medium wisely promoted that fact. Portable radios sold by the millions. There was a newfound interest in the ailing medium.

Programming reflected radio's utility. "WXXX, your constant companion"; "Wherever you go, 560 radio is by your side"; and "Whether at home, work, or play, the WXXX good guys keep you company," were representative of the slogans that embodied the new concept.

Prerecorded music, announcer chatter, and news, all with a local flavor, were the primary programming ingredients in the early 1950s. As stated earlier, the major networks had reduced the number of feeds to their

FIGURE 3.2
Today we take for granted the miniaturization of receivers.

affiliates due, in part, to the mass migration of programs and talent to television. This literally forced stations around the country to rely on their own resources to generate programming product. The age of the deejay was born.

The idea of radio programming consisting of recorded songs introduced by an announcer was not a unique concept. Two radio programs, *Make Believe Ballroom* and *Your Hit Parade* (dating back to the 1930s), employed the format.

Martin Block, host of *Make Believe Ballroom*, skillfully integrated recorded music with announcer discourse to create a blend especially resonant with the medium. Block's format provided the listener with the best of both worlds: hit music and interesting talk. (Actually, it was Los Angeles announcer Al Jarvis who originated the format in 1932, but it was Block who refined and popularized the concept.)

While the program approach proved very successful for many years, no one perceived it as the precursor to modern radio programming. Other enterprising broadcast voice performers, such as Bob Poole on New Orleans station WWL, emulated the format and found success as well.

LPs AND 45s

The innovation of long-playing albums (LPs), 33⅓ rpm recordings, was another bonus for radio programmers. They offered multiple selections per disk, better fidelity, and they significantly reduced the amount of storage space needed for the old 78 rpm disks.

The LPs generated record sales and listener interest. For stations concentrating on music, they were a windfall.

Another recording industry innovation, the 45 rpm single, would later serve as the primary source of music programming material for Top 40 radio stations.

The disk and the deejay became as inseparable as the stage and the actor. Without one, the other served little function.

SPECIALIZED PROGRAMMING

Although the transistor, LP, and 45 aided in the convalescence of radio, they alone did not effect a full recovery for the medium.

FIGURE 3.3
Martin Block, one of the first radio deejays. Courtesy WOR-AM.

Radio made its most significant forward motion when it adopted the "demographic" programming approach. Stations holding to a passe "all things to all people" programming philosophy found it hard going in a marketplace that had become increasingly competitive.

On the other hand, stations willing to focus on a specific segment of the listening audience discovered that they had a more viable product to offer advertisers. In other words, stations that could deliver listeners of a certain age group to an advertiser marketing to that particular demographic group were included in buys.

To accomplish this, stations had to specialize in a certain type of sound. For example, stations out to attract young people had to air popular, up-tempo music and deejays who reflected the mood and attitude prevalent among youth.

FIGURE 3.4
A 78 RPM photo disk (circa 1945), LP, and 45 RPM.

During the prerock era of radio specialization, the distinction between stations, except those offering country or classical music, was often less evident in the music than it was in the text and tone of the personalities. Big Band music, swing, jazz, and blues were popular among young people, but not alien to older adults. Stations often programmed a combination of several musical genres without disenfranchising anyone in particular. Rock 'n' roll music would precipitate the most profound audience fragmentation experienced by the medium.

THE TOP 40 DEEJAY

The era of format radio was legitimately launched with the introduction of Top 40 in 1954. As the story goes—one that has become legendary in the annals of radio programming history—two young programmers at KOWH-AM, Omaha, Nebraska, happened onto the idea of all-hit radio while imbibing at their favorite local tavern. At the end of a long and often frustrating day, Todd Storz and Bill Steward would commiserate about their station's poor ratings over an ale, as patrons of the bar played the same songs over and over on the jukebox.

At first neither took notice of this phenomenon, but one day it occurred to the two mirthless programmers that something unique was happening. Within minutes it also struck them that a possible solution to their woes had presented itself. What if the station based its playlist on the most popular songs of the moment, such as those repeatedly selected on the jukebox? This was the question to be put to a test.

Storz and Steward implemented the concept at their faltering station, and within weeks they topped their competition. Top 40 radio was officially born, as was true formula radio.

At the start, Top 40 playlists consisted chiefly of the highly orchestrated (big band) tunes and easy listening love ballads that sparked consumer interest. In 1954, the pop charts were the domain of artists like Rosemary Clooney, Tommy Dorsey, Harry James, Perry Como, Vaughn Monroe, The Mills Brothers, Les Paul and Mary Ford, Theresa Brewer, and Frank Sinatra.

By late 1955, the pop music charts and Top 40 stations had been infiltrated by a new form of music called "rock 'n' roll"—a term attributed to famed deejay Alan Freed. A metamorphosis of sorts soon took place. Top 40 playlists were dominated by rock singles, which were being scooped up by eager teens as fast as the record companies could press them. Clooney and Dorsey were being outpaced on the charts by Haley and Berry.

Among the most frequently played songs in the Fall of 1955 were those by rockers, such as Fats Domino ("Ain't That a Shame"), Chuck Berry ("Maybelline"), and Bill Haley and His Comets ("Burn That Candle").

Top 40 programmers, cognizant of their teen demographics, hired deejays who could relate in a manner most appealing to their young listeners. Chart hit deejays were the embodiment of energy and hipness, or at least came across that way. Rock 'n' Roll deejays sought to imitate the driving, throbbing, and pulsating rhythms of the songs they spun—rock jocks were the music incarnate.

The high-intensity, super cool deliveries of deejays like Murray the K, Bruce ("Cousin Brucie") Morrow, and Alan Freed became synonymous with Top 40. Young listeners tuned as much for their favorite deejays as they did for the latest recordings. Many rock 'n' roll station deejays achieved celebrity status as had the radio commentators of a previous generation of broadcast voice performers. When asked by audience surveyors what station they tuned, teens would often respond with the name of their favorite deejay: "The one with Cousin Brucie!"

As the 1950s moved toward an end, Top 40 stations were among the highest rated in the country, and the wild and zany deejays could claim a major role in this success story. Meanwhile, as Top 40 made its presence known in the radio marketplace, other formats did likewise.

NEW FORMULAS

Beautiful Music (BM), a format serving as a perfect counterpoint to the near manic sound of Top 40, arrived on the scene in 1959 at the coaxing of Gordon McLendon. Rather than scream, shout, and spin the hits, BM sought to sooth. "More relaxing music for the twilight hours on WYYY."

Obviously, stations employing this format strategy were not interested in the teen demographic stratum, but rather were intent on

FIGURE 3.5
Legendary pop-rock radio performer Cousin Brucie. Courtesy Bruce Morrow.

delivering the over-thirty crowd to advertisers, and this they succeeded in doing. Beautiful Music announcers did not operate under the gun, as did their counterparts in Top 40. Dead air was not viewed as a felony as it was by many Top 40 programmers. High-intensity deliveries were not compatible with the gentle orchestrations of Mantovani, Percy Faith, and Liberace. Thus announcers sought to match the flow and attitude of the music through their on-mic performances.

Deep voiced males dominated the airwaves at BM outlets. The sonorous baritone (or basso profundo) became the standard as program directors hired the type of voice they perceived as most complementary to the music, which consisted primarily of lush, full instrumentals and soft mood-inspiring vocals. The term "mood" was most closely associated with the format. The idea was to provide listeners with a shelter from the hectic pace common in other formats. The deep, often affected, delivery of BM announcers was consistent with this objective, at least from the perspective of programmers.

Over the years that followed the introduction of the format, announcers were often accused of sounding stilted and mechanical. Yet for almost two decades the BM announcing style would remain basically unchanged. In the late 1970s, as the consequence of format revitalization and updating, the bassy-voiced ideal gave way to the natural conversational style delivery.

The number of formats available to listeners tripled in the years between the inception of Top 40 and 1960. Specialization had paid off and radio was thriving despite television's continued success. The fact is, both mediums had found their comfortable niche.

Stations airing Middle of the Road (MOR), Top 40, BM, News, Talk, Country, and Classical were common in mid-size and large markets. Due to its broad base appeal, MOR remained the most prominent format in small markets.

FM EVOLVES

Meanwhile, as AM radio enjoyed the fruits of its realignment, FM remained in the shadows. Despite the fact that it had been on the scene since television's debut, audience interest verged on apathetic. Progress was uninspired, to say the least. The prevailing sentiment was, "Who needs another radio band?" Consumers were busy purchasing television sets and discovering the new formats on AM. FM was just not a priority to most Americans.

What further deterred FM's wider acceptance was its eclectic programming, which primarily resided within a cultural vein. That is, classical and fine arts programming were synonymous with FM in the 1950s and 1960s. Jazz, folk music, and educational features also filled the FM broadcast schedule.

Early FM voice performers brought to the airwaves their own distinctive sound. If BM announcers could be stereotyped as "voicey" and Top 40 as "hyper," then FM announcers could be described as "haughty." What fostered this image was the attitude that FM was the more culturally sophisticated, astute, and refined band—the "alternative." FM was the band listeners could tune to escape the banal excesses of pop culture so plentiful on AM. FM also offered better sound fidelity—music without static.

FM's competitive edge was sharpened in 1961 when the FCC approved stereophonic broadcasting. With its broader channels, FM was perfectly suited for side-banding or channel separation, wherein the incoming radio signal is fed to a left and right speaker for fuller, truer sound reproduction.

FM receiver sales increased as the listening audience became more interested in better sound. Stereo component systems became the hot "in" item to own, and stereo recordings began to supplant monaural.

Initially, stereo audio attracted fans of so-called "serious" music (classical), and recording companies responded. Cognizant of this, many FM stations featuring classical music adopted the new audio processing system. The format drew audiophiles with different musical preferences as well.

FM's reputation for superior sound fidelity grew significantly, although its audience increased only moderately. Nonetheless, strides were being made. However, employment for announcers on FM remained nominal.

In the year following the approval of FM stereo, 1962, the Commission imposed a partial freeze on AM station construction. Due to the hectic growth of AM, which brought with it interference problems, the FCC felt compelled to call a time out for an assessment of the situation. This resulted in refocusing attention on FM.

While the AM band had reached the saturation level, FM was still wide open. In effect, the FCC's action brought about an increase in FM frequency applications. Meanwhile, the most important legislation to impact the fate of FM was yet to come.

THE SEPARATION

Concluding that broadcasters holding combination (AM/FM) licenses were doing little to provide audiences with unduplicated programming, the FCC imposed a remedy in the mid-1960s. An AM and FM licensee in a market with a population of more than 100 thousand was required to originate separate programming 50 percent of its broadcast day. This was a landmark decision in the progress of FM stations, since 65 percent were tied to AM outlets.

To offset the expense of a separate on-air operation that would have required additional announcers, equipment, and substantial programming material, many combo stations resorted to the use of automation.

Because of its "more-music, less-talk" programming approach, the format most suited for automation was Beautiful Music. Thus, a considerable number of combo stations found themselves offering automated "good" music on their FMs.

Broadcasters expected little yield from these operations, hoping in many instances to simply break even until FM found its audience. To the surprise of many, this did not take long. Beautiful Music in FM stereo proved a winner. Within a couple of years, many FM frequencies out-performed their AM counterparts in the ratings. Beautiful Music was FM's first real commercial success in that it drew larger numbers than any other type of programming previously offered.

VOICES IN THE VORTEX

The 1960s was a decade like no other, and the country would be changed forever by its extraordinary events. Through it all the electronic media and its performers would play a unique role.

Television technology made world events much more immediate and vivid. Videotape recorders gradually replaced the conventional film and kinescope equipment and brought instant replay into the living room.

While technical innovations and expanded news capability enhanced television's appeal, they also made the terrible more obvious.

No American who ever sat through the Kennedy and Oswald assassinations can erase the imprint of the odious images that were endlessly replayed over a three-day period in November 1963. Nor can anyone forget the grief-stricken, incredulous expressions on the faces of network newsmen Chet Huntley and Walter Cronkite, who delivered the tragic news.

In 1965, another bizarre event of a much less tragic nature proved the indispensability of the battery-powered radio. As commuters headed home throughout the Northeast, a massive power failure occurred, leaving the most densely populated part of the country in the dark.

Radio station WBZ-AM in Boston was one of several major outlets that fired up an emergency generator in order to continue broadcasting. The station's talk show host, Bob Kennedy, began to report the event, as well as to provide confused and frightened listeners with crucial and, in some cases, life-sustaining advice. Throughout the ordeal Kennedy was a beacon of reason and calm to thousands with portable and car radios.

The blackout proved beyond any doubt radio's value in an age enthralled by the video image. It was one of radio's finest hours, as well as Bob Kennedy's, who received national acclaim and recognition for his superb performance.

FIGURE 3.6
President Kennedy's motorcade moments before the fatal shots. Courtesy Harry L. Kreshpane.

The latter half of the decade proved to be one of the most turbulent periods in the annals of U.S. history, and the TV camera and radio mic covered it all. The nation had barely regained its footing after the loss of a President when the tide of social upheaval swept in.

Under the leadership of Dr. Martin Luther King, Jr., the civil rights movement was at full throttle. Across the United States consciences were being jarred by the issue of racial equality. Massive nonviolent protests took place in nearly every major city, and the evening newscasts were chock-a-block full with details.

As 1967 approached, the nation was caught in the grips of yet another movement, this one in protest of military involvement in Vietnam. Stormy protests involving thousands of antiwar advocates were the subject of talk shows, newscasts, commentaries, and documentaries. The conflict became known as the "living room war," and scenes of bloody battles and reports of body counts accosted viewers nightly.

Drug use, in its multifarious forms, became a cultural preoccupation and another hot topic for broadcasters. Drug disciples, such as Timothy Leary, promoted the use of LSD and marijuana, much to the consternation of the authorities. Mind-altering drugs became the succor and inspiration of a subculture. Hippies and flower children roamed the city streets espousing the virtues of peace and "free" love.

The social and cultural ferment was heightened further by more assassinations. At the start of 1968, Dr. King was shot as he stood on the balcony of a Memphis hotel. Footage of the civil rights leader on the balcony moments before he was gunned down was aired countless times during the ensuing days, as was film of several U.S. cities ablaze as enraged blacks vented their pain and anger.

Viewers also witnessed a young senator and presidential hopeful, Robert Kennedy, consoling grieving blacks during the hours that followed the assassination. No one could have realized that he, too, would fall victim to an assassin's malice.

Most of the country awoke to the awful news that Robert Kennedy had been killed. Solemn voices and grim visages greeted the unknowing multitudes. Television and film cameras had captured the fallen senator as he lay paralyzed, eyes locked in a frozen stare, near death.

To many viewers it all seemed like a horrible case of déjà vu, as the same network reporters who had been present at President Kennedy's death eulogized his sibling. Radio and television reporters relaxed little during those harrowing days. The 1970s had to be better.

INTO THE 1970s

While the social and cultural upheaval of the 1960s provided unlimited text for the broadcast press, other programming genres drew audiences. On the FM side a significant departure from the conventional and formulated evolved—Progressive radio. Its existence was, in fact, a reaction to the prosaic programming formulas, in particular Top 40, that were dominant.

What Progressive radio sought to do was provide listeners a true alternative to the frenzied, ultrapop sound of hit radio. Music playlists were not drawn from the charts. In fact, initially, music programming was presented in a block fashion. That is, no primary format was featured. A typical broadcast day often included segments of jazz, folk, rhythm and blues, and so on.

Progressive deejays did not scream at listeners. They did not talk at an accelerated pace, but rather communicated in a low-key, conversational manner. The idea was to communicate on a super-casual, one-on-one level unusual for the times. It is perhaps inaccurate to refer to Progressive voice performers of the period as deejays, since the traditional concept of deejaying was antithetical to the philosophy espoused by the format. Progressive programming was distinctive. It did not fit neatly into the mold shaped by the previous generation of radio programmers, and not fitting in was its aim.

The Progressive brand of radio would impact nearly all subsequent programming approaches, however, and would help FM shake off the staid and parochial image that had stigmatized it.

Within a couple years of its 1966 introduction on New York station WOR, the Progressive format (or the majority of stations working the formula) had evolved into rock-based music outlets, known variously as Acid and Psychedelic. The progeny of Progressive, Acid rockers concentrated on airing music most allied with the drug movement.

The music on these stations was characterized by harsh, decibel-devouring guitar riffs by such notables as Jimi Hendrix. Acid rock stations, like Progressive, avoided the mainstream music charts as well as high-intensity deejays. If anything, Acid rock jocks served as direct counterpoint to pop-chart deejays. Whereas Top 40 deejays were the very symbols of hype and contrivance, Acid voice performers stood as models of calm and candor. So modulated were their deliveries that many listeners got the impression that they were as sedated (stoned or high) as the artists whose disks they spun.

Meanwhile, as radio deejaying styles became more diverse, television's introduction of the portable camera for taped and live on-the-scene reports fostered a demand for broadcast voice performers, namely news reporters. Television news departments swelled as technology enhanced its ability to cover stories with greater speed and efficiency. Concomitantly, viewership grew as the result of the improved service.

At the beginning of the 1970s, all electronic media appeared hale and hardy. Television was the established leader in home entertainment. AM radio had fully recovered from the effects of the video medium, and FM was making significant strides. By the end of the decade the fortunes of each would undergo a change.

SHIFTING BANDS

Top 40, MOR, Talk, and Country were the radio formats attracting the greatest number of listeners to AM in 1970. Beautiful Music, Album rock, and Classical drew solid audiences to the FM band, but AM still boasted the majority of listeners, most of whom tuned for music. The difference between AM and FM announcing styles remained one of intensity. Generally speaking, AM aired "wired" jocks, while FM offered "laid-back" ones.

A turning point in the evolution of FM occurred early in the 1970s when Top 40 was introduced on the band. Gradually, hit-chart listeners made the conversion to FM in order to hear the most popular songs. This effectively opened the flood gates. By 1975, FM offered every music format found on AM. Listeners were forsaking AM and tuning to FM in huge numbers because of its superior fidelity.

As a consequence of FM's embracing the mainstream formats, little distinction remained between the announcing styles found on the two bands. FM, too, had its high-intensity, super-charged jocks.

FM became the preferred radio medium in 1978, when a survey revealed that 51 percent of the listening audience tuned it. FM's ascent and AM's decline would continue into the 1980s. Today, approximately eight out of ten listeners are claimed by FM.

To counteract this trend, many AM stations have gone stereo in the hopes of reclaiming some music listeners. However, as of this writing, talk and information programming are most prominent on AM.

In the 1980s, cable converters had replaced the conventional television set tuning knob in one third of U.S. homes. The network's share of the viewing audience pie has shrunk from over 95 percent to less than 75 percent in the past half decade, according to some surveys.

Over sixty-five hundred cable systems make expanded video viewing options available to most Americans. Although the rise of the cable medium has altered television viewing habits, broadcast voice performing opportunities have not been significantly affected. That is to say, cable has not deepened the job pool to any great degree.

Unlike broadcast television, cable does not, as a general rule, hire booth or staff announcers. However, larger cable systems (those with many subscribers) often originate news and live on-camera reports; thus, cable has created some entry-level opportunities for voice performers.

SUGGESTED FURTHER READING

Bittner, John R. *Broadcasting and Telecommunications*, 2nd ed. Englewood Cliffs, N.J.: Prentice-Hall, 1985.
Busby, Linda, and Parker, Donald. *The Art and Science of Radio*. Boston: Allyn and Bacon, 1984.
Chapple, Steve, and Garofalo, R. *Rock 'n' Roll Is Here To Pay*. Chicago: Nelson-Hall, 1977.
Delong, Thomas A. *The Mighty Music Box*. Los Angeles: Amber Crest Books, 1980.

Lichty, Lawrence W, and Topping, M.C. *American Broadcasting: A Source Book on the History of Radio and Television.* New York: Hastings House, 1975.

Lujack, Larry, and Jedlicka, D.A. *Superjock: The Loud, Frantic, Non-Stop World of Rock Radio Deejays.* Chicago: Regnery, 1975.

MacFarland, David T. *The Development of the Top 40 Format.* New York: Arno Press, 1979.

Morrow, Bruce. *Cousin Brucie.* New York: William Morrow, 1987.

Passman, Arnold. *The Deejays.* New York: Macmillan, 1971.

Sklar, Rick. *Rocking America: How the All-Hit Radio Stations Took Over.* New York: St. Martin's Press, 1984.

4 ANNOUNCING IN FORMAT RADIO

FITTING THE FORMAT

Radio announcing styles vary according to station format. Why? Well, certain radio stations choose to soothe and relax their listeners; thus a high-powered announcing style would be inappropriate. Meanwhile, other stations aim to keep their listeners in a perpetual state of excitement. Therefore, an ultra-laid-back delivery would be out of context. The simple fact is radio formats possess their own unique personalities, and these personalities are reflected in deejay presentation.

In the 1980s and 1990s, dozens of radio formats (perhaps over 100 when all the subformat variations are counted) vie for the listening public. Narrowcasting and specialization produce diverse programming. There is something for nearly everybody. For instance, a fan who enjoys the very latest in country music is targeted by stations employing the Contemporary Country format, whereas the country music fan who prefers older standards would find sounds to her liking on a Traditional Country station. The Country format alone offers several programming variations, and each presents its own special approach to announcing. (More on Country format voice performance criteria later in this chapter.)

Let it suffice to say, the majority of formats offer permutations within the context of the product they offer. For example, there are "primary" formats, such as Country, Adult Contemporary, Easy Listening, and nearly all have "subcategories," like Country Hits, Lite Adult, Contemporary Easy, and so on. There also is a category of formats that may be called "specialty," under which would fall ethnic and religious stations, among others.

Several hundred radio stations devote themselves to programming of a religious nature, while an equal number broadcast in a foreign language. A couple dozen stations air programming designed for the exclusive consumption of American Indians.

The role of the broadcast voice performer is affected by format at most stations. Market size also has an impact on announcing presentation. For example, an Adult Contemporary (AC) station in a small town opts for heavy announcer presence to instill in its listeners a community involvement and good-neighbor image. This requires that announcers play a greater role on-air, due to the heavy volume of announcements and patter such a strategy imposes. Meanwhile, a major market AC decides to reduce deejay presence to convey a more music-oriented image. It assumes this position on the basis of its competition. Two other ACs work the local airwaves, and both program more chatter.

DEGREES OF ANNOUNCER PROMINENCE

One of three approaches to announcer on-air involvement is generally evident at stations. The approaches employed can be listed as (1) personality, (2) program (music) host, and (3) staff announcer. The first elevates its voices to celebrity status. At stations taking the "personality" approach, air people "are" the product. That is to say, they are a primary element of programming. These supernovas of the air are most prevalent during morning drive-time.

Humor and wit are the qualities most attributed to these voice performers. Morning personalities are the ratings getters and income generators, as is the case with luminaries such as Howard Stern, Rick Dees, Dave Maynard, Larry Lujack, Don Imus, and dozens of other ratings monarchs. They set the tone and tenor for the broadcast day and are accorded star status with six- and even seven-figure salaries and perks such as limousine service.

Morning personalities generally are the longest on experience at the station. In major markets they average a minimum of ten years before the microphone.

The most widely employed approach to announcer presentation in radio follows a somewhat lower profile path. While some personalities are given considerable latitude in the presentation of their shows, the majority of voice performers serve as extensions of the format. "Program hosts" are a part, an ingredient, of the program and not the program itself.

While program hosts convey personality, they do so strictly within the context of the station's overall sound and image. The vast group of radio voice performers adhere to a more rigidly defined set of rules pertaining to on-air discourse. Program or music deejays bridge the space or breaks between musical selections. They maintain the flow between programming elements. Ad-libs and humor are often a part of their repertoire, but economy is the operative term. "Say what you have to say, and get off," is the rule.

Program hosts often have name value, but not to the extent of their personality brethren. Few listeners tune into a station because a certain program or music jock is on. The contrary is true of the personality, who often is the main drawing card at a station.

The last category consists of "staff announcers." This group of radio voice performers is the least visible and seldom enjoys name recognition. Stations taking this approach deliberately deemphasize announcer presence to foster a more-music impression among listeners. Here the voice performer is viewed as secondary to music programming.

Staff announcers back-announce lengthy sweeps of music, read promo and liner cards, and provide brief informational statements, usually pertaining to the weather, temperature, and time. Many stations using this method are automated or satellite driven, and announcers are referred to as "op-assists" (operator) or "live-assists." The staff announcer at such stations is also responsible for operating the automation equipment. Ad-libbing and extemporaneous remarks or chatter are rare and are usually not expected of the staff announcer.

As this chapter looks at the ways certain formats affect announcing styles, the preceding approaches will be examined more fully. What follows is an assessment of the announcing criteria in several of today's most widely aired radio formats.

FIGURE 4.1A and B Adult Contemporary radio promotional pieces. Courtesy WMJX and W-Lite.

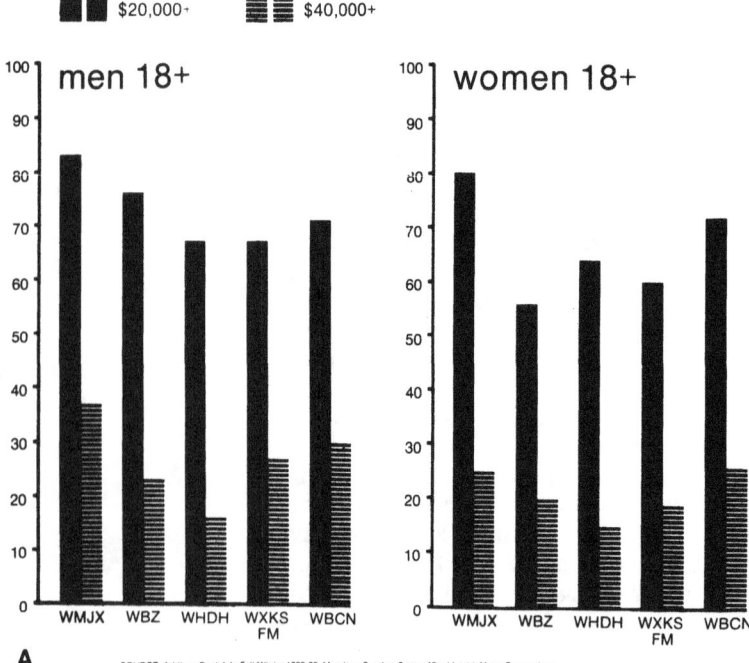

ADULT CONTEMPORARY

The Adult Contemporary format is the most frequently tuned in the United States. Nearly one out of every four radios are dialed to some form of AC programming. Adult Contemporary has been variously referred to as lite rock, soft rock, easy hits, and hot adult. While AC stations focus on today's music, they deliberately steer a course away from hard rock.

FIGURE 4.1 Continued

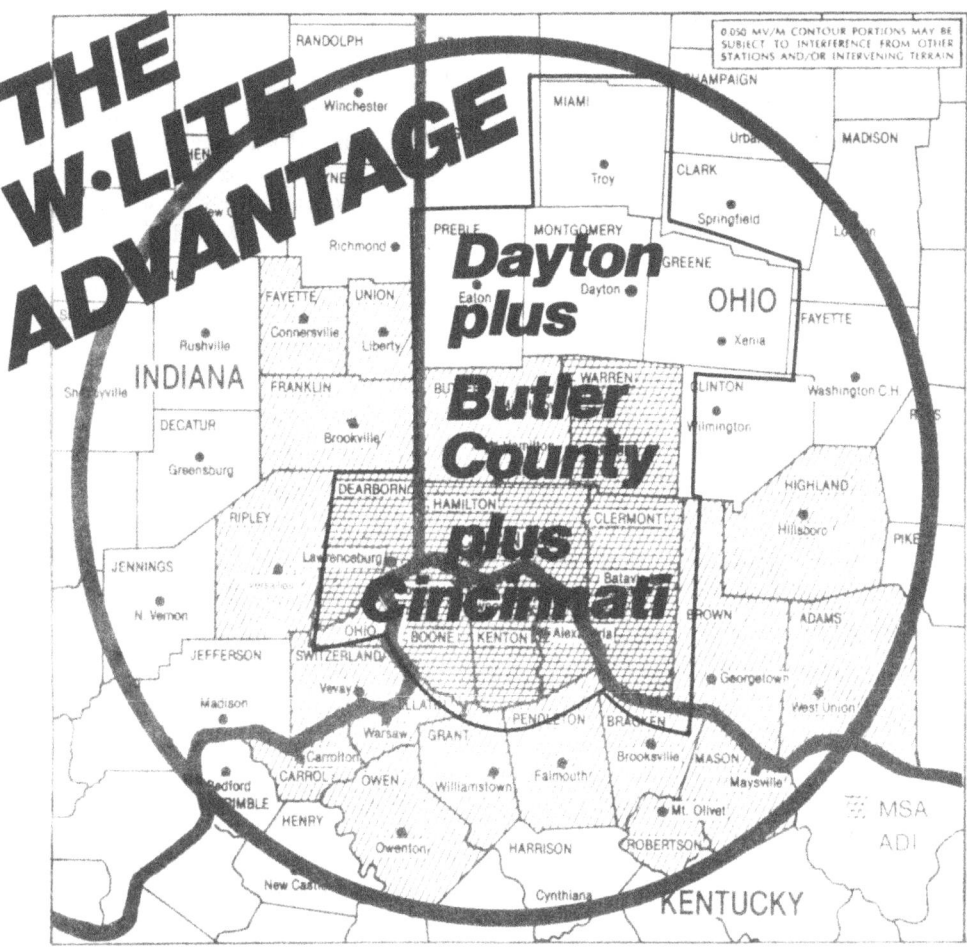

You already know that W•Lite is an excellent advertising vehicle for reaching Cincinnati adults 18-49, particularly women 25-49.

But, you may not know that because of W•Lite's unique tower location, a strong signal is broadcast into Dayton and surrounding areas. In fact, W•Lite is one of the most listened-to NON-Dayton radio stations in Dayton's Arbitron defined Metro Survey Area!

The W•Lite signal, covering both Cincinnati and Dayton, gives you "The W•Lite Advantage". Look what happens when the populations of the Cincinnati and Dayton MSA, plus the population of Butler County, are added! The combined population is greater than the nation's 13th largest radio market!

As a retailer with locations in Cincinnati and Dayton, or in between, you can benefit from "The W•Lite Advantage!"

CINCINNATI MSA 12+	1,155,600	#27 Population Rank
DAYTON MSA 12+	680,100	#48 Population Rank
BUTLER COUNTY 12+	214,878	
TOTAL POPULATION	2,050,578	Greater than #13! (St. Louis)

B

The age demographic pursued by AC stations is typically 24 to 39; however, many can boast more listeners at either end of the spectrum depending on how they skew their playlists and presentations. For example, a hot AC programming more up-tempo chart hits would attract a younger following than one airing mellower sounds.

Adult Contemporary is a music-intensive format. Music-heavy ACs present music in sweeps (blocks), wherein three to four music selections are followed by clusters (spot sets) of commercial announcements. The announcer involvement is obviously lower when music is the priority.

A substantial number of ACs are automated, thus announcers assume a support (live-assist) status rather than a primary on-mic role. In this case, live copy is rare.

One third of the radio stations airing AC emphasize news, information, and personality, as well as music. These stations are referred to as full-service ACs. Broadcast voice performers are accorded more airtime at full-service outlets, regardless of format. There are full-service Easy Listening, AC, Country, and Oldies stations, to name a few. At full-service operations, live copy delivery is often the rule rather than the exception.

Announcing Criteria

The one-on-one conversational delivery tops the list of announcing styles in AC, according to J. Carroll Buckley, Program Director, KXO-AM/FM, El Centro, California. "The ability to communicate on a personal, one-to-one basis is really central to our presentation and to this format wherever it is found."

Adult Contemporary programmer Stan Steel concurs. "You have to come across as accessible, not aloof. Actually, I look for

FIGURE 4.2A and B Sixty-second Adult Contemporary commercial copy. Courtesy WJR and KXO.

WJR AM RADIO 76
Stands for Detroit

2100 FISHER BUILDING
DETROIT, MI 48202

L-3953

CLIENT: NEVADA BOB'S
LENGTH: :60
EFF:

IT MAY NOT BE EASY TO TRADE IN YOUR GOLF GAME ON A NEW ONE, BUT HERE'S THE NEXT BEST THING...NEVADA BOB'S, THE WORLD'S LARGEST DISCOUNT GOLF STORE CELEBRATES TRADE-IN DAYS.

:10 — <u>TODAY'S THE FINAL</u> DAY TO TRADE IN YOUR OLD GOLF EQUIPMENT FOR GREAT SAVINGS ON BRAND NEW EQUIPMENT. ITEMS TAKEN IN TRADE WILL BE DONATED TO THE POLICE ATHLETIC LEAGUE'S PROGRAM TO HELP KIDS THIS SUMMER. THROUGHT THIS WEEKEND, TRADE IN YOUR OLD MATCHING SET OF GOLF CLUBS AND RECEIVE A BIG, 50-DOLLAR TRADE-IN ON A NEW SET! GOLF BAG SHOWING

:30 — ITS AGE?? TRADE IT IN AND GET 15-DOLLARS OFF ON A NEW ONE. PUTTER LETTING YOU DOWN? TRADE IT, AND GET FIVE DOLLARS TOWARD A NEW ONE. THOSE TIRED OLD GOLF SHOES, TOO, WILL FETCH TEN DOLLARS ON A NEW PAIR. BRING IN YOUR OLD GOLF BALLS. A DOZEN WILL BE WORTH TWO DOLLARS ON EACH NEW DOZEN YOU BUY. THEY'LL EVEN LET YOU HAVE ONE DOLLAR OFF, WHEN YOU TRADE IN YOUR OLD GLOVE ON A NEW ONE. SAVE MORE ON ALREADY DISCOUNTED PRICES DURING NEVADA BOB'S TRADE-IN DAYS, AND HELP PAL HELP KIDS. THEY'RE TRADIN'NOW AT NEVADA BOB'S, CORNER OF FORD AND TELEGRAPH IN DEARBORN...5TH AND MAIN IN ROYAL OAK...AND VAN DYKE AT 18 MILE IN STERLING HEIGHTS.

:60 —

A

FIGURE 4.2 Continued

KXO — EL CENTRO, CALIFORNIA

COPY

CLIENT: IMPERIAL STORES
LENGTH: 60 SECONDS
DATE:
REMARKS: INTEREST SALE #1

1. DOUBLE BARRELLED SAVINGS CONTINUE AT THE IMPERIAL FURNITURE
2. STORE, 945 NORTH IMPERIAL AVENUE, IN EL CENTRO. EVERYTHING
3. IN THE STORE IS REDUCED 10 TO 40%....AND IMPERIAL FURNITURE
4. WILL DEDUCT ALL INTEREST CHARGES FOR ONE FULL YEAR FROM ALL
5. HOME FURNISHINGS PURCHASES. YOU SAVE 2 WAYS...BECAUSE EVERYTHING
6. IN THE STORE IS ON SALE AND FOR THE FIRST TIME EVER, IMPERIAL
7. FURNITURE WILL DEDUCT AN AMOUNT EQUAL TO THE INTEREST CHARGES
8. FOR ONE FULL YEAR BASED ON A 12 MONTH CONTRACT...THE SAME
9. AMOUNT WILL ALSO BE DEDUCTED FROM ANY CASH PURCHASES....BUT
10. HURRY...THE SALE ENDS SUNDAY. HERE'S AN EXAMPLE OF THE SAVINGS.
11. A STYLISH, 5-PIECE OAK DINETTE SET WITH CANE BACK CHAIRS,
12. REGULARLY $599.00...NOW $399...PLUS, SAVE ONE FULL YEARS
13. INTEREST. IMPERIAL'S "INTEREST DEDUCTION PLAN" APPLIES TO
14. HOME FURNISHINGS PURCHASES OF $299 OR MORE, WITH NORMAL
15. DOWN PAYMENT AND APPROVED CREDIT...AT THE IMPERIAL FURNITURE
16. STORE, 945 NORTH IMPERIAL AVENUE, IN EL CENTRO. HURRY,
17. THIS SALE ENDS SUNDAY.
18.
19.
20.

This announcement was broadcast____times, as entered in the station's program log. The times this announcement was broadcast were billed to this station's client on our invoice(s) dated _____ at his earned rate of:

$____each for____announcements, for a total of $____
$____each for____announcements, for a total of $____
$____each for____announcements, for a total of $____

Signature of station official

(Notarize above)   Typed name and title   Station

B

communicators who are Renaissance men and women, with positive outlooks. I try to avoid placing announcers with extremely biased outlooks, since so much of the AC formats at the stations I program are made up of opinion, talk, and the processing and relaying of information. I want announcers to encourage progress in civilization, not regression."

Since the format's approach is fashioned to appeal to adults, maturity is a key ingredient, contends Jim Barrett, Assistant Program Director, WJR-AM, Detroit, Michigan. "By 'maturity' I don't mean announcers have to be older, just more mature sounding than those on CHR and AOR stations. Our listeners are generally 35 plus. You have to be able to relate to them in a manner they would find interesting and pertinent. Our listeners are also used to 'personality' radio. This is not a music-intensive station. It requires more work and research to give the audience what we provide. I think we invest more heavily than do some other stations, but that is our decision."

Doc Kirby, Program Director, WTBF-AM, Troy, Alabama, believes, as does Barrett, that a mature announcer style is important to the format. "We reach the adult listener, so we can't be silly or adolescent on the air. Our deejays must possess a willingness to enjoy music older than they are sometimes. We have a young on-air staff. An understanding of AC listener's lifestyles is essential, too. In other words, announcers must know who they're speaking to. They must actually care about listeners, all of them, not just the ones like themselves."

Due to the sophistication of the AC audience, KXO's Buckley perceives strong language skills as vital. "Our broadcast voice performers must possess a good command of the language and must be well read in a wide range of subjects. I have found it to be axiomatic that good readers are good communicators, and that is what we look for in announcers."

Basic verbal skills, such as pronunciation, diction, and articulation rank high, says Kirby. "Proper pronunciation and accurate articulation are important to on-air credibility. When a listener hears something mispronounced or slurred, she feels cheated. That is, she thinks she's getting an amateur. Clients are especially intolerant of bad pronunciation."

KXO's Buckley agrees: "A deejay should not open the mic until he or she is absolutely sure of the way a particular word is correctly said."

WJR's Barrett observes that the lack of these essentials will keep a person off the air in a big market. "You don't break into the majors with a weak performance. Announcers at this station have a good command of the English language. They must be easily understood."

Accents are nearly always perceived as negatives to on-air performance. "Regional accents are a distraction to the listener and generally unappealing," notes Kirby.

Dialects suggest inexperience, contends Stan Steel. "Listeners are accustomed to polish, and a regional dialect sounds unrefined and even a bit crude. Furthermore, accents often cut down on listener comprehension."

Voice quality is a factor when WJR's Barrett hires. "An announcer must have a pleasant voice, okay. That's basic. The timber and texture has to be right. A good, naturally resonant voice is most appealing to the ear." Kirby agrees, adding, "The quality of the voice is certainly a primary consideration. A shrill, cacophonous voice doesn't belong on the radio. On the other hand, the ultrabassy voice is not the only one that is effective on the air."

According to programming consultant Jay Williams, the ability to concentrate is vital to solid on-air presentation. "A radio station control room can get pretty crazy at times, what with sales people, traffic and copy people, and other announcers coming in and out, not to mention the occasional equipment problem that harkens the engineer. Distractions are a part of the game, so the ability to concentrate keeps you from sounding flustered and uncentered on the air."

As in any other profession, practice makes the difference, says Steel. "A good performer knows what is happening around her. The control room should feel like your own backyard for starters. Confusion and uncertainty are revealed quickly. The mic seldom lies. Copy should also feel familiar. A good habit is to go through the copy book before each shift and become acquainted and reacquainted with all the commercials it contains. Practice reading copy aloud before actual on-mic delivery. It's just unprofessional to air copy cold."

WTBF's Kirby subscribes to the same thinking. "Preparation is extremely necessary no matter how experienced you are. Establishing good habits from the start accelerates development. By good habits I'm talking about preparation. Plan and rehearse before going on. Don't stop practicing once you leave the station. For instance, continue to work on the voice to develop better control, range, and power. Read, read, read—not just copy, but billboards along the highway, signs, magazine advertisements, movie theater marquees. You get the idea. This is the way to improve. Airchecking or taping yourself keeps you informed of bad habits, too."

The benefits to be derived from self-critiquing are manifold. As far back as radio's golden era, would-be announcers have been advised to listen to themselves. In *Effective Radio Speaking* (New York: McGraw-Hill), Ralph L. Rogers recommends that announcers assess their performances by airchecking themselves. "To hear one's own voice work is worth many critical suggestions on the part of others. All radio speakers should use recordings of their broadcasts to improve their work." The book was published in 1944.

Complacency is the enemy of broadcast voice performers, believes Stan Steel. "Air people should constantly strive for excellence. Don't become satisfied. Aircheck yourself. Listen to yourself objectively, and seek out other opinions. Success involves the pursuit of excellence."

Self-evaluation is a defense against weaknesses, says WJR's Barrett. "It takes a while to develop a style that is natural and comfortable. It's good to find out what your weaknesses are and work on them. Work is the remedy. We all have a tendency to want to do what we do best and avoid the problem areas. I would recommend that the first thing an aspiring announcer do is work on how to be 'himself.' It's my experience that this is one of the toughest things to do."

In the things to avoid department, KXO's Buckley suggests not using slang and bad grammar. "The latter is bad in all formats, but slang really doesn't fit in adult formats such as ours."

Clichés are also unwelcome, notes Barrett. "Worn out clichés and repetitiveness turn off listeners. There is no need to do breaks the same way all the time. There are a variety of ways to do the weather, call letters, time, and so on." Barrett also cautions against the use of crutches. " 'Umms' and 'ahhs' can also be very distracting if they occur often. How many times have you heard someone say 'you know' without being aware of doing so? Things like that are insidious. They creep into conversation undetected, but the listener hears them. Believe me." Steel agrees, saying, "Word whiskers like 'uh' to fill time are irritating to listeners. 'Wallpapering' or excessive use of words or phrases like 'the temperature is currently 76 degrees on the outside' instead of simply stating 'it's 76 degrees,' create clutter."

Steel also warns against giving misinformation. "Giving incorrect information as fact, like saying it's 76 degrees when it's actually 82 degrees, goes against industry ethics. The announcer should always aim for accuracy, even if it means inconveniencing himself. If you know the thermometer is off, go to another source. Don't just guess."

WTBF's Kirby says beware of apathy. "Not really caring about the listener is the quickest way to lose listeners. Never be rude, impatient, or indifferent. The listener is what keeps the station in the black. Granted, long on-air hours can take their toll, but never short change the audience. Stay motivated. You work better and come across better when you are 'up'."

The unnatural manipulation of the voice makes the 'don't' list. "I can't stand hyped-up voices! It's great to have an upbeat style, but not if it's unnatural. Contriving a deeper voice is equally unappealing. Announcers shouldn't lower their voices unnaturally. Making the most of what you have will bring out the qualities that will provide success," says WJR's Barrett, and KXO's Buckley agrees. "I'm opposed to a contrived or phoney delivery. Announcers who speak too fast or too slow for effect strike me as bush league. The natural pace and rhythm of conversation works best. Running off at the mouth generally decreases understandability. Enunciation suffers. Word endings are lost, and words overlap and intersect."

As a rule, programmers warn announcers against allowing their egos too much rein. "An overactive or swollen ego can get in the way of a good performance and can alienate listeners and colleagues alike. My best advice to any broadcast voice performer is to keep perspective and not get swept away by the feeling of inflated self worth. The listener is the person who matters most," offers Kirby.

KXO's Buckley sums up this section on AC announcing criteria: "Again, keep in mind that this is an adult format, so an intelligent, mature sound is basic. Moreover, the style of delivery most appropriate is the conversational, one-on-one. Shouting and jive talk are qualities indigenous to other formats, not Adult Contemp."

CONTEMPORARY HIT RADIO

No format is as chart conscious as Contemporary Hit Radio (CHR). As mentioned in an earlier chapter, CHR was founded on the supposition that airing the best selling songs would attract a large audience. At its inception, hit song radio was called Top 40 and was originated by Todd Storz and Bill Stewart and later refined by programmers such as Gordon McLendon, Bill Drake, Mike Joseph, and Rick Sklar. New pop songs are the bread and butter of CHR outlets.

Many CHR stations confine their playlists to fewer than fifty titles, whereas others allow for older chart-toppers dating back a few years. Rarely do strict CHRs dig back into the music bins more than five years. These are stations focused on what is hot in music "now." Consequently, their audience is the youngest tuned to radio.

Although CHRs claim a much broader demographic group (18 to 34 years), their prime following usually falls within the 14- to 21-year-old age range. This, of course, affects the style of on-air delivery. Energy characterizes CHRs better than any other term. The objective is to keep things going at an exciting, if not breakneck, pace around the clock. Upbeat deejays, hot promotions, and super-charged jingles give the sound an intense and vital quality.

Up to the late 1970s, CHR was a big winner for AM stations. Since then the format has taken up residence on the FM side of the street, and only a relatively small percentage of AM outlets offer chart hits. According to *Radio and Records*, CHR was the second most listened to format in the United States in 1986, with nearly 18 percent of the radio audience. A slight decline in these figures was noted the following year as formats such as Classic Hits, Urban Contemporary, and Album-Oriented Rock made strides.

The original formula format, CHR adheres as closely today to a programming schematic. Hot clocks outlining the music hierarchy, the order in which songs are aired, are traditional. Of all formats, CHR is the least inclined to air lengthy sweeps of uninterrupted music. It is more commonplace for

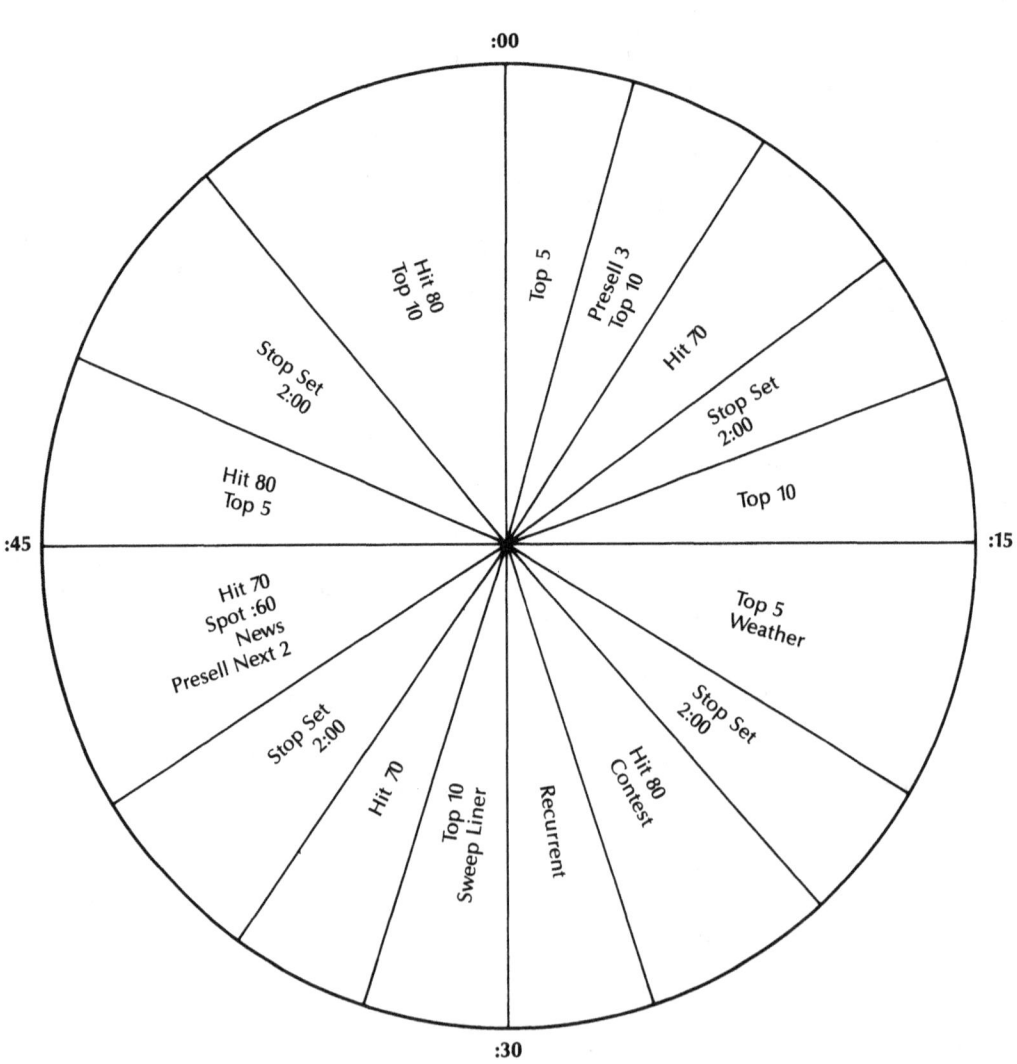

FIGURE 4.3
A Contemporary Hit Radio format clock.

these stations to break between hits. However, a segue (two or more songs played in succession) is a familiar technique for attracting and retaining listeners.

News is seldom regarded as a primary element of programming at CHR outlets. This has mostly to do with the conventional wisdom that kids tune for the music, not the news. In fact, many chart-hit station programmers have regarded news as a tune-out factor since the format's introduction. That is not to say that news is not offered by CHRs. To be certain, the majority do program news, but seldom to the extent that adult-oriented formats do.

Announcing Criteria

Above all else, CHR deejays need to communicate excitement and energy. "For CHR-format stations like ours, an energy level approaching the high end is a necessity. On a scale of one to ten, with a one being the lowest register mumble and a ten being an outright scream, a nice seven will create the sound of excitement that makes you come across as happy and upbeat without being grating. Because of the nature of the hit music in this format, CHR jocks have to maintain at least a seven or eight level between songs or continuity is broken. Besides, who wants to hear anyone on the air who sounds lifeless or dull, that is, someone with an 'anywhere but here attitude'," observes David E. Atwood, Program Director, KQID-FM, Alexandria, Louisiana.

The proper on-air attitude is very important in CHR, contends O.C. Everett, Program Director, WAYS-FM, Macon, Georgia. "A winning attitude is infectious. Listeners become engaged by it. This is an upbeat, positive format. Deejays must exude positivity. It is a necessary quality to succeed in CHR."

Social extroverts make good CHR personalities. "Outgoing personalities, people likers, if you will, come across best here," says Mark Bolke, Program Director, KRXY-FM, Denver, Colorado. Other CHR programmers concur. "I look for outgoing, gregarious personalities with down-to-earth attitudes. Specifically, I seek individuals who feel completely comfortable with the audience, people who can genuinely interact with the listener," says Charles Phillips, Program Director, WAIL-FM, Key West, Florida.

Bolke feels it is imperative that the CHR deejay relate to the music the format airs. "My jocks must honestly enjoy the music. This is the principle reason people tune CHR. The deejay should be into the music as much as the listener. You can't sell something if you don't believe in it yourself. Ultimately, those of us on the air are salespeople in a sense. We must be convincing in our appreciation of the product."

Possessing a desire to entertain is important to the CHR deejay, says WKWF's Phillips. "This format survives on glamour and glitz. It is show biz, and we rely on our air talent to get this over to the public."

Basic language skills top the list of criteria at the audition stage. "When screening job applicants, I generally look for the basics. This includes a decent command of the English language, which, amazingly, is lacking in 50 percent of those I interview," says Phillips.

Clean speech is fundamental to on-air positions, contends KQID's Atwood. "Enunciation is basic, of course. As a listener and broadcaster, I want to hear every syllable. A job candidate with a language deficit, such as a lisp, is at a serious disadvantage. Above all else, I'm alert to this problem."

Atwood cites voice quality as another criterion. "Good overall tonal quality is very important. I look for voices that won't be too 'muddy' when sent through the heavily processed audio chain."

The would-be CHR voice performer should exhibit self-assurance. "Generally speaking, I feel that aspiring announcers should achieve a high degree of self-assuredness. The deejay should truly believe that he or she is adding an element to the programming that music alone cannot. The 'beginner' should spend the majority of his or her time on simply becoming comfortable in front of the mic. At first, this may seem to be no problem. However, it is not as easy as it looks. Above all, a person should never allow others to 'set him back' emotionally," says WKWF's Phillips.

Determination and the ability to take directions are of great importance. "A deejay really must be able to follow directions and be capable of understanding what is required of him. Of course, you may possess all the acumen in the world, but if you haven't got the raw material to work with, it doesn't matter. I've also seen instances of a person possessing the talent to succeed but lacking in

FIGURE 4.4A and B Two sixty-second CHR commercials. To time the length of a spot, figure that one line of copy generally takes about three seconds to read at a medium pace. Therefore, twenty lines of copy would time out to one minute. Read aloud one of these commercials and time yourself. If you run long, read the spot again at a slightly accelerated pace. Should you time out short of sixty seconds, reread the spot at a slower pace. Try this same exercise with the other commercials in this chapter. Proper timing is crucial to the broadcast voice performer, regardless of format. Courtesy KRXY and WAYS.

```
Y108 KRXY   CLIENT WM DISTRIBUTING/ROBBIE NEVELL    FOR EMI/MANHATTAN
            AM___ FM _X_ AIR DATES FROM ___ TO ___ LENGTH :60 CART # 585

 1  BLUE SPRUCE BRINGS YOU GREAT SPRING SAVINGS WITH THE HOT NEW
 2  DEBUT RELEASE BY ROBBIE NEVELL, CALLED ROBBIE NEVELL, FROM
 3  EMI/MANHATTAN, NOW FOR SIX-TWENTY-NINE, CASSETTE OR LP!
 4  (MUSIC UP: "CEST LA VIE" - ROBBIE NEVELL)
 5  ROBBIE NEVELL, THE NEW, UP-AND-COMING ARTIST FROM EMI/MANHATTAN...
 6  YOU'LL WANT TO KEEP YOUR EYES AND EARS ON HIM...WITH HIS DEBUT
 7  ALBUM ROBBIE NEVELL, PRODUCED BY ALEX SADKIN...THE TOP PRODUCER
 8  WHO'S BROUGHT YOU HITS BY THE THOMPSON TWINS, FOREIGNER, DURAN
 9  DURAN, SIMPLY RED AND MORE.
10  (MUSIC UP: "CEST LA VIE" - ROBBIE NEVELL)
11  ROBBIE NEVELL, A REKNOWNED SONGWRITER WHO'S WRITTEN HITS FOR
12  EL DEBARGE, THE POINTER SISTERS AND SHEENA EASTON, HAS A SURE
13  FIRE WINNER FOR HIMSELF WITH HIS DEBUT RELEASE ROBBIE NEVELL...
14  FEATURING THE TOP TEN SINGEL "CEST LA VIE"...AND THE NEW
15  SINGLE ON IT'S WAY TO THE TOP OF THE CHARTS, "DOMINOES".
16  (MUSIC UP: "DOMINOES" - ROBBIE NEVELL)
17  ROBBIE NEVELL'S DEBUT ALBUM, ROBBIE NEVELL, FROM EMI/MANHATTAN
18  FOR SIX-TWENTY-NINE, CASSETTE OR LP AT BLUE SPRUCE 27875 HIGHWAY
19  74 IN EVERGREEN, 1153 HIGHWAY 74 IN BERGEN PARK, AND 23697 CONIFER
20  ROAD IN ASPEN PARK!  (MUSIC OUT: "DOMINOES" - ROBBIE NEVELL)
```

THIS ANNOUNCEMENT WAS BROADCAST _____ TIMES, AS ENTERED IN THE STATION'S PROGRAM LOG. THE TIMES THIS ANNOUNCEMENT WAS BROADCAST WERE BILLED TO THIS STATION'S CLIENT ON OUR INVOICE(S) NUMBERED/DATED _____ AT HIS EARNED RATE OF:

$_____ EACH FOR _____ ANNOUNCEMENTS, FOR A TOTAL OF $_____
$_____ EACH FOR _____ ANNOUNCEMENTS, FOR A TOTAL OF $_____
$_____ EACH FOR _____ ANNOUNCEMENTS, FOR A TOTAL OF $_____

Signature of Station Official
LESLIE K. HUGHES CONTINUITY DIRECTOR KRXY AM/FM
(Notarize above)   Typed Name and Title   Station
7075 West Hampden Avenue • Denver, Colorado 80227 • (303) 989-1075

A

the will to succeed. There is no easy path, but a person who does not discourage easily has the best shot," says WAYS's Everett.

Empathy for the listener's point of view puts the on-air performer out in front of the one who lacks it, holds KRXY's Bolke. "Understanding the mindset of your audience is imperative. An on-air person must be sensitive to her listener's needs and desires. Announcers should learn the consumer's side of radio—how, when, and why they use it."

Topping the list of "don'ts" in CHR is the use of cliches and crutches. "This is a trendy, hip format. Using words and phrases that are archaic is regressive, not progressive. To me, the worst habit in announcing is the 'crutch.

1314 GRAY HIGHWAY
P.O. BOX 5008
MACON, GEORGIA 31213

AM / (912) 741-9494 FM / (912) 741-9999

Spot Length: :60   Client: PENN. HOUSE GALLERY THE HOUSE OF OAK
Effective Date: _____   Copy By: RAMAGE

USE 10 SEC. JINGLE FOR INTRO:

AMERICA'S PREMIER LINE OF SOLID CHERRY, OAK, AND PINE FURNITURE AWAIT YOU AT THE PENNSYLVANIA HOUSE GALLERY. FROM THE MOMENT YOU FIRST ENTER THE PENNSYLVANIA HOUSE GALLERY, THE FEELING OF ELEGANCE OVERWHELMS THE SENSES. THE AROMA OF SOLID CHERRY, OAK AND PINE FILL THE AIR. THE SMOOTH TOUCH OF FINE WOOD LETS YOU KNOW YOU'RE SHOPPING AT A FINE QUALITY SHOWROOM GALLERY. THE PENNSYLVANIA GALLERY OFFERS FINE FURNISHINGS IN CHIPPENDALE AND QUEEN ANNE DESIGNS FROM COUNTRY TO ELEGANTLY FORMAL SETTINGS. DISCOVER AN EMACULATE GALLERY FULL OF FINE DECORATIVE PIECES AND ACCESSORIES FOR YOUR BEDROOM, LIVING ROOM, DINNING ROOM, OR ANY ROOM OF YOUR HOME. THE DISCOVERY BEGINS AT THE HOUSE OF OAK-PENNSYLVANIA HOUSE GALLERY...ACROSS FROM MACON MALL NEAR TOYS 'R US.

B

Anything other than call letters that are said automatically without really engaging the thought processes is a crutch. The most common for new announcers has to be the ol' 'time and temp' syndrome. This is deadly to an announcer. The first time you notice anything on your tape being repeated too often, call letters the exception, dump it, and I mean fast! This means dopey, tiresome clichés, too. Remember, a groove can turn into a rut very fast. Flippancy is inappropriate on air, too. There are a lot of jocks who confuse rudeness with wit. Everything said should be concise, pertinent, and, above all else, relatable to the listener. Leave the private jokes and negativism outside the control room door," says Atwood.

Predictable patterns are boring to the listener, contends consultant Jay Williams. "Falling into predictable, day-in, day-out patterns invites audience tune-out. Creativity and diversity are essential in radio."

Failure to think through what is going to be said on the air leads to trouble. "Deejays in this format or any other should never throw open the mic without knowing exactly what to say. Since this format is especially tight, jocks cannot dawdle on the air. It throws off the flow. A deejay who stumbles or gropes for something to say sounds amateurish and makes the whole station sound unprofessional" notes WAYS's Everett.

Finally, CHR programmers caution against affected presentation. "I believe most p.d.s dislike exaggerated deliveries. Hyperbolic pronunciation is a by-product of this. The general public does not speak with flawless perfection. Precision speech is okay for formal recitations, but it's a good practice in this business to talk like you're addressing a friend, not sixty people attending a reading of Wordsworth in a university assembly hall," offers radio expert Donna Halper.

COUNTRY

Over twenty-three hundred radio stations offer country music. This makes Country the most executed format in the United States. This was not true a couple of decades ago. In the 1960s, Country, while popular in the South and Midwest, was almost nonexistent in the North. What happened to change this was the crossover ability of a number of country music artists, such as Glen Campbell and Johnny Cash, whose songs jumped from the Country charts to the mainstream pop charts, raising the awareness of the general public regarding country music.

The further popularization of country music continued into the 1970s with the rebel rock sound epitomized by artists like Marshal Tucker, Lynyrd Skynyrd, and the Allman Brothers.

The number of Country stations doubled by 1975 as the format made significant inroads into the northern markets. Enhancing Country radio's wider acceptance was the diversification of its product (with artists such as Dolly Parton and Kenny Rodgers).

Today, the Country format can be divided into three general categories: Traditional, Middle of the Road (MOR), and Contemporary Country. Remember, these are only generalizations. Country comes in a variety of configurations.

Traditional Country outlets offer old-line country music with a folksy, rural sound more akin to stations prior to the crossover trend. These are stations tuned by hard-core country music fans, who mostly reside in the South and Midwest.

MOR Country stations assume a less traditional posture, while avoiding sounding too modern as well. As the term suggests, stations employing this format avoid extremes. MORs mix their playlists to reflect a broad range of Country styles, from Bluegrass to rural rock.

The most recent Country progeny takes an exclusively up-to-date approach. Contemporary Country focuses on present and recent chart toppers and can resemble CHR, especially at those stations skewing their playlists toward up-tempo sounds. These stations are sometimes called "Hot Country." Some Contemporary Country stations opt for a mellower, albeit modern, sound by airing "lite" hits. Many Contemporary Country stations taking this approach refer to themselves as "Lite Country." These stations resemble ACs in that they steer clear of hard sounds and frequently present lengthy music sweeps. This latter approach has become popular on the FM band in the 1980s, whereas Traditional and MOR remain pretty much AM oriented.

Announcer involvement in Country is dictated by programming approach. For instance, Traditional stations usually heavy-up on personality. Air people play a vital role and have high visibility. This also applies to many MOR Country stations, although decreasing announcer participation outside of drive-time periods is a common practice. In the Contemporary Country category a couple of announcing approaches are dominant. Lite Country outlets often minimize announcer involvement, while up-tempo Hot Country stations generally allow for more deejay play.

Many outlets airing soft country music are automated or satellite service affiliates, and thus go the operator/live assist announcer route. This system of presentation became increasingly popular in the 1980s.

The demographics for Country radio have shifted dramatically since the 1960s, when the bulk of listeners fell into the low-income, blue-collar stratum. Since Country has become more sophisticated and cosmopolitan in its presentation, it now draws a more upscale clientele. It is no longer true, if it ever was, that only Southerners or the poor and uneducated tune. Country can also boast one of the broadest age groups listening to radio. Young and old alike find Country radio programming appealing.

Announcing Criteria

Country programmers seek broadcast voice performers who know and appreciate the music. "Air people here must have a knowledge of the history of Country music with respect to the styles and careers of artists. They should be up on current data as pertains to the music stars. You can't be strictly a voice in this format as you can in others," says Don Wray, Program Director, WSGG-AM, Scottsboro, Alabama.

Country programmer Bob Fruen (KMSL-FM, Magnolia, Arkansas) requires that announcers have a thorough understanding of the medium itself. "A person can't really get the most out of something if he only half understands it. You have to possess a solid concept of the medium before you can hope to be a fully actualized on-mic performer. Too many broadcasters know format but really don't know *radio*. As pertains specifically to my station, I expect my people to be radio experts and to thoroughly know the music and the folks who sing it. Deejays should become a part of the music they play. In different words, they should inhabit the same world—blend into the format, not sound like they're outside it because they may not truly appreciate the type of music programmed. I suppose any air person operates from a disadvantage if he or she does not enjoy and relate to the format in which they work."

Country radio requires dynamic performers, contends W.C. Stedman, Program Director, KNEW, Oakland, California. "To be honest, I think that there are very few really good communicators out there. To be memorable, and that is what you want to be, you have to stock the airwaves with compelling personalities. Weak or wishy-washy deejays don't belong on Country, or on any station for that matter."

A chief quality sought after by most Country programmers is warmth and friendliness. "I don't believe any other format requires a more down-to-earth, neighborly announcer style than ours. Country deejays have to be able to talk *to*, not *at*, an audience. They never should talk down to an audience, either. Personalities here must come across as fellow citizens, not as outsiders or radio stars. That doesn't wash in this format. Connectedness is fundamental to what we do on the air. A knowledge of local issues and civic functions establishes this link, among other things," says WSGG's Wray.

When it comes to basic verbal skills, Country programmers are no different than their counterparts in other formats. "Regardless of format, broadcast voice performers must have the ability to pronounce effectively, especially when dealing with names. You want to turn off an audience? Mispronounce a widely known name. New announcers in an area should spend a lot of time becoming familiar with local pronunciations, even colloquialisms unique to the coverage area of the station," says Wray.

Getting the mechanics of language down is the first step toward success in Country announcing, says KMSL's Fruen. "You don't belong in front of a microphone if you can't speak clearly. That's just for starters. Beyond that you need to possess the talent to communicate 'poignantly' with the listener—a fancy term that means hitting the bull's eye when opening your mouth. Using the right words prevents confusion and frustration among listeners. Another thing, a jock, no matter how friendly sounding, doesn't communicate effectively with a head or mouth full of marbles."

In preparation for an on-air career in Country radio, Fruen suggests monitoring the medium as much as possible. "The aspiring Country announcer had better listen to radio. Tune in the major market stations and try to pick up on voice styles, phrasing, humor, whatever. If you listen to the best, it will help you become a better announcer faster."

Conscientiousness and the desire to do the best possible job are of paramount importance, says Dave Ross, Music Director, WBOS-FM, Boston, Massachusetts. "A deejay has to want to do the job correctly all the time—to sound good every minute that he or she is on-mic." Fruen agrees, but cautions against perfectionism. "One thing an announcer has to understand is the fact that he or she can't be perfect all the time. Things are going to

FIGURE 4.5
Country radio two-voice commercial.
Courtesy KMSL-FM.

KMSL FM — 100
724 SO. JACKSON
MAGNOLIA, ARKANSAS 71753
PHONE (501) 234-7790

Advertiser: Ivan Smith Furniture

Begin: _____ End: _____

Prepared by: _____

Spot No.: _____

BOB: Hey, Lori, what's going on at Ivan Smith Furniture, everywhere I go people are tAlking about it. All I hear is Ivan Smith and sale prices.

LORI: Well, Bob, everybody is talking about Ivan Smith because their anniversary sale is still going on, and everything is sale priced--at substantial savings, too. Like an England sofa and love seat--the regular price is $1300, it's sale priced now for $888.

BOB: Gosh, that's a savings of $412!!

LORI: Yeah, and you can also buy a Broyhill bedroom suite for $649, normally priced at $900--and that's a savings of...

BOTH: $251.00!!

BOB: At those prices I'd love to do some refurnishing, but you know I just spent all my extra money on my new sports car.

LORI: Bob, Ivan Smith has easy credit terms that are no hassel, so you can just finance it, and if you need some new appliances, Ivan Smith has a full line of Hotpoint appliances.

BOB: So, I can still have my sports car, and new furniture, too, with easy financing.

LORI: Yep.

BOB: Now I know why everybody is talking about Ivan Smith Furniture and that's where I'm going right now, to Ivan Smith on North Jackson in Magnolia.

This announcement was broadcast __44__ times as entered in the station's program log. The times this announcement was broadcast were billed to this station's client on our statement dated _____ at his earned rate of:

$ _____ each for __44__ announcements, for a total of $ _____.

$ _____ each for _____ announcements, for a total of $ _____.

Sworn & subscribed to me this

_____ day of _____ 19 _____

_____
Bookkeeper, KMSL FM

Notary _____

---

screw up. That's the charm of a live medium. There are going to be glitches, and when there are, you can't be too damning of yourself. Learn, and move on. Of course, the desire to do the best in all situations is another matter."

Fruen says the way to ensure against on-air blunders is to acquire excellent reading and interpretive skills. "The announcer should constantly work on reading spots and news copy. I've noticed, too, that the broadcast voice performer who reads a lot for pleasure is better at copy interpretation, not to mention the fact that he or she is simply better informed and knowledgeable as a consequence. The moral: Read!"

In the "things to avoid" department, insincerity scores high. Fruen adds, "This is the straight-from-the-holster format. Being pretentious sounding on the air doesn't cut the mustard. Putting on a 'sound' is a bad practice. Be genuine. The audience relates to sincerity, especially in Country. Of course, a deejay had better not be too 'homey' or 'man-on-the-street'-like, if that's possible. You don't want to sound like everyone else, either. This is an entertainment medium, after all. Carving out an honest style that accurately reflects your personality in its sharpest and liveliest form is the way to go. Another dreaded 'no-no' to keep in mind: Don't cough or clear your throat on mic. Hit the 'kill' switch, hack, and get back on. Live TV performers don't have much choice, but radio announcers can flip the toggle for a brief second without much notice."

Insufficient control of the vocal system creates innumerable problems, too, says Wray. "For example, improper breathing affects voice quality, not to mention copy interpretation, and manipulating the voice box by lowering it beyond its natural range produces negative results. In the first instance, taking a breath at the proper place is essential, and in the second instance, straining the voice is abusive and amateurish."

Wray cites another "don't." "The 'just get by' attitude is poison in Country, and in any format for that matter. Lack of desire shows. Who wants to listen to a deejay who sounds like he'd rather be fishing or chopping wood? You have a responsibility when you open that microphone to sound like you love being with your listeners."

EASY LISTENING

Easy Listening radio was conceived as Beautiful Music in 1959 by programmer Gordon McLendon. The format has not changed significantly since its inception. The idea then and now is to offer listeners relaxing, easy sounds and more music than anyone else. "Wall-to-wall" music is a term often ascribed to Easy Listening (EL) outlets.

Originally a major AM format, EL made the conversion to FM in the late 1960s. A couple of factors precipitated the switch. In the mid-1960s, in a move to improve FM's status, the FCC forced larger market AM/FM combo operations to originate programming on their FMs at least 50 percent of their broadcast day. Many of the dual operations simulcast (duplicated) their AM broadcasts for the sake of simple economics. It was cost smart. Pressed to separate signals, many combo stations went the automated route to avoid staffing demands. The Easy Listening formula was the most adaptable to automation, due to its emphasis on uninterrupted music and little live announcer participation.

Another factor inspiring the wider presentation of Easy Listening/Beautiful Music was stereo. FM was capable of broadcasting in stereo, and as a "more-music" format stressing fidelity, broadcasters found this a marketing asset.

Today Easy Listening is almost exclusively an FM offering, and about six hundred stations air the format. According to *Radio and Records*, EL attracts 11 percent of the tuning public. In nearly every major market, an Easy Listening station appears somewhere near the top of the ratings. Boston is a good example. Easy Listening station WJIB-FM has managed to position itself among the top five rated stations for nearly two decades. This is not an isolated example either.

Since the quintessential focus of EL outlets is music, sweeping is the natural modus operandi. Ten- to twelve-minute blocks of music followed by spot clusters (spot sets) is the typical approach, except during drive-time periods when the audience is interested in receiving a greater amount of information, such as news, weather, sports, traffic, and stock reports.

Program syndicators, many using satellites to distribute their products, find EL stations eager subscribers. In fact, this format relies on syndicated programming more than any other. Again, the more-music formula makes EL fertile ground for syndicators. Consequently, announcer presence is usually low, certainly lower than in most formats. As stated earlier, Easy Listening outlets marketing "all-music, all the time" allow for few announcer interruptions, which are usually in the form of music recaps (backsells), brief weather statements, and time and temperature checks.

The prime listening group for this format

is between thirty-four and fifty-nine years of age, with the larger chunk of the audience found in the upper end of that demographic cell.

Announcing Criteria

Of course, it follows that voice quality is important in radio, but during the early years of Easy Listening, voice quality, that is, timbre and depth, took precedence over all other considerations. Voice quality remains a major criterion today, but not to the degree it once was. "A deep, resonant voice blends well with this format, no doubt, but it is not the only reason for hiring announcers. A smooth, medium-paced delivery is what you're after in this format," says Charles C. Castle, Program Director, WAPR-AM, Avon Park, Florida.

Making the most out of the material at hand yields the best results in this department, offers Dennis Hare, Station Manager, WTAY, Robinson, Illinois. "Learn to maximize what you have, to control your voice, rather than manipulate it. Regard it as an instrument, and learn to play it like a virtuoso. Cultivating the voice box to its ultimate output should be the broadcast voice performer's key objective."

Easy Listening programmers want their announcers to possess a comprehensive understanding of the English language as well as a knowledge of world and local affairs. "You'll hear this from every radio p.d., but I'll repeat it because it cannot be overstated. You have no business being on the air if you can't use the language the way that it is designed to be used. Lately, however, you hear the language being slaughtered practically every time you turn on the radio. God, that gets to me! Another gripe of mine is deejays who haven't got the slightest idea of what they are reading or what is going on around them. It's clearly negligent to me not to understand, or make an attempt to understand, what you are reading on the air. As broadcasters we all have the obligation to be informed," says Hare.

Jay Richards, Public Affairs Director, WBYU-FM, New Orleans, Louisiana, agrees with Hare, adding, "Never be caught unprepared. Read and digest everything that is to be aired before airing it. EL is a mature format. You can't fake intelligence with our listeners. They know when you're out in left field trying to catch a ball hit to right."

An affinity for Easy Listening music must exist. "Despite the fact that many ELs are regarded as background or subliminal music services and are automated or satellite driven, an air person should appreciate the type of music presented. You're in the wrong place if you're a hard-core rocker. Staying connected with the air product is vital. You can't hate something and be enthusiastic about it at the same time. As in any format, the important thing is to be at home with the music," says Richards.

In years past, Easy Listening/Beautiful Music announcers were often criticized for their affectedness and stiffness. This, to a large extent, has changed. "Stilted deliveries, that is, the stiff-collared BM announcers, are pretty much extinct. Exaggerated enunciation and diction sound peculiar in this day and age. I personally try to colloquialize as much as possible, while maintaining grammatical integrity. The two are compatible. I don't believe pronunciation, articulation, and diction need be exercised to the 'nth' degree. I've always felt that while one should try to speak accurately and with a degree of precision, one doesn't have to emulate a Shakespearian actor in order to communicate effectively in Easy Listening. A slight amount of formality is not horrible in this format, but too much and you sound officious; then the contact level with listeners drops," observes Richards.

According to EL programmer Charles C. Castle, announcers must come to grips with the concept of "match flow." "The announcer in this format, perhaps more than any other, has to match the tone and tenor of the surrounding programming and production values. Deliveries must reflect the music, not clash with it. To get what I want in this area, I hire people who can take direction and criticism. In other words, adapt to the format or get another job. I can overlook many errors if the person is trying hard and is loyal to the format and the station."

On a final note, Castle speaks for all programmers, regardless of format, when he states the importance of developing a sense of timing. "Maybe it hasn't been brought up by other p.d.s, but I know they feel as I do that broadcast voice performers have to have a sense of the clock. This is a business that sells 'time'; don't forget it. We deal in increments of time—thirty- and sixty-second commercials, five-minute network news feeds, fifteen-second donut drop-ins, ten-

```
WTAY
1570 AM – 101.7 FM
CONTINUITY
```

COPY NO. _____
PROGRAM: 7AM NEWS
SPONSOR: M & M AUTO SALES
DATE BEGIN: _____ DATE END: _____
COPY BY: DENNIS G HARE
LENGTH: 60 SEC

10 GO SEE THE FRIENDLY SALES STAFF AT M & M AUTO SALES, ON THE
    FRIENDLY CORNER. THEY CAN SHOW YOU SO MANY QUALITY PRE-OWNED
20 CARS AND TRUCKS, BOTH DOMESTIC AND FOREIGN, THAT IT WILL BE EASY
    TO FIND WHAT YOU'VE BEEN LOOKING FOR. AFTER A TEST DRIVE, OF
30 SEVERAL OF THEIR MANY CARS ON THE LOT, WE'RE SURE THAT YOU;LL FIND
40 THE CAR FOR YOU. BUYING A PRE-OWNED CAR SAVES THE TROUBLE OF
    "BREAKING IN" AN AUTOMOBILE AND SAVES THOUSANDS OF DOLLARS. BUY
50 A PRE-OWNED CAR AT AFFORDABLE PRICES, AT THE BEST USED CAR DEALER
    IN THE AREA. GO OUT TO M & M AUTO SALES, MONDAY THRU FRIDAY, 8 TO
60 5 AND SATURDAY, UNTIL NOON, AT THE FRIENDLY CORNER INTERSECTION
70 OF ROUTE ONE AND THIRTY-THREE, JUST EAST OF ROBINSON. THEY CAN
    FIND YOU A PRE-OWNED CAR THAT YOU'LL BE PROUD TO DRIVE. STOP
80 BY M & M AUTO SALES, AT THE INTERSECTION OF 1 & 33, AND TALK TO
    THE FRIENDLY SALES STAFF TODAY.
90

Remarks:

FIGURE 4.6A and B Easy Listening copy. Courtesy WTAY and WAPR.

A

second promos, and on and on. To the incoming announcer, I say learn timing. Practice reading copy with a stopwatch or a clock with a big sweep hand. Time *is* the essence in this business."

ALBUM-ORIENTED ROCK

Top 40 radio was the impetus behind the debut of Album-Oriented Rock (AOR), which upon its inception in 1966 was called Progressive. The idea was to break with convention and offer the listening public a programming alternative—one that was not so rigidly formulated as the hit chart stations dominating the airwaves at the time.

Rather than air a single or primary format, Progressive chose to block program, to offer a variety of music genres. By the late 1960s, many of these stations had abandoned the block approach in preference for all rock,

FIGURE 4.6 Continued

WAPR AM/14

P.O. BOX 1390 — 813/453-3139
AVON PARK, FL 33828

RADIO COPY

DATE_____ NUMBER_____

Advertiser COLOR RITE RENTAL
Product APPLIANCE & FURN. RENTALS
Salesman KIM FILEGER
Begin Broadcast_____
End Broadcast_____
Composer KIM FILEGER

Date	Annc.	Sec.	
		0	SOME PEOPLE CALL IT THE "BOOB TUBE". COLOR RITE T V AND APPLIANCE RENTAL PREFERS TO REFER TO IT AS TELEVISION. OF COURSE YOU COULD BE A "BOOB" BY SPLURGING WHEN YOU CAN RENT TO OWN. COLOR RITE HAS
		15	NO CREDIT CHECK, NO LONG TERM OBLIGATIONS, NO REPAIR BILLS, NO HASSELS AND NO BIG DOWN PAYMENT. AND THE FIRST WEEKS RENT IS FREE. COLOR RITE T V CARRIES BRAND NAMES. TV'S, STEREOS, APPLIANCES, VIDEO PLAYERS,
		30	AND FURNITURE. STOP IN AND SEE TOM FOR HELPFUL ADVICE. AND WHILE YOU'RE THERE YOU CAN REGISTER TO WIN WAPR'S DINNER FOR TWO. SO COME ON IN AND SEE THE FRIENDLY PEOPLE AT COLOR RITE T V ON RIDGEWOOD DRIVE IN THE
		45	THRIFTWAY PLAZA IN SEBRING.
		60	
		75	
O.K.			

B

predominantly of a nonhit nature. The album rock format was firmly in place by the early 1970s. Psychedelic and Acid rock radio were variations on the album rock format, which focused on music inspired by the drug movement of the era.

From its start in the 1960s, AOR has almost exclusively resided on the FM band. The format brought a younger demographic stratum to FM and, in so doing, paved the way for wider listener acceptance.

In the 1970s, album rockers became more mainstream and formulated in their presentations. Far less was left up to chance. Format clocks were installed, and deejays were given less latitude on the air and in the selection of music. This was done in an effort to expand on the listener pool and station revenues.

Throughout the 1970s, AOR's popularity increased, but late in the decade and in the early 1980s, the format experienced listener erosion. This was the result of chart radio crossover hits by several artists who had traditionally been aired by AOR. The Police, Talking Heads, David Bowie, and countless other performers enjoyed immense success on CHR stations. Album-Oriented Rock playlists suffered from age and stagnation; thus, many listeners headed for CHR stations.

In the late 1980s, AORs regained much of their strength by revising and updating their playlists. Approximately 12 percent of the radio audience is loyal to AOR. The strongest demographic cell is males, 18 to 34 years old, but the format has gained some ground in recent years in attracting female listeners.

The sweep method is most prevalent at AORs, and spots are clustered as they are at other stations emphasizing "more music." Like most stations targeting younger listeners, news is not a primary marketing tool. Whereas AORs, like everyone else, air more information-based material during commuter periods, music generally tops the marquee the remainder of the day. The fact is, news is relatively scarce outside of drive-time slots on AORs.

Announcer styles run the gamut from heavy personality, nearly always an ingredient of morning drive, to the program host or op/assist approach. The middle-ground deejay presentation is most in evidence on AORs. For the most part, announcing is kept down so that the music remains the focus.

Announcing Criteria

A pedestrian knowledge of music is unacceptable in AOR. "This format requires that air personnel have an in-depth schooling in the music programmed. Deejays have to be amply familiar with a song's heritage, the musician's background, and the instrumentation—meaning what instruments are used and the significance of the arrangement, and so on," says Art Farkas, Program Director, KKDJ-FM, Fresno, California.

Album-Oriented Rock programmer Dennis Constantine, KBCO-AM/FM, Boulder, Colorado, agrees with Farkas. "More than in any other format, with the exception of Classical, perhaps, a super knowledge of the music is expected from the air talent. AOR listeners are very much into what is played. They know their music and expect deejays to know and appreciate the music as well."

A natural, conversational delivery is expected of AOR voice performers. "A good natural delivery is what most AOR p.d.s are after, I believe. For the most part, this is an unpretentious format. 'Straight ahead' is the idea. Hype exists in AOR, as it does in most formats, but here I want real people who can relate behind the mic," says Constantine.

Album-Oriented Rock programmers look for performers who exemplify the attitude and image of the format. "You can't be just an announcer in AOR. I hire air people who see themselves as personalities and who are AOR listeners themselves. In order to really connect with an audience, I think you have to live as they do, that is, relate to the same life-style trends and activities. You have to live AOR to do AOR. That is the formula," says Jose Diaz, Program Director, WNCM-FM, Lewiston, Maine. Diaz places ad-lib skills on his list of announcer criteria. "It takes time to develop effective ad-lib skills, but it is worth it. Too many air people cannot talk off-script. Have you ever been tuned to a station when something goes wrong, say a piece of equipment breaks down, and the deejay suddenly acts like he has amnesia because a glitch is not in the script? I find this rather sad. All radio people should be capable of ad-libbing."

Innovative and imaginative air people are the type KKDJ's Farkas is interested in hiring. "Free-flowing creativity tempered by an understanding of the disciplines necessary to the job make for the best air talent. I want a person with a strong desire to entertain but within the established parameters."

KBCO's Constantine says air people must possess off-air skills, too. "My deejays know their way around a production studio. Most mix spots and promos, so they have to operate a studio with authority as well as a sense of mixdown aesthetics." Constantine contends that deejays must be attuned to all the broadcast equipment in the control room, too, whether it is a part of normal operations or not. "Equipment can be intimidating. It's important to get past any anxieties in this area. Make the effort to find out what every-

FIGURE 4.7A and B (A) A sixty-second AOR commercial and (B) accompanying production order. Courtesy KKDJ-FM.

Advertiser Category: JOURNEY PROMO
Script Number: START
Length of Spot: :60

:10 — DUE TO THE OVERWHELMING RESPONSE FOR JOURNEY TICKETS, KKDJ HAS ANOTHER BIRTHDAY SURPRISE FOR YOU -- BY POPULAR DEMAND, KKDJ HAS ARRANGED TO BRING JOURNEY BACK TO SELLAND ARENA FOR A <u>SECOND SHOW</u>, FRIDAY NIGHT, JANUARY

:20 — SECOND. NOW'S YOUR CHANCE TO GRAB GREAT SEATS TO THIS ADDITIONAL SHOW. IN THE MEANTIME, WE'VE STILL GOT TICKETS TO GIVE AWAY TO THE FIRST JOURNEY

:30 — SHOW, DECEMBER 29TH AT SELLAND. SO, AS ALWAYS, STAY LISTENING AND BE THE 16TH CALLER ANYTIME YOU HEAR US PLAY JOURNEY AND WE'LL GIVE YOU TICKETS

:40 — TO THE FIRST SHOW. PLUS -- GET THIS -- WE TALKED TO STEVE PERRY AND HE WANTS TO INVITE SIXTEEN OF OUR TICKET WINNERS BACKSTAGE AFTER THE SHOW TO SAY HI!

:50 — SO, IF YOU WIN TICKETS FROM US, YOU COULD BE CHOSEN TO GO BACKSTAGE, TOO! DETAILS COMING UP ON A SPECTACULAR NIGHT WITH JOURNEY, FROM THE HOME OF ROCK 'N ROLL...106-KKDJ!

:60 —

A

thing does, even if you don't have to use it during your shift. There may come a time when you have to operate a piece of equipment that is not a part of normal daily operations, and you'll be on top of things. When you're at home with equipment, you can concentrate on communicating."

Learning to be at ease and comfortable on the air is essential, says Constantine. "Sounding at ease is very important in AOR.

FIGURE 4.7 Continued

```
                    KKDJ
                    106              COMMERCIAL PRODUCTION ORDER

    Date into Production: _____       Producer:   JEFF RIEDEL
    Date Needed: _____               Acct. Executive: AR
    Account: JOURNEY CONCERT PROMOTION       Co-op: _____

            INSTRUCTIONS:    PLEASE CUT WITH UPTEMPO DELIVERY;
                             USE LIVE JOURNEY TRACKS FOR SPLICE-UP;
                             BIG ENDING, PLEASE.

    Recorded Tag : _____
    Music: _____ Jingle: _____ Cut: _____

    Cart Label instructions:     :60   1      :30 _____
    Start Date: _____ End Date: _____ Cart#: 146
                                             Replace Cart#: 146
    -----------------------------------------------------------------
    Producers Instructions:
    Business Name: _____ Phone: _____
    Location: _____ Owner: _____
    Type: Humorous _____ Straight _____ Hard Sell xxx Other _____
    Essential Information: (Products, Business hours, Target audience, etc....)

                    PLEASE WATCH FLIGHT DATES.  THANKS!

    pacific quadracasting inc. 3636 north first street suite 135, fresno, california 93726, (209)226-5991
```

B

If the jock is relaxed on the air, the listener will feel it. It's important to keep in mind that there is only 'one' person listening. All speaking on the radio should be directed to one person. Treat the microphone like a living, breathing human being. Using phrases like 'Good evening, everybody' excludes the person listening to radio by himself, and that is the majority of listeners. My advice to jocks is to keep communications on the personal level. Instead of a sea of listeners, imagine one person at the other end of the mic, and talk to her. The thought of speaking to only one person, rather than the multitudes, aids in relaxation, too."

Listening to other AOR deejays provides a helpful point of reference, says Diaz. "Don't isolate yourself to your own show. I mean, listen to your colleagues and to other radio personalities. The great part about working in this business is that it literally surrounds you, and all you have to do to gain some insight into your profession is flick the switch. Try to enlarge on your ability to listen objectively to others. Don't copy their strengths. Emulate their good qualities, and retain your own identity."

Over the years AOR has become less tolerant of verbose air people. This was not true during the early days of the format when performers were sometimes permitted to talk at great length. "Most AORs have adopted the maxim 'say what you've got to say, and get back to the music.' Using too many words to say something that can be conveyed using fewer is a bad habit as far as I'm concerned. In this format, the audience tunes for the music. A gabby, windy deejay just keeps people from getting what they want. Diversity in what you say keeps things more interesting to the listener, too. We all have heard deejays drone on for what seems an eternity without really saying much of anything, and we've heard deejays repeat the same inane comments over and over again," says Constantine.

According to Diaz, sloppy execution decreases the value of the air product. "Air people who can't run a tight board, who have lots of dead air, overlap, and bad levels, hurt a station. Listeners expect a professional presentation from small stations as well as large."

Lack of pride and the unwillingness to learn from mistakes are roadblocks to success. "Lack of concern about bad habits or an attitude that keeps people from learning about themselves and their performance are real negative forces for everyone, the station included. If I bring bad habits, such as clichés, poor commercial deliveries, dead air, and sluggishness, to the deejay's attention, I expect he or she will exert a sincere effort to make constructive adjustments. Another point I think worth mentioning is that anything that moves the jock's delivery away from the AOR arena will ultimately hurt his relationship with the listener. Bottom line: Listen to yourself and others, and stay on track," says KKDJ's Farkas.

CLASSICAL

New York City station WQXR-AM began airing a daily schedule of classical music in the 1930s, making it one of the first to do so. In the 1950s, the Classical format took up residency on the fledgling FM band. The superior fidelity of FM made it better suited than AM for the presentation of classical music.

The next major step in the progress of Classical radio was stereophonic sound, which came to the medium in the early 1960s. Stereo brought more listeners to FM and the Classical format. Although Classical radio attracted modest audiences compared to other formats, it was a mainstay for FM.

The size of the format's following has grown steadily over the past two decades, although fewer than two dozen commercial stations offer classical music on a full-time basis. While commercial radio has been slow to embrace the format, non-commercial broadcasters have made the format more available to audiences. Today, noncommercial stations are the greatest proponents of the Classical format.

Government-subsidized Public Radio stations are among the largest supporters of classical music. Many of these stations are affiliated with colleges and universities. Commercial Classical stations are most likely to be found in metropolitan markets, whereas noncommercial Classicals are located in small to larger markets. Both attract up-scale, educated listeners—what advertisers and underwriters refer to as a "blue-chip" audience.

It is the music that is marketed in this format. This means that all other programming elements are secondary to the music selections, which frequently are ten to fifteen minutes long. One cut of classical music often constitutes what other formats call sweeps. Both commercial and noncommercial Classical stations cluster announcements.

Of all nonmusic ingredients, news is afforded the greatest amount of air time. Similar to other formats, Classical increases news coverage during drive-time periods, especially morning commuter hours. Many noncommercial stations air National Public Radio's afternoon, ninety-minute-long news feature *All Things Considered*.

In recent years, many Classical stations have expanded the role of their on-air people. Personalities were a rarity until the late 1970s. Today, rather than the laconic music host of the past, who scarcely did little more than deliver title and composer data, Classical broadcast voice performers commonly interject more of themselves into their programs. "What distinguishes us from other Classical stations, and certainly those of yesterday, is that we combine the elements of 'personality' radio with our basic product—classical music. Our audience has grown significantly since adopting the approach. The wit and charm of our air staff serves as a bridge between the casual classical music listener and the music itself, which can be pretty austere," says Paul Teare, Program Director, WGMS-FM, Baltimore, Maryland.

Announcing Criteria

The one universal criterion that Classical on-air personnel are expected to possess is a knowledge of the music the format offers. "An intelligent, knowledgeable presentation of classical music is absolutely necessary.

Your credibility is on the line, so your air staff has to exhibit a level of sophistication when it comes to the playlist. Along with this, a complete mastery of the English language is a given. Classical air people also need some foreign language skills. You seldom open the microphone without having to pronounce a foreign name or title," says Marilyn Heltzer, Vice President of Programming, Minnesota Public Radio.

WGMS's Teare agrees with Heltzer. "I'd say above all I look for a sound grasp of classical music and its performers and a command of whatever language one must announce. I'd add to the list the ability to deliver a good commercial. In commercial radio it is not enough to talk the music; you must also be able to sell the product that generates revenue."

Not unlike Easy Listening, Classical has a taste for the resonant, mature voice. "A good voice, a radio voice, mixes best with Classical production values. A lower register female or male voice sounds really good here. As far as style of delivery, I desire something that is warm and friendly but not 'smarmy'— a friendliness and certain intimacy of style. An announcer is talking to 'one' other person, not to the world at large, so he or she should reach home, so to speak," says Heltzer.

Good communicators are hired at WGMS, says Teare. "Personally, I would rather do away with the term *announcer* altogether. Especially in a Classical music format. The very word conjures an image of the old-fashioned, stereotypical, detached style of broadcasting. I look for 'communicators,' people with genuine personality, warmth, and a strong desire to transmit their enthusiasms and interests—people who enjoy serving as catalysts in the process of unifying a body of listeners. Pronunciation, articulation, diction, phrasing, modulation are all essential qualities which contribute to good announcing, but one may possess all of these, that is, master the skills, and still fail miserably as a communicator."

MPR's Heltzer has further advice for aspiring Classical radio broadcast voice performers. "Get a lot of practice. Educate yourself in the body of music the format airs. Find a mentor who will work with you. If you don't improve FAST, give it up, and move on to something else. To be blunt, some people have a knack for this business. Some don't. If you've got 'it,' you can start out being simply terrible and three months later sound terrific. But if it takes much longer than that to 'get good,' not 'great,' but 'good,' then look for an alternative occupation. Pick your mentor/station carefully. You may acquire habits that will serve you poorly."

Preparing for Classical on-air duty is a process that also includes formal education. "A college education with a music component establishes the foundation. To be on the air in Classical you have to know more than current hit chart information. There is a deep historical heritage to classical music. The music in this format runs very deep. It is complex and rich. Classical broadcast voice performers seldom succeed with only a pedestrian knowledge of the music," says Teare, who adds, "I, too, have alerted the aspiring Classical radio announcer against wordiness. It's nice to know a lot about something, but don't overdo. Some Classical air people perceive themselves as musicologists and the audience as students. Be concise when you give general information, too. Don't say, 'The time now, according to the clock on the wall, is five minutes before the hour of four P.M.' It is much better to say 'The WGMS time is three fifty-five.' It never hurts to get the call letters in."

Another point by Teare has to do with the lack of preparedness. "This often results in speech pattern interjections that are used to kill time to avoid dead air. As the performer searches her brain for the next word or phrase, things like 'uh,' 'em,' 'hm,' and 'you know' fall from her mouth. Oh, yes, also to be listed in the 'negative' column is the show-off interviewer. We all know him. He's the guy who spends more time demonstrating to both guest and audience his in-depth knowledge of the topic than he does drawing out his guest. This is an obvious ploy to direct the attention to himself. Yet instead of praise from the audience he inspires contempt for his inability to subordinate himself to the subject and interviewee."

Heltzer advises announcers to get right to the point when they open the microphone. "Talking too much is a bad habit in any situation or venue, but especially on the air. With our format it is important to get on with the music. An announcer with a wonderful voice can fall into the trap of simply loving to hear herself talk. Simply put, leave your narcissism at home. A couple of other things to be avoided are laziness and the inability

FIGURE 4.8A and B
Two Classical radio station commercials. Courtesy WGMS-FM.

WGMS 570AM-103.5FM
WASHINGTON'S GOOD MUSIC STATIONS

One Central Plaza, 11300 Rockville Pike, Rockville, MD 20852   (301) 468-1800

THOROBRED MOTORCARS

Once upon a time Italy created a masterpiece legend: the Maserati. A legend on the Grand Prix circuit and a legend on the road. Test drive the new Maserati Biturbo at Thorobred Motorcars, the exclusive Maserati dealer in Washington dealer in Washington and Northern Virginia. The Biturbo is quite simply the most exciting 4-passenger sports sedan you've ever driven. Sink into the luxury of soft Italian glove leather upholstery...then feel the power of the twin turbo engine that accelerates from 0 to 60 in 6.8 seconds...so fast it leaves the Porsche 944 and BMW's far behind. It's $26,000 worth of pure excitement backed by a 2 year, 24,000 mile factory warranty. A 7 year financing plan is available. See the Maserati Biturbo at Thorobred Motorcars, at the corner of Wilson and Washington Boulevards in Arlington. Call them at 522-4844. 522-4844. And drive away in a Maserati Biturbo.

RKO RADIO
RKO General, Inc.

A

to accept criticism. Falling into rote behaviors in announcing eventually leads to unemployment, and an oversensitivity to criticism can create real difficulties. Too many announcers regard criticism and comments as a personal attack, even when it is done with the greatest of diplomacy. You must realize that feedback comes with the territory and can be very constructive and helpful."

VINTAGE

Hundreds of radio stations devote their air time to music of the past. There are several different Vintage format approaches. Among the most prominent are Oldies, Nostalgia, and Classic Hits. These formats are often referred to as *Gold*, as well.

Oldies stations focus on the pop-chart hits of the early days of rock, drawing their play-

```
                                               CATHEDRAL CHORAL SOCIETY




Every English Monarch since George II has been crowned to the

glorious sounds of Handel's Coronation Anthem, ZADOK THE PRIEST.

(Music up)

This majestic anthem will highlight the Cathedral Choral Society's

TRIBUTE TO HANDEL concert, opening its 44th season at the Washington

Cathedral.  This Sunday, Music Director J. Reilly Lewis leads the

Cathedral Choral Society, orchestra and soloists in a Handelian

celebration featuring the Utrecht Jubilate and the opulent Ode for

St. Cecelia's Day.

Join the Cathedral Choral Society in their birthday tribute to

Handel, this Sunday October 20th at 4 p.m. at the Washington

Cathedral.

(Music God Save, etc...)

Tickets at the Cathedral Museum Shop, or at the door.  For information

call 966-3423.  966-3423.
```

B

lists from the 1950s and 1960s. The Oldies format is the elder statesman of the Vintage genre, having surfaced in the mid-1960s.

Nostalgia is also known as Big Band in some markets. The format is the concept of programmer Al Ham, who began marketing his programming idea in the late 1970s. Nostalgia concentrates on music dating as far back as the 1930s and 1940s, as well as the 1950s. These stations also incorporate contemporary compositions—by artists such as Linda Ronstadt—that are viewed as compatible with the overall sound.

The most recent Vintage manifestation is Classic Hits. A product of the 1980s, this Vintage variation airs top pop-rock charters from the late 1960s through the mid-1980s. In 1986, the number of Classic Hits outlets tripled as audiences found the format an appealing alternative to contemporary hit stations. The Classic Hits format is mostly found on the FM band, although an increasing number of AM stations have found the formula effective as they tried to win back music listeners in the 1980s.

Nostalgia, too, is most likely to be found on the FM band, although it has been, and remains, a successful AM offering.

Of all Vintage formats, Oldies is the most steadfast resident of AM. However, in the 1980s, the number of Oldies operations on FM increased sizably.

Nostalgia is the least personality oriented of the Vintage formats, as it is often affiliated with a program syndicator and automated. Oldies stations have always been proponents of the air personality, whereas Classic Hits station voice performers usually assume a somewhat lower profile.

The age levels of the Vintage audience varies. Oldies attracts an over-thirty listener, and Nostalgia draws an even older demographic stratum, usually over forty. Of the three Vintage categories, Classic Hits stations appeal to the youngest crowd—a group mainly in their twenties and thirties, and often younger.

Announcing Criteria

The Vintage formats recruit people who have a keen affection for the past. "We air rock history, so we're all music historians, to a point. A love for the music and artists has to show on the air. I don't hire announcers just to fill slots. Air people reflect the attitude and feel of the oldies music. No 'time and temp' jocks in this format," says Glenn Colligan, operations manager, WDRC-AM, Hartford, Connecticut.

An appetite for the period makes for the most effective air person. "In this format, programmers search for someone who is more than mildly acquainted with the period. Our listeners relive the era from which the music is derived, so our deejays, regardless of their age, talk oldies with authority and affection. You can't fake it. There are thousands of intelligent and informed listeners tuned, so you've got to know your stuff," observes Jim Stowe, Program Director, KEZC/KJOK, Yuma, Arizona.

Jim Byard, program director of Oldies station WRXJ-AM, Jacksonville, Florida, says that after basic announcing skills, knowledge of the oldies music library is essential. "You can't get by with just announcing titles in this format. Listeners want background and want to believe that the air person is educated in the music. In terms of deejay delivery, friendliness and warmth rank high. This is a 'good-time' format. People tune to revive old memories. You have to treat the music with love and respect or you offend the memories of your listeners. Deejays must 'converse' with the listener. He or she must be polite with call-ins, too. Another thing that I require of my air people is the ability, or flexibility, to work in different time slots. I want to be able to switch a person around if I have to and know that he or she can adapt to the different daypart and sound good."

KEZC's Stowe attempts to fill his Oldies air schedule with broadcast voice performers who can ignite an audience. "The capacity to charge and stir listeners, to get them involved and excited, is gold in a deejay. Put that kind of person on the air with the right mix of oldies music and you have a winning sound."

WDRC's Colligan bemoans what he perceives as a lack of literacy in prospective air people. "I can't imagine anyone hoping to talk over a mass medium, such as radio, without sufficient reading comprehension skills. If you can't read, you can't talk on the radio effectively, and if you can't speak effectively, you have no right opening the mic switch. Understanding what you are reading, be it a spot or news copy, allows you to communicate it to the listener."

Having a distinctive on-air persona keeps a deejay in the minds of his listeners. "Anybody wanting air work in Oldies, or any format really, should develop their own personality or character. Don't try to mimic someone else. There are enough clones out there already. You are you, and it is that person you should develop and be able to convey to an audience. In other words, give your listeners the warm and real YOU," advises WRXJ's Byard.

WDRC's Colligan concurs, "Work on being your own person, not at trying to be someone else. Use other people's good qualities and work them into your own style. Once you get an air person to be his own person, the rest is a matter of practice."

Oldies programmers cite writing skills as essential. "I believe an announcer should be able to write effective commercial copy. Not only does this broaden his or her value to the station, but it gets the individual's cre-

FIGURE 4.9
Two-voice Vintage commercial with tag. Courtesy WRXJ-AM.

```
LENGTH :60                COPY # 1
CLIENT STRICKLANDS  MAYPORT
START SPEC SPOT           END
INSTRUCTIONS
APPROVED BY CLIENT AS PROD.____ DATE____
```

1. FRANK: (SFX WAVES LAPPING) HEY JOE SURE IS A NICE DAY TO BE FISHING.
2. JOE: SURE IS FRANK, PASS ME ANOTHER COLD ONE. (SFX: LEFT TO RIGHT CAN FLYING INTO HAND) THANKS.....
3. FRANK: JOE, REMEMBER LAST YEAR WHEN WE WENT FISHING AND DID'NT CATCH ANYTHING
4. JOE: YEA, BUT WE SURE MADE UP FOR IT AT STRICKLANDS ALL THAT FRESH FISH DAILY WHAT A A CHOICE, BETTER THAN ANYTHING WE COULD CATCH.
5. FRANK: WE DEFINATELY HAD A GREAT TIME ESPECIALLY AT THE OYSTER BAR...BOY THEY TASTED GOOD.
6. AND THE VIEW WAS FANTASTIC.
7. JOE: I HEAR THAT.-DURING THE MONTH OF SEPTEMBER, WHEN YOU ORDER A FRIED SHRIMP DINNER AT\. $8.95...A FREE SHRIMP COCKTAIL IS INCLUDED.
8. FRANK: SURE GIVES YA AN APPETITE..TOSS ME A SANDWICH.(RIGHT TO LEFT SANDWICH TOSSED)..THAN
9. JOE: FRANK, ARE YOU THINKING WHAT I'M THINKING
10. BOTH: STRICKLANDS AT MAYPORT
11. FRANK: GOOD IDEA JOE....LETS GO (SFX: GETTING OUT OF BOAT ON TO DOCK WALKING AWAY)
12. JOE: I CAN'T WAIT TO SAVOR THAT MOUTHWATERING FRESH FISH
13. FRANK: I'M HEADING FOR THE GREAT VIEW AND OYSTER BAR.
14. JOE: YOU KNOW FRANK WE SURE SAVE A LOT OF MONEY WHEN WE GO FISHING.
15. FRANK: YEA, HOW?
16. JOE: WE NEVER USE ANY GAS.
17. TAG: STRICKLANDS AT MAYPORT, FLORIDAS LANDMARK FOR SEAFORD FOR FIFITY YEARS OPEN DAILY AT 5 PM AND AT NOON SATURDAY AND SUNDAY. TAKE FLORIDA HIGHWAY A1A 15 MINUTES NORTH OF JACKSONVILLE BEACH.

```
PRODUCTION ALBUM#____ SIDE____ CUT____ TITLE OF CUT____
SECOND LP USED   ____ SIDE____ CUT____ TITLE OF CUT____
SOUND EFFECTS _____ JOX____
```

ative juices flowing, which is what is needed in this business—on or off the air," says Byard.

KEZC's Stowe recommends daily vocabulary exercises. "Air people have an obligation to themselves and their audience to work toward a mastery of the language. For starters, keep a dictionary at your side. A handy pocket dictionary is useful. Build on your word power, not to impress listeners but to communicate more effectively—with depth and variety, not pretentiousness. Open the dictionary each day, and learn a new word. You know what they say, 'use a word three times, and it's yours forever.' A deejay who does not comprehend what she is reading can't communicate with complete credibility. You have to learn to converse, not simply read aloud."

Colligan adds to Stowes' statement: "If you have educated yourself in the language, you are able to pick up words and phrases spontaneously. Sight reading, the ability to understand what is on the printed page in-

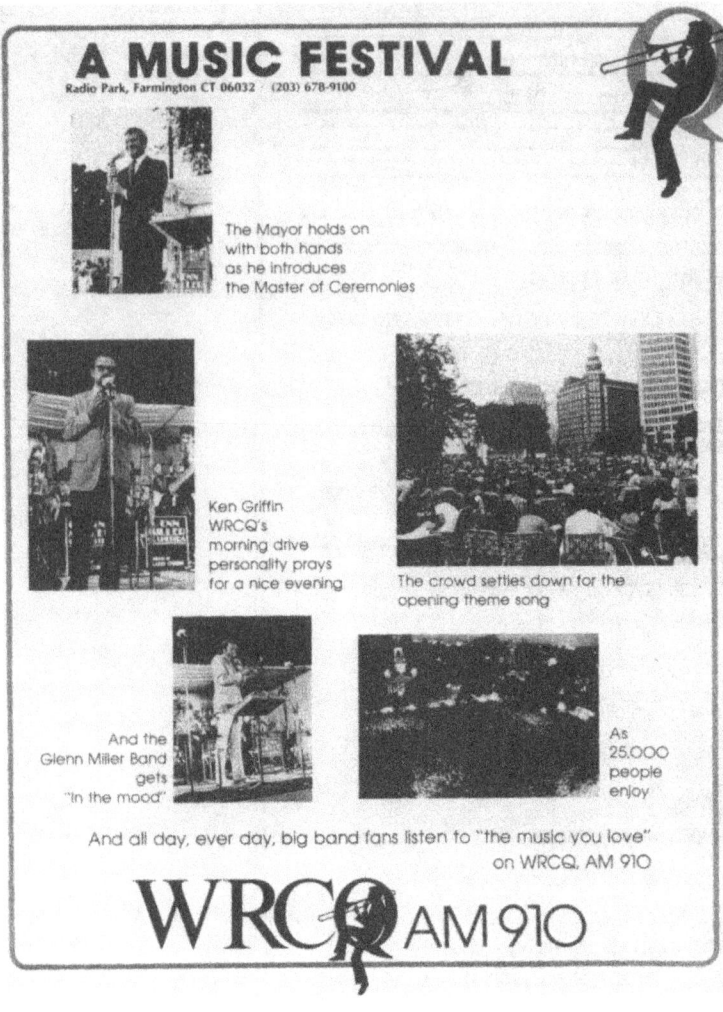

FIGURE 4.10
Vintage (Big Band) station promotional piece. Courtesy WRCQ-AM.

stantly, without hesitation, is what distinguishes the pros from the neophytes."

Colligan asserts, too, that "Complacency is anathema to broadcasters. The worst thing for an air person to suffer from is indifference. I know you've heard this from other p.d.s, but it bears repeating, I think. Sitting back and accepting that what you did is the best you can do is counterproductive to growth, and we all have room to grow, even the top personalities in the mega-markets. Strive to be better. Work at your sound daily. The oldest pro will tell you that he is still learning."

Another item in the Vintage format minus column has to do with mood and attitude. "The Vintage formats are very genial and upbeat. A deejay can ill afford to let his or her personal feelings carry over onto the air. I'm talking about gloom and cynicism. It is the air performer's job to keep the listener in a positive frame of mind, so smile when you open that mic, despite the burden of your personal problems," advises programming consultant Jim Smith.

ANNOUNCING IN OTHER FORMATS

The formats examined up to this point employ nearly 70 percent of the radio industry's broadcast voice performers. The balance work in formats such as Religious, Middle-of-the-Road, News/Talk, Urban Contemporary, and Ethnic, among others.

Religious

Mike Landry, operations manager for Religious station KFEL-AM, Pueblo, Colorado, discusses announcing criteria in his format. "We have a very loyal audience. They stay with us for a long period. Therefore, our air staff must consist of people who wear well. First off, they must project 'believability.' My first criterion for hiring an announcer is air presence. Usually this means that a job seeker needs to possess a combination of good voice and sound diction. Of course, there are people without the standard 'radio voice' who are able to project a personality and a likeableness.

"Another indispensable quality that I find appropriate in air people is intelligence. It doesn't take much to parrot words on the radio. I want a pro who can be cool in the face of adversity, someone with smarts. We're a commercial station, so another essential for air people here is sales ability. You can overlook a nonstandard voice if a radio personality can sell the goods on the air. Witness the success of radio legends Paul Harvey and Arthur Godfrey. They could sell ice to Eskimos and neither has a traditional radio sound.

"Let me also add that you should develop your strengths and downplay your weaknesses. Charlie Martin of KHOW in Denver does not have a standard radio voice, but he's pulling down a six-figure salary. Tom Brokaw has a slight impediment or nasality, but he has been able to compensate in other areas.

"One last thing, ad-lib statements need to answer the 'who cares' test. In other words, why am I saying this? To inform? To entertain? To help? And if I know why I am saying this, will anyone really care, and can I pull it off effectively?"

News and Talk

News and Talk radio stations have been drawing listeners for nearly thirty years. Today these nonmusic formats are the main entrées on the AM menu, although only a handful of FM stations air all News. Marni Pingree, program director of News and Talk station KTAR-AM, Phoenix, Arizona, offers these observations regarding on-air performance in her format. "Due to the fact that we are in the information business, I require that a person be very informed about the local community, as well as the nation and world. You have to be up on current events, in particular. The specific qualities which I feel are basic to good announcing at my station are voice quality, the ability to speak effectively on-mic in our native tongue, as well as the talent to communicate one-on-one, as though the listener were in the studio. Enthusiasm, liveliness, and eagerness are important. In other terms, does the announcer sound as though he or she cares about what they are doing and saying? Ad-lib skills are very valuable, too. Empathy, also. Does the performer sound like someone you would like to spend time with?"

Middle-of-the-Road

In an attempt to reach the broadest demographics, the Middle-of-the-Road (MOR) format offers a diverse mix of programming. The granddaddy of format radio, MOR has been around since the early 1950s. Like News and Talk radio, MOR is primarily an AM offering. Personalities typically play a large role in this format, which frequently airs chatter in equal proportions to music.

Mianne S. Mitchell, program director of MOR station WMCW-AM, Harvard, Illinois, explains announcing criteria from her format's perspective. "Versatility is important here. MOR is a variety format, so air people need depth of skills and general knowledge. I expect my air staff to know a little about a lot. Our people must be able to conduct solid interviews involving topics as disparate as farming and politics. They must be able to write and report news and sports. One of the main qualities I look for is a 'happy' voice. It reflects a happy person, and it comes through as such on the air. We're a small market station, and our listeners really feel a closeness to our announcers. Their attitude establishes the proper mood and atmosphere. I look for people who sound upbeat and conversational. Our air talent 'visit' with our listeners.

"A habit I dislike immensely is verbosity—running on long after the point has been made. My rule is, 'Say what you have to say, and move on to the next element'."

As this chapter has demonstrated, a station's format does affect announcing criteria. Anyone planning a career on the air in radio needs to become aware of the unique characteristics that distinguish one format from another.

Of course, it should be evident, too, that there are qualities basic to all formats. Programming consultant Donna Halper observes that once all the trappings are stripped away, the audience wants to know that a flesh and blood person is at the other end of the radio. Echoing the sentiment of several other programmers in this chapter, Halper says, "Be you! Yes, adapt to the format environment, but be you. That is, in fact, the biggest 'do' of all today. Radio voices and phoney images no longer work for the audience. It wants you as you really are—a friendly person who loves radio and enjoys entertaining folks each day. So be yourself."

SUGGESTED FURTHER READING

Armstrong, Ben. *The Electronic Church*. Nashville, Tenn.: J. Nelson, 1979.

Cliff, Charles, and Greer, A. *Broadcasting Programming: The Current Perspective*. Washington, D.C.: University Press of America, 1974 to date, revised annually.

Hall, Claude, and Hall, Barbara. *This Business of Radio Programming*. New York: Billboard Publishing, 1977.

Keith, Michael C. *Radio Programming: Consultancy and Formatics*. Stoneham, Mass.: Focal Press, 1987.

———, and Krause, Joseph M. *The Radio

Station. Stoneham, Mass.: Focal Press, 1986.

Orlik, Peter B. *Broadcast Copywriting,* 2nd ed. Boston: Allyn and Bacon, 1982.

Routt, Ed, McGrath, James B., and Weiss, Frederic A. *The Radio Format Conundrum.* New York: Hastings House, 1978.

5 THE BROADCAST NEWS VOICE

RADIO IN THE NEWS

In *The Radio Station* (Focal Press, 1986), I made the statement that "The medium of radio was used to convey news before news of the medium had reached the majority of the general public." Marconi's wireless telegraphy was first and foremost a medium of information. A young David Sarnoff demonstrated the value of Marconi's curious new electronic communications device to a throng of intrigued onlookers at Wannamaker's department store in New York by receiving wireless distress messages and information pertaining to the sinking *Titanic*. The year was 1912, and the wireless had recently been installed on all ships transporting fifty or more passengers as a means of calling for help in a crisis such as that which befell the *Titanic*.

Ship-to-ship and ship-to-shore communications were transformed by the wireless. As mariners entered the twentieth century, they no longer had to face the anxiety of being incommunicado while at sea. The wireless telegraph made it possible for them to remain in touch with the world. As ships traveled the high seas they were able to transmit and relay news and information over the great expanses of water to other journeying vessels and foreign ports.

During World War I, the military recognized the value of the wireless and encouraged the government to award it exclusive use of the medium, which it received. During the war years, nonmilitary use of the new communications device was prohibited by federal law.

It was at the onset of the United States' involvement in the war that David Sarnoff wrote his historic memo proposing domestic use of the radio medium. It would be several years after the war before Sarnoff's plan would be fully implemented.

In 1920, several million home receivers were being manufactured, and in November of that same year Pittsburgh radio station KDKA aired the Harding-Cox Presidential election returns, beginning the age of broadcast coverage of key news events. Soon thereafter stations around the country exerted efforts to report on important local and national news topics. The profession of broadcast journalism was slowly evolving.

RADIO GOES TO PRESS

The earliest radio news voices were recruited from various fields but most frequently from the press. Most broadcasters had backgrounds in newspaper writing and reporting, and many maintained their involvement with the print media while moonlighting in radio.

As the medium established itself in the homes of Americans, news features became somewhat more common, but not commonplace. The role of news would be advanced with the introduction of the networks (NBC and CBS) in the last half of the 1920s.

In 1930, the first regularly scheduled network news report was aired by NBC. Lowell Thomas anchored the five-times a week, fifteen-minute news broadcast. Thomas would continue his newscasts for the network until 1976. Other newscasters, such as H.V. Kaltenborn, Edwin C. Hill, and Boake Carter, soon joined Thomas in regularly scheduled news reports.

As the networks were attempting to launch their broadcast news services during this pe-

FIGURE 5.1
Early network newscaster H.V. Kaltenborn. Courtesy CBS.

FIGURE 5.2
CBS News special correspondent Charles Collingwood reported on World War II for the network. Courtesy CBS.

riod, they relied on the wire services, which were controlled by the newspaper industry. This arrangement culminated in a crisis when the print media began to perceive radio as a competitive threat. The wire services were advised to discontinue their flow of information to the electronic medium. In the ensuing months of the copy blackout, radio resorted to various means of in-house news gathering.

By 1933, an agreement was struck with the print media that provided for a resumption in wire service to radio. However, the agreement seriously limited radio's news broadcast capability, and within a few months several independent news gathering operations, chiefly Transradio Press Service, were formed to provide news copy to stations not bound by the agreement. Transradio Press Service's success prompted the Press-Radio Bureau (International News Service, United Press, and Associated Press) to lift all strictures for fear that it would ultimately lose revenues gained by selling news to radio.

With the wire service dilemma settled, a more stable environment allowed for the continued growth of the broadcast journalism field. However, in the 1930s, radio remained primarily an entertainment medium, despite the aspirations and efforts of many news reporters and commentators to elevate the status of news programming. Until the late 1930s, most radio managers were content to let the newspapers handle the task of informing the public.

THE WAR IS NEWS

Broadcast news really did not come into its own until World War II. Radio newscasters delivered reports on the progress of the war, and correspondents from the battle zones filed observations and comments on the conflict, which touched the lives of every American. The radio became the primary source of immediate information about the war. The networks shifted their focus to coverage of the war, because the audience wanted as much data as the medium could supply.

With the extended coverage, radio's status as an information medium soared, as did its overall credibility. Networks increased the size of their news staffs and broadened their news budgets. All told, the networks (NBC, CBS, MBS) doubled their scheduled newscasts between 1940 and 1945. By 1944, network news programs constituted nearly 20 percent of the networks' weekly broadcast schedules.

News reporters such as Howard K. Smith, Charles Collingwood, Eric Sevareid, Webley Edwards, Edward R. Murrow, Robert Trout, and others became household names as they brought the latest information on the war into homes on a daily basis.

TELEVISION NEWS

Following the war, the arena for broadcast news was expanded with the introduction of television. In the late 1940s, the networks (NBC and CBS) aired a nightly fifteen-minute newscast. John Cameron Swayze greeted viewers on NBC's *Camel News Caravan*, and *Douglas Edwards with the News* informed viewers tuned to CBS television. Years later Walter Cronkite would bring his charismatic presence to CBS, adding further acclaim to the network that had gained the most prestigious image in electronic journalism.

Cronkite's former newswriter and producer at CBS, Ed Bliss, attributes the news anchor's success to a unique combination of warmth and authority. "Cronkite's warmth of personality was reflected in his voice. This, I am sure, contributed greatly to his success. But, I believe, it was his experience, earnestness, and enthusiasm about news—his seriousness about news—that, more than anything else, made him 'the most trusted man in America.' His serious approach to the news showed in his delivery of the news. The viewer sensed that here was news being delivered by a conscientious, honest-to-God newsman, a reporter with credentials."

While Cronkite became the centerpiece of CBS news, Chet Huntley and David Brinkley assumed nightly network news broadcasting chores at NBC. The delivery styles of Huntley and Brinkley often inspired comments and even parodies by entertainers and satirists. While Chet Huntley projected an austere and even solemn image, his co-anchor was dubbed "Twinkly Brinkley" by *Newsweek* magazine because of his Alfred E. Newman, "What me worry?" on-camera presence. Each served as perfect counterpoint to the other, which contributed significantly to their audience popularity and long run on NBC.

FIGURE 5.3
Early television news anchorman Douglas Edwards. Courtesy CBS.

The Documentary

The television news documentary added to the credibility and stature of electronic journalism in the 1950s and 1960s, most notably under the guidance and genius of Edward R. Murrow, who formed CBS's Documentary Unit. Programs covering important news stories and social issues, such as *See It Now*, co-produced by Murrow and Fred Friendly, would spawn numerous features of a similar ilk on television and radio. Murrow's last documentary for CBS, *Harvest of Shame*, focused on the abject conditions facing the migrant worker. The program raised a furor among government bureaucrats but received accolades from practically everyone else, including the print media.

Murrow's ethics and sense of fairness also inspired him to rebuke Senator Joe McCarthy

FIGURE 5.4
David Brinkley—one half of the popular 1960s television news team Huntley and Brinkley. Courtesy ABC.

for his blacklisting tactics against alleged communist sympathizers. During two of his *See It Now* programs, Murrow exposed the menace behind McCarthy's methods and actions. Many historians view Murrow's broadcasts as the arrow in the Senator's Achilles' heel. During one of his broadcasts, Murrow observed "This is no time for men who oppose Senator McCarthy's methods to keep silent." It was not in Murrow's nature to remain taciturn in the face of injustice.

The documentary format that Murrow innovated remains intact and healthy today, although it has seldom reached the rarefied heights that it did while under his brilliant direction.

FORMATTING THE NEWS

As television overtook radio as the prime home entertainer, the latter medium shifted to a more local news emphasis. Station formats dictated news delivery styles and content. For example, Top 40 stations seeking young listeners often expected newscasters to deliver copy in a manner indistinguishable from deejays' hyped lead-ins to pop records. Many Top 40 outlets adopted a "hyped-heads" (headlines) approach to news presentation—the idea being to keep it short and sensational.

Consequently, the content of newscasts was often equated with the yellow journalism tabloids of the day, due to their inclination to focus on the bizarre and tragic. I recall a newscast on just such a station that featured a news story about the unsuccessful surgical separation of Siamese twins. The story, which topped the newscast, was delivered very melodramatically and was accompanied by reverb (voice echo).

Other formats imposed different presentation criteria on newscasters. Middle-of-the-Road stations aimed for a more conversational, one-on-one presentation, whereas Beautiful Music and Classical stations insisted on a more formal and conservative news style. Country stations favored a down-home, neighborly sound.

As radio moved further into the age of spe-

FIGURE 5.5
Boston news anchors Jack Hynes and Uma Pemmaraju. Women co-anchors became popular in the 1970s. Courtesy WLVI-TV.

cialization in the 1960s and 1970s, newscast delivery styles became somewhat less affected by formatics. Most stations adopted a standard approach, whereby news was presented in a more generic, that is, direct and unaffected, manner. This is not to suggest that the "screamers" and "sleepers" no longer exist. They do. But for the most part, radio news has a more neutered, less self-conscious sound than it did during the early years of format specialization.

LOCAL NEWS

While radio news adapted to the requisites of tailored programming, television news coverage grew on the local level. The networks provided affiliates fifteen-minute national and world news coverage nightly, and many stations originated local news blocks, usually fifteen minutes in duration, to round out the half-hour.

In the 1950s, television stations were less concerned with the journalistic credentials of on-camera reporters than they were with their appearance. Frequently, station staff announcers would deliver newscast copy as well as serve in various other capacities, such as program emcees and hosts. At one station the evening newscaster also performed as a clown on a Saturday morning children's show.

Later in the decade local television programming became a more serious enterprise. Stations sought news personnel with training in reporting. Credibility became an important factor as stations began to promote and market their news offerings. With news perceived as an income generator, stations became more willing to invest in their news operations.

By the 1960s, the majority of local newscasts had been extended to a half-hour format that included on-scene reporting and comprehensive weather and sports coverage. The networks, too, had extended their nightly news broadcasts to a half-hour. Between 1950 and 1965, television network news staffs had increased manifold times, and local television news had grown from infancy to young adulthood.

FIGURE 5.6
Television station newsroom. Courtesy WJAR-TV.

NEWS BROADCASTS TODAY

Television and radio news presentation continued to grow in the 1980s, perhaps more as the consequence of the proliferation of broadcast signals than out of a desire to offer more comprehensive coverage. In fact, a slippage in the actual percentage of local radio news presentation has been detected by the Radio and Television News Directors' Association (RTNDA) since the Federal Communications Commission's elimination of news and public affairs programming requirements in the early 1980s.

While practically every radio station (12,000) in the United States airs news, the average amount of time a station devotes to it daily is about 125 minutes. (This figure obviously does not apply to all-News format operations.)

Meanwhile, the television networks have made several unsuccessful bids to lengthen their nightly newscasts to one hour, but affiliates have resisted such proposals, not willing to cut into the lucrative local revenues their own news shows generate.

On another video front, cable has added significantly to the electronic news menu. For example, the Cable News Network (CNN), based in Atlanta, offers cable subscribers twenty-four hour news and information coverage, and a recent study revealed that the round-the-clock news service has cut into network news viewership. At the same time, many local cable systems offer viewers evening news programs.

There is clearly a preponderance of news available via the electronic media. In fact, in most portions of the country a person is only a flick of the switch away from up-to-the-minute reports on local, national, and world events. For a majority of Americans, broadcast (cable) news is the primary source of information about what is happening around the block and around the globe.

THE ELECTRONIC NEWSROOM

Technology has revolutionized nearly every aspect of the broadcast field, and the newsroom has not been untouched. Indeed, the broadcast newsroom has undergone some of the most dramatic changes. Computers and satellites have virtually swept electronic

FIGURE 5.7
Statistics on radio news listenership. Courtesy RAB.

RadioFacts

Radio Is The First Morning News Source

Morning (6 AM-10 AM)	Radio	TV	News-papers	Other/None
Persons 12+	49%	29%	15%	7%
Teens 12-17	60	21	12	7
Adults 18+	48	30	16	6
Adults 18-34	53	28	13	6
Adults 25-54	50	29	16	5
College Grads.	46	27	22	5
Prof./Mgr. Males	55	19	20	6
F/T Working Women	56	27	11	6
$50K+ Income	49	28	18	5

Radio Is The First News Source At Midday

Midday (10 AM-3 PM)	Radio	TV	News-papers	Other/None
Persons 12+	36%	24%	14%	26%
Teens 12-17	30	24	17	29
Adults 18+	37	24	14	25
Adults 18-34	43	19	18	20
Adults 25-54	41	18	15	26
College Grads.	36	17	15	32
Prof./Mgr. Males	36	9	23	32
F/T Working Women	48	9	12	31
$50K+ Income	44	10	17	29

Radio Is The Major Source of News

Morning (6AM-10 AM)	Radio	TV	News-papers	Other/None
Persons 12+	42%	31%	18%	9%
Teens 12-17	54	29	9	8
Adults 18+	41	31	19	9
Adults 18-34	45	28	20	7
Adults 25-54	43	29	20	8
College Grads	38	24	30	8
Prof./Mgr. Males	48	16	27	9
Working Women	49	28	15	8
$50K+ Income	45	21	27	7

Radio Is The First Source For Local Emergency News

	Radio	TV	Other/None
Persons 12+	50%	48%	2%
Teens 12-17	50	49	1
Adults 18+	50	48	2
Adults 18-34	50	49	1
Adults 25-54	54	44	2
College Grads.	56	42	2
Prof./Mgr. Males	57	40	3
F/T Working Women	51	47	2

journalism into a new age of speed and efficiency. "The electronic newsroom is here. It is a fact of life, and not just in major markets. Computers and satellites are becoming as much a part of a station's news operation as the telephone and tape recorder," says Judy Smith, News Director, KAPE-AM, San Antonio, Texas.

Typewriters have been replaced by desktop computers at many stations, both large and small, throughout the country. Boston all-News station WEEI-AM has computerized its operation from stem to stern—from its on-air studio to its newsroom—with Media Touch Systems' Touchscreen 2000 series automated assist system, which is driven by an IBM computer. On-air operators simply touch items displayed on the monitor to call up or activate elements.

In the newsroom, staff members work off minicomputers to write and rewrite stories and to store and retrieve data. Numerous computer data banks and bulletin board services provide outstanding sources for the newsperson. At some stations, newscasters actually announce their copy directly off video display terminals, foregoing hand-held copy.

In the 1980s, television has increased its reliance on satellite technology in the newsroom. Electronic news gathering (ENG) minivans outfitted with satellite dishes give field reporters greater live-feed capability and increased mobility. "Satellite and computer technology has transformed the TV newsroom and field mobile units. News people can do more now and with significantly enhanced quality than they could a decade ago. Television news is, if anything, high-tech, and more is on the way," observes David Graves, News Director, WPRI-TV, Providence, Rhode Island.

The new and evolving technologies impact news personnel. "News people and those aspiring to careers in this business should really bone up on the new technologies, es-

FIGURE 5.8 Touchscreen 2000 automated assist system. Everything at the touch of a newsperson's finger. Courtesy Media Touch Systems.

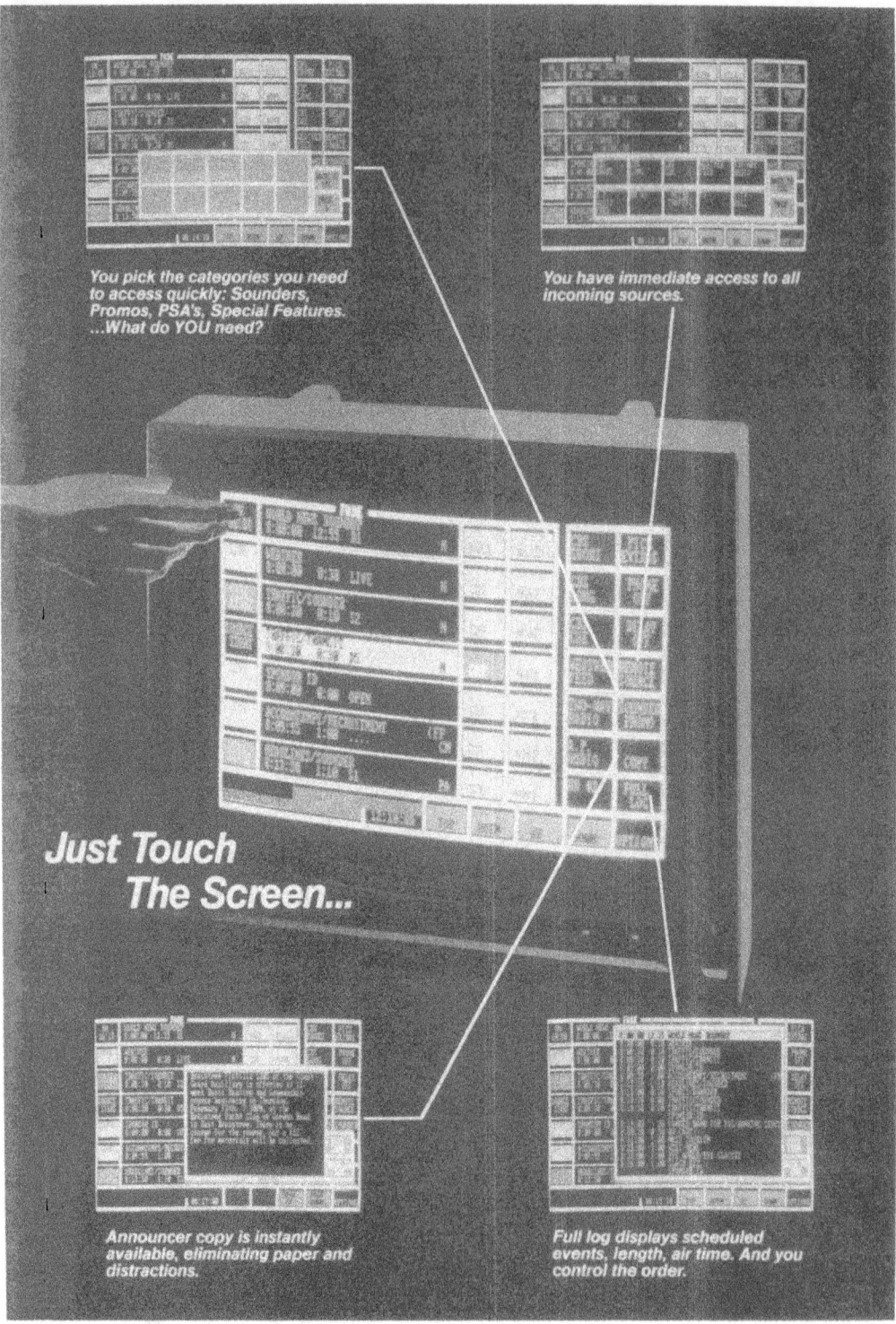

pecially computers, because they are fast becoming an integral part of the profession. It used to be that typing skills were enough. Not any more. Equipment is very sophisticated, and it requires a sophisticated person to handle it," notes Larry Jewett, News Director, WTOD-AM, Toledo, Ohio.

NEWSCASTER CRITERIA

As broadcast voice performers, newscasters must bring special skills and qualities to the microphone. Credibility, confidence, and authority are top criteria among news directors hiring on-air reporters. "Of course, a newscaster must have a clear, easy to take speaking voice, plus a pleasant but animated style of delivery, and an appearance that does not distract viewers from the message being presented. But most importantly, he or she must have credibility. Credibility comes from experience, plus the impression the newsperson gives the audience that he has done his homework. Viewers must believe the person reporting the news is not just reading copy. Viewers can quickly determine if an anchor-person knows his or her subject. Credibility is a fragile thing. A mispronunciation can crack the glass of credibility," says Larry W. Price, News Director, KSTP-TV, Minneapolis/St. Paul, Minnesota.

R. "Bob" Gishard, News Director, KAYN-FM, Rio Rico, Arizona, shares Price's position on credibility. "One of, if not, *the* most important qualities a newscaster must get across to the viewer or listener is credibility. To accomplish this, good speech is an absolute necessity. A newsperson must enunciate properly, speak clearly and naturally, and be familiar with his or her copy. Credibility requires a command of the vocabulary, that is, names and places, both local and universal. If you pronounce properly, that's instant credibility."

Delivery can strengthen or weaken credibility, contends Bill Yarbor, News Director, WYER-AM, Mt. Carmel, Illinois. "Newspeople must be capable of displaying credibility in ways other than just having the facts straight. Through the vocal delivery the listener is able to form an opinion as to whether the newscaster knows what the hell he is talking about. Too many times I have heard newscasters deliver stories as if they were reading and interpreting at the same time. The result was a muddled, unconvincing sound and the loss of credibility. We all stumble over a word or two from time to time, but we have to sound like we know what we're talking about or it's all out the window. Preparation and practice make the kind of delivery that convinces the audience."

Yarbor contends that confidence is another important on-air quality for newscasters. "Don't sound as though you're afraid of the mic or act like you're testifying before a senate subcommittee on news ethics. Timid is one thing a newsperson cannot be. Be confident in your ability, and it will come through on the air. Don't confuse confidence with cockiness, however. Both show through, and the results in terms of audience acceptance to each is quite different. Nobody likes a smug or egotistical news anchor."

Without confidence a newscaster cannot communicate authoritatively. "Sounding confident is essential," states Monica Brooks, News Director, KPWR-FM, Los Angeles, California. "Even when I was a deejay I had offers from competing stations to do news for them. They would always say they liked my confidence and authoritative delivery of whatever I was doing, even if it was

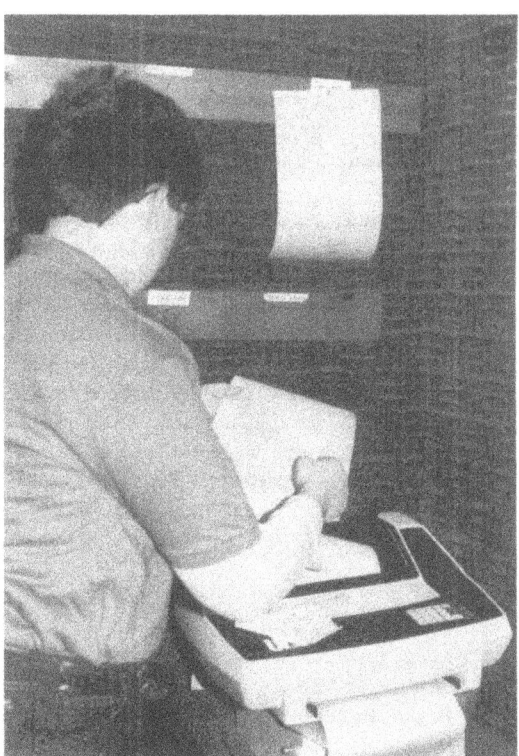

FIGURE 5.9
Newscaster assembling news for upcoming broadcast.

just a p.s.a. I believed in myself, so I created an authoritative image. Now I am doing news at the top station in one of the world's foremost cities. An authoritative delivery helps a listener or viewer establish trust—an important element. A good reader, one who doesn't stumble a lot, also makes a good broadcaster. It helps you sound like you know what you're reporting. Listening to someone who doesn't read well can be very annoying."

An authoritative presence is what the audience expects from a newscaster, believes Richard Bird, News Director, WCIL-AM, Carbondale, Illinois. "The first thing most broadcasters look for in a news announcer is someone whose delivery has weight and substance, someone who commands respect. Although most people think of this as only coming from someone with a deep-throated rumble of a voice, it actually has more to do with how the voice is used than what kind of voice someone has. Even slight speech impediments can be overcome if the delivery is convincing, as demonstrated by broadcasters such as Barbara Walters and Tom Brokaw. A news announcer must be able to sound conversational and authoritative, intense but not excited, informed and intelligent but not overly intellectual, and concerned yet objective. A newscaster also needs to be able to deliver a story not so much without a mistake in reading but in such a way that the listener doesn't think about it. When the uncertain announcer trips up, the whole audience takes notice, and to a negative effect."

According to Steven M. Hodges, Program Director, KCWD/KNWA, Harrison, Arkansas, a relaxed voice communicates command. "A calm voice gives an authoritative impression. A newscaster should work on breathing and pitch. A breathy, thin, or shaky voice does not instill an image of confidence and control in the listener's mind. News is a serious matter and must be told by someone who sounds together and stable. Pay attention to your pitch when you're reading. Strive for some consistency. Don't warble the news."

News directors hire intelligent and educated on-air personnel. "For me, and I don't think I'm unusual in this respect, the most important attribute in prospective newscasters is intelligence, both on and off the camera. To be blunt, the would-be news announcer better understand what he or she is reading, or no sale. Without this basic quality, almost any viewer will reject the reporter," says John Carpillio, News Director, WHJJ-AM, Providence, Rhode Island.

Other news directors concur with Carpillio. "It is imperative that behind the voice there is a brain. News requires a degree of intelligence and sophistication in worldly affairs. For one basic thing, this translates into proper pronunciation of foreign names and places," says Donald C. Keyes, owner, WTAL-AM, Tallahassee, Florida.

"A thorough grasp of copy content is necessary," says Jack Baty, News Director, KCEE/KWFM, Tucson, Arizona. "Newspeople must read the 'sense' of the story. Patterns won't do." KMOV-TV's news director, Michael Castengera, agrees. "Of all the attributes a newscaster has to have, the ability to read for sense and not for sound ranks highest, at least from my perspective. In other words, the newscaster/broadcaster must be capable of reading a sentence so that it makes real sense to the audience, not so it just sounds good. You have to read beyond the symbols of the language, the words, to get to the meaning—the essence. Talking with, not to, the viewer increases intelligibility and understanding. To relate, the conversational delivery is best. Have a conversation about the news with your audience. Embrace your viewers."

Jeanne D. Jackson, News Director, KARQ-FM, Ashdown, Arkansas, adds a note of caution about the conversational approach. "Conversational delivery does not mean flippantly going through your copy. It means talking *to* your listeners, not *at* them."

Steven Hodges of KCWD/KNWA expands on Jackson's cautionary note. "The ability to 'read for conversation' is an attractive attribute. A person should be able to read a script and talk it on the air. A 'reader' is boring to listen to. But conversational doesn't mean lazy or sloppy sounding either. Articulate conversation is the aim, of course."

Voice Quality

Voice quality, as in any area of on-air performance, is a major consideration when news directors look for employees. "Another important factor in the hiring process is an appealing voice. It need not be the so-called 'big voice' that a lot of announcers, particularly in radio, seem to feel they have to have in order to attract listeners. A pleasant sounding voice fulfills this criterion. If the person also has rich timbre and depth in his or her voice, so much the better," says John Carpillio.

KARQ's Jackson agrees with Carpillio. "A pleasant voice, not necessarily a 'good set of pipes,' will create the impression that you have command of the content of your 'cast. Deepening your natural tones may be desirable if you have a nasal sound (this sometimes eliminates that quality) or if you are a female with a particularly high-pitched voice. In most cases the deliberate dropping of the voice to a lower register is undesirable. It sounds contrived. Besides, lowering your voice register seldom gives you the authoritative sound. Knowing what you're talking about and delivering it concisely and intelligibly will give you authority, regardless of the depth of your voice."

Clarity

Clarity of vocal presentation is enhanced by good inflection, diction, and emphasis. "Let's face it, a news announcer must be understood from the first word to the last if he or she is to make it in this profession. This is the most basic of all requirements, but sometimes the most problematical. In my opinion, speaking clearly is the primary requisite behind the mic. Newspeople, especially beginners, need to aircheck themselves and listen with a critical ear. Misplacing the emphasis on a word or phrase or faulty inflection can warp the meaning of a story. You must be able to interpret with accuracy the substance of your copy. Personally, I've found that a background in drama (basic theater) is excellent training for major market news delivery. It teaches all the basics in breathing, projection, diction, and so on. Of course, the more you read the better able you are to speak. That's what my philosophy teacher would call 'axiomatic'—an immutable fact. Good readers, that is, people who read a lot for pleasure, are usually more articulate," observes J.E. Reiplinger, Vice President and General Manager, WYNG-FM, Evansville, Indiana.

Interpretive skills are needed to achieve clarity, says WTAL's Keyes. "The ability to read interpretively through the use of inflection and emphasis—this includes the 'coloring' and 'shading' of the voice as it relates to the subject matter—is an indispensable attribute and central to clarity. Read with understanding, and you'll be understood. It's not a complex concept."

KCEE's Baty suggests developing certain techniques to increase clarity. "Learn to use pauses and changes of inflection to make stories clearer and for the sake of variety. However, don't seesaw or bounce around. Establish a level of evenness. Shoot for smooth with a pinch of spice." Baty also points to the importance of projection while on-mic. "Remember to project. This is the 'alive' sound that most easily distinguishes the beginner from the expert. Even laid-back announcers project."

Be "On" When You Are On

Projection is no less important on-camera, notes KSTP-TV's Price. "Whenever that red light is activated, you're on, and *on* is the operative term. The news anchor must stoke up the engines and project. Another point: the anchor must be able to smile at the appropriate place. He or she must not come across silly, but as warm and friendly, so don't 'torpedo' project. If an anchor can't convince the viewer that he is a nice person, so to speak, he or she probably won't succeed. You have to be serious at the appropriate time, too. I guess when you get right down to it, I would quarrel with the term *announcer*. For my money, the best broadcasters do not announce, but communicate. The style years ago called for *announcing*. Walter Cronkite, Douglas Edwards, and the great newscasters of TV's first generation had a definite announcing style when presenting the news. It was quite different from casual conversation and, yes, quite successful at the time. The trend in the second generation has been away from the more formalized to the conversational and less affected. Tom Brokaw's style is certainly more conversational and casual than Cronkite's. Brokaw's delivery is more relaxed and 'at-home.' Of course, both gentlemen project a strong image."

Fitting and Ad-Libbing in Format

News directors expect their on-air people to reflect the station's sound, as well as ad-lib when the situation warrants, says Ken Conlin, News Director, KRED-AM, Eureka, California. "You hire news voices that mirror the station's format. We expect newscasters to be simpatico with the station's image. It makes sense. You don't want a Top 40, hyped news delivery on an adult music station. I tell my news people to align themselves with the surrounding production values. This sometimes involves ad-libbing along with our personalities—you know, the back-and-forth banter around newscasts. Under deadline situations, the newscaster should also have the ability to effectively ad-lib, while maintaining the factual integrity of a story. Deejays are not the only broadcasters who need to develop sharp ad-lib skills."

Newscasting Versus Deejaying

News directors make a clear distinction between newscasting as a form of broadcast voice performance and announcing or deejaying. "The newscaster tells the audience what he or she has learned about a given story or stories. He or she is not given to forming public opinion on issues and individuals. A newscaster should not be a part of the news, but should simply deliver the goods. A disc jockey can poke a little fun at a story or newsmaker and get away with it. A newscaster, however, must not toy with the news, particularly when dealing with local news in a small market. The audience takes the news quite seriously, and any sort of deviation from what they perceive as the norm can be costly in terms of your credibility," contends WYER's Yarbor.

KCWD's Hodges adds to Yarbor's position, "Newscasting is the 'passing along of information.' A radio deejay creates his or her own information. A newscaster should not lean one way or the other on an issue. Neutrality is crucial."

In order to maintain this important distance, newscasters generally are kept from commercial announcing. "Since a key factor in news credibility is neutrality, a good newscaster will never voice spots. Most stations establish this as policy anyway, but on occasion I have heard a news voice on a commercial, and it is not a desirable situation. Ultimately, this is a damaging error. News of the Persian Gulf and Artie's Furniture Sale-a-thon don't mix well coming from the same person," says WYNG's Reiplinger.

KMOV-TV's Castengera believes as Reiplinger that commercial delivery by newscasters has a negative effect on listeners. "I see on-air delivery as falling into two categories—commercial and news. I am not able to deal with the first except to say that it appears the general audience is willing to accept the falsity that this kind of announcing projects—false enthusiasm, false bravado, false concern, etc. In newscasting the person must be perceived as 'real.' There can be no falsity. Most of the time the successful newscaster comes across as sincere and honest. It is imperative that this be so. Anything that jeopardizes this must be eliminated."

Newscasting is not designed to be entertainment. "You are not there to entertain listeners. You are informing them of what is happening out there. Present the news to them, not the 'bull.' They will form their own opinions and interpretations. You cannot do that for them. Try it and it will eventually backfire. Today's audience has exposure to so many sources of news information that they are not looking for someone to tell them *how* the news is, but *what* it is and what *effects* are possible on their daily lives as a consequence," observes KARQ's Jackson.

Newscasting is very serious business, says WCIL's Bird. "News announcing is neither selling, as in a commercial, nor cajoling, as in deejaying. Newscasting is relating the facts of a story—sometimes grim, sometimes upbeat, sometimes maddening, and sometimes bizarre. Newscasters must not be flamboyant." WDWS's Talbot adds to Bird's statement: "To offer a theatrical distinction, where announcing allows for melodrama, overt comedy, and the like, news reporting is a much more understated presentation, more like a formal address than a humorous monologue."

Unlike deejays, newscasters must live with the constant pressure of deadlines, contends KPWR's Brooks. "Newscasting is different, too, because you're not on the air in a sustained manner like the disc jockey, and you're always under a deadline, with stories changing and developing every minute. Records don't change as fast. There is new material every second in a newsroom. This makes the newsperson's job a twenty-four-hour thing, because there's always something happening that is newsworthy."

INTERVIEWING

News personnel must know how to conduct an interview. Reporters spend a great deal of time questioning figures related to news stories. Preparation is half the task, says Daryl Borden, News Producer, WRGB-TV, Albany, New York. "Do your homework. Know what is going on. Research as much as possible before you conduct an interview. I shudder when I see a reporter corrected by an interviewee. This is tantamount to saying to the audience, 'This reporter is ill-prepared.'"

KARQ's Jackson says that reporters have to develop listening skills if they hope to do a good interview. "Pay attention to what your subject is saying, and react accordingly. Some of the best questions in an interview are inspired by comments from the person being interviewed. One other piece of advice: Don't ask 'dead-end' questions. These are questions that elicit a 'yes' or 'no' response. Pose questions that force the interviewee to respond at length. Ask innovative and inspired questions, and ask questions you know the audience wants answers to."

Do not overwhelm, bully, or intimidate the person being questioned. "Avoid being too pushy or aggressive. Don't play 'Mr. News Reporter.' Put your guest at ease. You'll get a lot more from her," advises KSTP-TV's Price. He adds, "Retain control of the interview, too. Just as you don't want an interviewee to be in awe of you, you shouldn't be intimidated by the person you're interviewing, regardless of the person's status or fame. Stay in charge."

Bill Porter, Program Director, WROL-AM, Boston, says to practice by conducting interviews with friends or relatives. "Like anything else in this business, the more you work at it the better you get. Take a tape recorder or camcorder to friends' or relatives' homes and conduct impromptu interviews. Try an MOS (man-on-the-street) interview. Ask some questions that you feel will inspire good responses. Test yourself. Put yourself on the line. This will sharpen your skills. Oh, and always check to make sure your equipment is operating correctly and that you have enough tape on hand."

PREPPING FOR THE NEWSCAST

Read

The importance of credibility has been stressed numerous times, and several news directors have commented that sounding tentative on the air undermines credibility. KSTP-TV's Price advises all would-be newscasters to master the art of oral communi-

FIGURE 5.10
News reporter interviews an eyewitness.

cations or storytelling prior to sitting behind a microphone as a means of overcoming the feeling of uncertainty. "Newscasters are storytellers in a way. So I suggest working on your storytelling skills. People are always interested in hearing a good story. If you can tell a story in an interesting and captivating style and can do so in a natural, forthright way, you're on your way to becoming a credible news presenter."

KCWD's Hodges suggests that newscasting students read aloud newspaper stories. "I think one of the best ways to practice for eventual on-air duty is by reading items from the newspaper out loud each day. This a person can do anytime. I tell aspiring newscasters to set aside time daily to announce newspaper stories in private. When they gain confidence, they should read aloud to friends or family. Establish a routine, and practice at every possible opportunity."

Reading aloud from works of literature is another way to develop announcing skills, claims WDWS's Talbot. "Reading from literature enriches a person's sense of pacing, inflection, intonation, not to mention vocabulary. Actually, news copy is too limiting, and confining your practice to it does not provide you with the kind of initial exposure that is most beneficial. Reciting literature is a 'stretch.' The more written material that a person can manipulate to good effect, the less the chances are that he or she will be stumped on the air."

Preread

News directors expect their reporters to preread copy before airtime. "Traditionally, you preread your copy. Never go on cold. You're asking for trouble. Go through the copy and underline or highlight the most important points of a story, then if you run into time problems during a newscast you have a way to effectively get the point of the copy across without panicking or ending a story prematurely," says KARQ's Jackson.

KCEE's Baty requires his newscasters to announce copy in the news booth before actual airtime. "No grabbing news copy seconds before airtime. I instruct my staff to read and reread their news scripts before hitting the airwaves. Practice using the actual air copy helps you hit the mark and find your rhythm before the 'you're on' cue. It's policy here to get in the news booth several minutes before airtime and read copy out loud, as if you were actually doing a newscast."

Taping

Tape recording practice sessions is helpful, notes WTAL's Keyes. "Tape yourself reading news copy, then critique yourself. Try to be objective. This is the tricky part. Have friends comment on your performance. If you are not yet in the business, go to a station and ask a broadcaster to assess your tape. You will find people in the business willing to give you good pointers. Remember, they were beginners, too."

WCIL's Bird believes that analyzing taped performances is one of the most effective ways of overcoming bad habits and mistakes. "Tape doesn't lie. Listen to yourself, and have others listen and critique your performance. Be careful, though. Don't be overly critical of yourself, and don't try to change too much too soon. Work piecemeal. Eliminate weaknesses one by one, methodically. Depend most heavily on those who are in the 'know'— the p ofessionals."

KARQ's Jackson observes that professionals commonly tape themselves for the purpose of analyzing their own performances. "Most newscasters, at least the conscientious ones, aircheck themselves, so it makes good sense for you to tape yourself as a way to prep for on-air work. When you tape yourself, listen to your delivery and decide if you are making yourself completely understood. Have someone listen to your tape. See if they arrive at the same conclusions that you have. Push your ego aside. Listen with an open mind, and don't be overly sensitive to their opinions. The idea is to get better. Not be flattered."

Listen

Take the time to observe and listen to the experts as they perform. "You can learn a lot simply by tuning those already in the business. Take what you like best from each performer, and develop your own style," says KPWR's Brooks. Bird adds, "Listen to other broadcast voice performers, good and bad. Decide why the good ones are good and why the others just don't cut it. Then incorporate the exemplary qualities into your own repertoire and become alert to those negative qualities evident in the weak performers. For news announcers, the classroom is only as far away as the tuning knob."

KRED's Conlin expands on Brooks' classroom analogy. "The radio and television receivers are rather like in-home campuses. I mean, the world of broadcast voice performance comes to you and without tuition, so tune in and study. It's my opinion that the best way to prepare to announce news is to study the deliveries of the 'experts.' For example, study the way in which, say, Dan Rather delivers his news on television. Although Paul Harvey has an unusual and very distinctive style, studying his performance is valuable, too. Watch and analyze. Be attentive."

Quick Read

Due to the time constraints usually facing newscasters, news directors seek persons capable of broadcasting copy at a first glance. "A hot breaking story may come across the wire while you're on the air. You have to be able to read stuff on the spot in certain instances, that is, without the benefit of a preread. This ability takes time—hard work and practice—to cultivate," says KARQ's Jackson, who continues, "A late breaking story may hit the wire seconds before you go on or even during your newscast. A practiced reader can present a piece of copy cold. Learn to rip and read, not to get out of working your own stories from start to finish, but to learn to read cold. Dealing with wire copy you will inevitably come across mistakes, so you'd best know how to cope with them. Besides, when you go for job interviews, you may have a rip and read situation thrown in your lap. You may be handed a stack of copy as a mic is pushed in your face. Without having a chance to review what's in your hand, you are given the cue to deliver. Stay up on wire pronunciation guides, even if you don't do national and world news. You may just end up having to deliver copy you've never dealt with before, and without preparation time either. If you haven't access to a station wire machine, drop by a station and ask for some old wire copy that you may use to practice with."

Copy Consistency

KCWD's Hodges advises newscasters to be consistent when preparing copy to avoid foul-ups and uncertainty on the air. "Prepare the news script to reflect your own personal habits. For example, use pencil marks throughout the copy to serve as pause markers. Adapt the script to suit your own particular needs. Use symbols of your own device, but be consistent. Establish your own road signs, so to speak. Set up your own cue sheet so that you have a clear idea of what is needed by you at a specific point in the copy. Of course, don't mark up copy that will be read by someone other than yourself. Just keep in mind that the news copy you prepare should be comfortable and predictable. Don't cross yourself up by changing a pattern minutes before you go on. If you have been underlining a word twice to denote emphasis, don't suddenly place the word in brackets. All you'll accomplish is confusion."

Inner Rhythm

Find your own comfortable pace and rhythm, advises WYER's Yarbor. "Don't try to copy Paul Harvey or Peter Jennings, but develop a pattern that best fits your own individual traits. Find your own inner clock and work from it. Cultivate your own distinctive on-air 'self.' You will sound simpatico and natural—synchronized. When you sit behind the mic to deliver a newscast, whether it's a one-minute update or a fifteen-minute roundup, work from within yourself out. Don't work from the surface, but from deep down. Don't hurry when the on air light flashes. Keep your presence of mind. Stay conscious and aware. Be in touch with yourself."

Prepped-Out

Overpreparation can create problems, too, notes KMOV-TV's Castengera. "You can dupe yourself if you are overwound and hyper-prepped. In a sense, the best way to prepare for 'announcing' the news is not to prepare. Yes, practice reading news copy for its aural impact, but first make sure you understand the copy. Don't overprepare yourself from 'saying' the news. Don't psyche yourself out. Don't be so overfocussed on performance that you lose connection with content. Your job

FIGURE 5.11 Humorous commentary is a legitimate ingredient of network news programming. Courtesy CBS.

is to communicate information. A verbal vaudeville act is not necessary."

Foundation

Newscast preparation begins long before an individual enters the station, says WPRI-TV's Graves. "A formal education provides a person with the basics needed to progress to the newscast preparation stage. Education is the foundation on which rests a professional presentation of a news program. My advice to a person aiming for a career as a broadcast newsperson is to get a solid liberal arts education and never stop reading about everything and everybody."

NEWSCASTING PROS AND CONS

Heeeere's the News!

On the "do" and "don't" checklist, news director Bill Yarbor includes the following: "Don't take what you're doing lightly. Don't clown around with the news. It's okay to read a humorous story toward the end of a newscast, if it's acceptable policy, but don't break up laughing over it. The audience might not find it funny, and if that's the case, they'll start to have some doubts about you." Fellow news director Steven Hodges concurs. "Don't circus it up. News should always be perceived as a serious thing. The 'sane' corner, if you will. A little levity in a story, perhaps, but no 'Bozo the newscaster.'"

KSTP-TV's Price cautions against losing perspective. "Only use humor if it fits, if the 'environment' is right for it. Be wary of any tendency to be Woody Allen. Be friendly, but not silly. Share something lighthearted with your viewers, but don't 'thwart the venue' or 'throw the baby out with the bathwater.' That is to say, don't forget that you are a broadcast journalist and not a runner-up in a Henny Youngman impersonation contest."

Who Is That Masked Voice?

Contrived vocal performance makes the "don't" list. "Don't try to turn your voice into something that nature never intended it to be. Recall the ridiculous newscaster Ted Baxter on the old *Mary Tyler Moore Show?* He, of course, was a fabulous parody of the terribly misguided and self-consumed news anchor," says WRGB-TV's Borden.

WDWS's Talbot conveys a similar sentiment. "Never use false intonation and inflection, and don't drop your voice. Speak as you naturally speak, with the appropriate or natural timbre your voice contains. In other words, don't phony it up. Something else on a similar theme, never emotionally color a story. Laughing, crying—recall the reporter portrayed by William Hurt in the movie *Broadcast News?*—any melodramatic reaction, if not totally spontaneous and sincere, shoots holes in your credibility. Leave the dramatic stuff to the actors."

KARQ's Jackson says not to use the voice as a weapon. "Don't clobber the listener with your voice. Avoid coming on too strongly or sounding like 'Mr. Voice.' You are the vehicle of information, not a steamroller. 'Say' the news, never 'shout' it."

And in My Opinion

Expressing bias is clearly something else to be avoided in the newscast, says WTAL's Keyes. "Never make editorial comments while giving the news. Remember that you are a reporter, not a commentator. Obviously, it is acceptable to lend a light touch to a funny story, but other than that, delivery should remain a matter of fact."

KRED's Conlin regards opinionizing as a major transgression in newscasting. "Newscasters are not supposed to have an opinion on the air. They are communicators of facts, who should not express their own biases. Editorializing violates the basic ethics of broadcast journalism. It is not a newscaster's function to make personal observations."

Do You Believe What I Just Did?

Broadcast news reporters should never highlight errors but rather make necessary corrections and move on. "Quickly correct mistakes, if possible. Don't linger with long apologies—unless you've messed up terribly. Just get it right and forge ahead. For example, if you say governor when it should be senator, say 'rather, Senator Smith said . . .' not 'I'm sorry, that obviously should be Senator Smith, not Governor. . . .' Just simply correct and move on. On the other hand, saying 'guilty' when the person is not guilty requires the newsperson to make greater amends. Repeat and correct the verdict or plea twice to make certain it is changed in the minds of your listeners," says Jackson.

"Talk About Stupid. . ."

Never offend or insult an audience, says KSTP's Price. "Don't make snide or inane comments or use condescending language. Never put down somebody or make a scurrilous comment about the area or the people in it. People will tar and feather you in their minds and get their revenge by tuning you out. Arrogance is an especially effective turnoff. Put-down humor can really have a chilling effect, too. Viewers resent it."

"Groovey" News

Price also considers the use of clichés and colloquialisms as tuneout factors. "Keep away from weary clichés and trite expressions. The other day I heard a newscaster use the 1960s term right-on, while he conversed with the deejay. It dated the newscaster and the station, which happened to be programming contemporary hits. The overall effect was embarrassing. I'm sure it slipped from the newscaster's lips quite unconsciously, but you have to stay alert. As a general rule of thumb, newscasters should avoid old, as well as current colloquialisms. The newscaster doesn't have to come across as hip—just informed."

Oh, What's the Use?

The final item on the "con" side of the ledger has to do with the lack of patience and perseverance. "Don't give up. It takes time and maturity for most of us to develop the smoothness and authority that make a good newscaster. One last point, too: never develop the thinking that you can't improve or get better. Never stop working at refining your presentation. Regard each day as an opportunity to sharpen your sound," advises WCIL's Bird.

Get the Story?

On the "pro" side of the ledger, KARQ's Jackson says an understanding of a story's meaning and content makes for a better presentation. "Do have some idea of what you are reading. Believe me, it helps. If you have no idea of what the story is referring to, ask! And keep asking until you have some inkling as to what is going on. You'll deliver it much better with an understanding rather than a vague notion. Uncertainty feeds on uncertainty. You may get away with not understanding what you're reading occasionally, but one day the audience will get the impression that you don't have an understanding of what you're saying, and it will drop you."

WCIL's Bird agrees with Jackson. "Do read the story through for meaning. The most common mistake among beginning announcers is placing the emphasis on the wrong word or phrase, thus shifting the point of the story. Like Jackson, I think newscasters should know everything they can about what is happening in the news. News is more than just talking on the radio or television. It is people and events, and you should know what you are talking about, not just how to talk."

Take the Time to Do It Right

Planning and preparation rank high on the "do" column. "For starters, arrive early enough to completely edit the news copy. While you may pride yourself on your ability to read 'cold,' there will come a time when you'll trip up and sound amateurish on the air. I've always practiced what I call 'pencil' editing. I go though copy and underline key phrases or verbs to give them full value on the air," says WTAL's Keyes.

Newscasts should never be delivered extemporaneously, contends WYER's Yarbor. "Do plan your newscast. Planning is a critical part of the process. It leads to a better newscast. Give yourself plenty of time. You can't redo a live broadcast."

As stated earlier in this chapter, part of the preparation process includes checking copy for accuracy. "For example, check copy for pronunciation. If you're unclear about something, ask around the station, make a call, or consult a dictionary. This goes back to what I said earlier; sound like you know what you are talking about," says Yarbor.

A Two-"Cah" Accident

KARQ's Jackson advises future newscasters to rid themselves of any accents. "Do lose any regionalisms, like the dropping of "r's," if you're from New England, or a Southern twang or drawl. You really want a generic sound in this business. Listeners should not be distracted by an accent. Another thing, too, a contrived accent sounds put-on and doesn't add anything to your on-air persona. Be yourself, and speak as if you were broadcasting nationally."

Ann Droid with the News

On a final note, KAYN's Gishard recommends that newscasters not forget that radio and television are *human* media. "Be human on the air, not mechanical just because you are announcing something as serious as the 'news.' Do keep in mind that there are people at the other end of the equipment, and that they are the ones you are broadcasting for in the first place, not the VP in charge of programming."

RADIO VERSUS TELEVISION NEWSCASTING

The addition of the visual dimension adds several factors to on-air news performance. "You can wear a Hawaiian shirt and jogging sweats while newscasting on radio and still come across as 'Ms. Authority.' Not so in television. In this medium, looking the part is nearly as important as sounding the part," observes Betty-Jo Cugini, News Assignment Editor, WJAR-TV, Providence, Rhode Island.

In the early days of television, many radio newscasters attempted to make the transition to the visual medium only to find that their appearance kept them from winning a job before the cameras. How they "looked" was crucial in *sight-radio*, a term used to describe the video medium at its onset.

The grey-haired, avuncular image served as the primary model for television newscasters for over two decades. In the 1970s, television shifted its preference to a more youthful look. The old-line television news anchor was gradually replaced by young adults with strikingly attractive physical attributes.

Today, "looks" continue to play an important role in television newscasting. However, the near obsessive preoccupation with "pretty" people that characterized the medium in the 1970s and early 1980s has diminished to some extent. Whereas news directors are still drawn to the under thirty-five, "Hollywood" face, youthfulness and sculpted good looks do not always win out.

A resurgence of the mature male newscaster took place in the late 1980s. Unfortunately, age still remains a barrier to the hiring of female television anchors and reporters, despite claims to the contrary.

On-Camera Newscasting

General appearance, aside from natural physical qualities, comes into play before the camera. Posture, facial expressions, movements, and eye contact must be properly cultivated for maximum effectiveness.

The way a newscaster sits before the camera can project a negative or positive image to the viewer and affect delivery as well. For example, a performer who slouches comes across as sloppy and indifferent. Slouching also causes the diaphragm to twist and fold, impeding breathing. Meanwhile, a performer who sits in too erect or rigid a manner conveys nervousness and tension. The middle ground between the two positions is most appropriate and conducive to a fluid delivery.

Posture should be natural but befitting the situation. Obviously, a person presenting news on camera is not sitting on a sofa at home, and that is not the image that should be conveyed. News is serious business, and it should be communicated in a serious manner. However, affected posture can detract from the message, and that is counterproductive.

Jerky or contrived movements create a distraction, too. Overwrought or melodramatic gestures are amplified by the camera and make a newscaster look unprofessional and even silly. On the other hand, a frozen figure appears lifeless and dull. Strike a balance. Here again the term *natural* expresses best the role of movements. "Be yourself—animated—but keep in mind the medium, that is to say, the camera before you. Don't lunge out of the shot or range of the camera. Also, stay alert for any little ticks or unconscious movements. Tape yourself, and watch how you move," advises KMOV-TV's Castengera.

It is unsettling to the viewer to sense he is not being directly addressed. Eye contact, like good posture and movement, enhances presentation. The lack of eye contact creates in the viewer a feeling of disenfranchisement—the feeling of being outside the circle of discussion. "When the tally light is on, announce to that camera. Keep your concentration. Know where the 'live' camera is. Pay attention to the floor manager. Don't stare at the camera, though. That can make viewers uncomfortable," notes Castengera.

Facial expressions influence the viewers' perception of the message being broadcast. The camera misses very little. Therefore the newscaster must coordinate "expression" with "story" to ensure that the message is received as intended. Smiling during a story about an air tragedy would seem sadistic and macabre, while a stoic expression would detract from a story about a pie-eating contest. Again, strike a balance, and keep in mind the camera's unique eyeview.

The role of the camera in broadcast voice performance is examined in greater detail in Chapter 6.

NEWS COPY

Newscasters gather and organize news copy. This involves several steps. At small market radio stations, newscasters are usually responsible for collecting stories outside the station. This entails on-scene reports and interviews, which are integrated into newscasts back at the station. Larger stations typically employ field reporters for outside news chores and in-studio newscasters, who assemble and broadcast copy.

Television copy may be written by individuals hired exclusively as news writers. These people rarely have on-camera responsibilities. The anchor often serves as news editor and supervises the preparation of the news program.

The primary source of news information at the majority of broadcast outlets is the wire service (United Press International or Associated Press) teletype machine, which spews forth a steady stream of news and information.

Small stations generally subscribe to one wire service, whereas larger and more prosperous stations frequently subscribe to numerous news sources, including both UPI and AP.

The bulk of the writing at stations centers around local news events, which the wire services sometimes treat in a cursory or limited fashion. Wire service copy is routinely updated from newscast to newscast to keep it sounding fresh.

The writing style of electronic news jour-

FIGURE 5.12
Station wire service machines.

THE BROADCAST NEWS VOICE   93

nalists differs from that of print journalists. In radio, the listener has to understand what is said immediately. The news broadcast is fleeting and does not hang around for leisurely scrutiny as does the newspaper. If a listener fails to catch the meaning of a story, it is lost, whereas the print news reader has the luxury to linger over a story until its meaning is fully digested.

With this distinction in mind, broadcast news copy must be written clearly. News directors express a preference for a conversational style. "Write to communicate in an immediate and direct way. Don't try to impress with your literary prowess. You will do yourself and your audience a disservice. An everyday intelligent, conversational style is what to strive for. This doesn't mean copy has to be written without color and pizazz. Write intelligently, but not too eloquently, and write using the active voice and in the present tense," suggests KSTP-TV's Price.

KCWD's Hodges warns against writing over the heads of an audience. "Remember, your listeners are not news professionals or may not be professional people, period. Write for the average person. Don't use pretentious five-syllable words. Utilize language that is the most universally used and comprehended. The newscaster's job is to communicate information, not create confusion. This does not mean you have to compose stories in monosyllables, either. Your audience is not dumb. It is the nature of the medium that requires copy to be succinct and intelligible when it is verbalized by the announcer."

Castengera of KMOV-TV sums up his newswriting philosophy in three words, " 'Keep it simple.' That's my advice to broadcast writers. Don't use ten words when five will do."

Many stations require newspeople to rewrite wire copy and adapt it to the general flavor of the overall programming. "I think it is a good idea to get into the routine of rewriting everything. But the main reason to rewrite is to align copy with station sound and to keep newscasts fresh and vital. Obviously, rewriting is also done to clean up awkward copy and to rid it of tongue-twisting phrases and incomprehensible words and sentences," says KCCE's Baty.

Getting all the pertinent information into the story is a primary goal of the news copy writer. The "five W's" rule is a simple way for ascertaining a story's comprehensive-

```
CHILD MONEY/reed.....FRI PM....3/4.........wf

THREE STATE LEGISLATORS TODAY LAUNCHED A CAMPAIGN TO FUND
SERVICES FOR EMOTIONALLY-DISTURBED CHILDREN. CRANSTON STATE
REP. JOHN REED TODAY JOINED HIS COLLEAGUES IN FILING
LEGISLATION TO APPROPRIATE $5-MILLION DOLLARS FOR VARIOUS
SERVICES. REED SAYS THERE IS ALREADY THE CHILDREN"S MENTAL
HEALTH CARE PLAN ON THE BOOKS.....

        CART::::::: reed #2#2 :12 secs "actual services"
TAG::::::: REED SAYS SEVEN-MILLION DOLLARS WAS
EAR-MARKED FOR THE PROGRAM IN 1984....BUT ONLY $600-THOUSAND
DOLLARS HAS BEEN APPROPRIATED TO-DATE. THERE IS NO NEW
FUNDING....EXCEPT FOR $375-THOUSAND DOLLARS FOR STAFFING
RESIDENTIAL TREATMENT CENTERS.


PANAMA CHAFEE/CHAFEE...JAP  AM SAT  3-5

SENATOR JOHN CHAFEE SAYS THE U-S WILL MOST LIKELY COME UP
WITH A DEFINTIE POSITION ON HOW TO DEAL WITH THE SITUATION
IN PANAMA...THE SENATOR SAYS UP UNTIL NOW WASHINGTON'S POSITION
HAS BEEN A LITTLE FUZZY WITH PRESIDNET REAGAN AND SECRETARY
OF STATE GEORGE SHULTZ BOTH OUT OF THE COUNTRY...HOWEVER,
CHAFEE SAYS WHATEVER OUR POSITION IS CONGRESS AND THE PRESIDNET
SHOULD WORK TOGETHER..

CART'40-Z  O/C;COORDINATED POSITION  ;14

CHAFEE SAYS PART OF OUR POSITION SHOULD BE TO GET MILTARY
STRONGMAN GENERL MANUEL NORIEGA OUT OF POWER..


ABORTION/CHAFEE...JAP   AM MON   3-7

SENATOR JOHN CHAFEE IS LAUDING A BOSTON COURTS RULING THAT
IT IS UNCONSTITUTIONAL TO BAN DOCTORS IN FEDERAL FUNDED FAMILY
PLANNING CLINICS FROM ADVISING WOMEN ABOUT ABORTIONS...

CART;40-C  O/C; PRENATAL PHASE  ;14

CHAFEE LED A CONGRESSIONAL PUSH TO STRIKE DOWN REGULATION
ISSUED BY THE DEPARTMENT  OF HEALTH AND HUMAN SERVCIES TO
RESTRICT DOCTORS FROM DISCUSSING ABORTIONS...
```

FIGURE 5.13
Local station news copy. Courtesy WICE-AM.

ness. A story should answer "who," "what," "when," "where," and "why." An omission of one of these creates a question in the audience's mind. "Make sure your copy doesn't lack vital data. You'll leave the listener dangling, and he'll tune elsewhere to get the full scoop. A story that lacks the facts misinforms, and that is not what a professional news broadcaster does. When you have the facts down, don't stop there, either. Go that extra step to corroborate your information. You can always talk to or interview one more person to make your story better than the rest. Regretfully, many reporters these days get by by the 'skin of their teeth,' because they know they aren't expected to fill more than one minute anyway. Don't assume someone else's facts are correct. Call and check for yourself," says KPWR's Brooks.

Television news writers must take into account visuals (photos, film clips, and video) when they prepare a news story. Copy has to be written to coincide with pictures that depict news events. "It's a matter of balance. Let the pictures tell the story when and where you can. When you don't need spoken copy, drop it. You'll find you seldom can allow much time to elapse without audio, though. After a relatively short span, say five seconds, voice becomes conspicuously absent. Copy and visuals should complement each other and assist in the understanding of a story. Write what you need to write, given visual material, to communicate the event with clarity and precision," offers WRGB-TV's Borden.

Scholar and ABC News political consultant Irving Fang offers the following news copy guidelines in his widely used book *Television News, Radio News* (Rada Press, 1985): "1. Always be prepared to revise copy. 2. Edit for brevity. 3. Look for deadwood. 4. Trim adjectives and adverbs." These are points that have also been raised by several news directors in this chapter, and they certainly are well worth committing to memory. Remember, a good piece of news copy is always characterized by its economy, whether it has visuals or not.

FIGURE 5.14
Two-column television news copy.

STORY: Bromwell Speech

TIME: Eleven News (20 SEC.)

WRITER: Peg McKenna

VIDEO	AUDIO
Chroma key PIC of Bromwell	KANSAS SENATOR BROMWELL WAS IN TOWN TODAY TO ADDRESS THE YOUNG FARMER'S ASSOCIATION. THE SENATOR ENCOURAGED HIS AUDIENCE TO BECOME BETTER EDUCATED IN THE AREAS OF BUSINESS AND TECHNOLOGY AS A WAY TO PREPARE FOR THE REALITIES OF A CHANGING INDUSTRY. SENATOR BROMWELL CONCLUDED HIS SPEECH BY ASSURING THE YOUNG FARMERS THAT THE NATION WOULD ALWAYS BE IN NEED OF THEIR SERVICES. WE'LL BE BACK WITH SPORTS AND THE WEATHER.

COPY FORMAT

Broadcast news writers observe certain criteria when putting copy to page. For the sake of readability and consistency, news copy is generally set up with these points in mind:

1. *Type.* Copy is never hand-written. Words are typed or word processed in UPPER CASE throughout the story. (There is, however, another school of thought that prefers that copy be typed in upper and lower case with sound bites or visuals typed exclusively in upper case.) When using all upper case letters, insertions, such as instructions for sound effects and bed music, are done in upper and lower case.

2. *Double Space.* For ease of reading, copy is double spaced. "Losing your place is less of a danger when you put a blank line between lines of copy," says KARQ's Jackson.

3. *Margins.* Keep a consistent space (one inch) on both the right and left side of the page. Don't break words at the end of a line by using a hyphen. Take the whole word down to the next line.

4. *Insertions.* In radio, place any "insertion" materials (actualities, sound bites, etc.) within parentheses and at the point they are to be aired. In television, visual material is noted on the "video" side or column of the script (see Figure 5.14).

5. *One Story Per Page.* Do not put more than one story on a page, regardless of a story's length. For the sake of clarity and organization, this is the most sensible approach. Since newscast copy generally is reorganized for use in subsequent broadcasts, it is easier to excerpt a particular story if it is written on a separate page.

6. *Phonetic Spelling.* Difficult or unfamiliar words are written phonetically. Phonetic spelling involves writing words the way they are actually pronounced—MERINGUE (MER-ANG). The phonetic spelling of a word is parenthetically inserted after the actual spelling of the word.

7. *Layout.* Radio news writers use the full page, that is, they type across the full width of the page from margin to margin. Television news writers split the page, designating one side for copy and the other for visual material (video, film, etc.) to be run during the story (see Figure 5.14).

8. *Punctuation.* Use the basics, and use them correctly. Semicolons, hyphens, and ellipses, while important grammatical symbols, are often dispensed with in broadcast copy because they can impede flow and cause hesitation and confusion. The same is true of commas, says KSTP-TV's Price. "Don't over comma. It can throw off timing and pacing. Use grammatical marks accurately and sparingly. Put a period where a period belongs and a comma where it belongs. Frankly, you don't need much else."

9. *Numbers.* There are several schools of thought on the presentation of numbers in copy. In general it appears that most news directors prefer that actual numerical symbols be used, with certain exceptions. For

FIGURE 5.15 A and B Wire service daily pronunciation guides. Courtesy AP and UPI.

```
RU

AP-PRONUNCIATION GUIDE (SATURDAY)

  NEWS
ABSECON -- AB-SEE'-KUHN
ALGONA -- AL-GOH'-NAH
MIKHAIL GORBACHEV -- MIK-KAH-EEL' GOR-BAH-CHOV'
MIR -- MEER
BRIAN MULRONEY -- MUHL-ROO'-NEE
MIGUEL OBANDO Y BRAVO -- OH-BAHN'-DOH EE BRAH'-VOH
HUMBERTO ORTEGA -- OOM-BAYR'-TOH OR-TAY'-GAH
DONA PAZ -- DOHN'-YAH PAHZ
JAVIER PEREZ DE CUELLAR -- HAH-VEE-EHR' PEHR'-EHS DAY KWAY'-YAHR
JIANG QING -- GEE'-YUNG CHING
YITZHAK RABIN -- YIT'-SAHK RAH-BEEN'
YURI ROMANENKO -- YOOR'-EE ROH-MAH-NEHN'-KOH
EL RUKN -- ROO'-KIN
EDUARD SHEVARDNADZE -- SHEH-VAHRD-NAHD'-ZEH

  SPORTS
VIJAY AMRITRAJ -- VEE'-JAY AHM'-RIH-TRAJ
KRANJSKA GORA -- KRANS'-KUH GOHR'-UH
MICHEL GOULET --MIH-SHEHL GOO-LAY'
ALI HAJI-SHIEKH -- AHLEE HAH'-JEE-SHEEK
ANDERS JARRYD -- YEHR'-REED
KARCH KIRALY -- KUH-RY'
JARI KURRI'S -- YAH'-REE KUR'-EES
CLAUDIA KOHDE-KILSCH -- KOH'-DEE KIHLSH
JANA NOVOTNA -- NOH-VAHT'-NAH
GAYLE SIERENS -- SEER'-IHNZ
JAY SCHROEDER -- SHRAY'-DUR'
MATS WILANDER -- VEE'-LUHN-DUR
SAMMY WINDERS -- WYN'-DURZ

AP-BX-01-02-88 0746EST


B080
    RU

   AP-ADVISORY

   AP NEWSPOWER, APTV, THE AP RADIO WIRE, AP HEADLINES, AP NETWORK
```

A

NNVN.... ZCUPIUPR

ZO585NNVN.
D V WORLD-PRONO-GUIDE 0493

-5-
   ALGONA (AL-GOH'-NAH), IOWA
   AQUINO, BENIGNO (BEH-NIHG'-NOH AH-KEE'-NOH), SLAIN FILIPINO OPPOSITION LEADER
   AQUINO, CORAZON (KOH'-RAH-ZOHN AH-KEE'-NOH), PRESIDENT OF THE PHILIPPINES
   ARIAS SANCHEZ, OSCAR (OHS'-KAHR AH-REE'-AHS SAHN'-CHEHZ), COSTA RICAN PRESIDENT
   BARCO, VIRGILIO (VEHR-HEE'-LEE-OH BAHR'-KOH), COLOMBIAN PRESIDENT
   BEIJING (BAY-JIHNG'), CHINA
   BERRI, NABIH (NAH'-BEE BEH'-REE), SHIITE MOSLEM MILITIA LEADER IN LEBANON
   BOTHA, PIETER (PEE'-TEHR BOH'-TAH), SOUTH AFRICAN PRESIDENT
   CHUN DOO HWAN, (CHUHN DOO HWAHN), SOUTH KOREAN PRESIDENT
   GERASIMOV, GENNADI (GEH-NAH'-DEE GEH-RAH'-SEH-MAWF), SOVIET FOREIGN MINISTRY SPOKESMAN
   GORBACHEV, MIKHAIL (MEEK'-HIGH-YEHL GOHRB'-AH-CHAWF), SOVIET LEADER
   HAMADEI, MOHAMMAD ALI (HAH'-MAH-DAY), ACCUSED T-W-A HIJACKER (SOURCE: FF)
   HOLOMISA, BANTU (BAHN'-TOO HOH-LOH-MEE'-SAH), TRANSKEI ARMY COMMANDER WHO BECAME CHIEF OF STATE IN A BLOODLESS COUP
   HORMUZ (HOHR'-MOOZ), STRAIT OF, CHANNEL CONNECTING PERSIAN GULF WITH GULF OF OMAN
   KABUL (KAH'-BUHL) CAPITAL OF AFGHANISTAN
   KHAMENEI, SAYED ALI (SIGH-EED AH-LEE KAH-MAY-NEE), IRANIAN PRESIDENT
   KHOST (KOHST), AFGHANISTAN
   KIM DAE JUNG (KIHM DAY JOONG), SOUTH KOREAN DISSIDENT
   MECHAM (MEE'-KUHM), GOVERNOR EVAN, ARIZONA REPUBLICAN
   MIR (MEER), SOVIET SPACE STATION
   MONONGAHELA (MUH-NAHN-GUH-HEE'-LAH), RIVER
   MORTON THIOKOL (THIGH'-UH-KAWL), MAKER OF SOLID-FUEL ROCKET BOOSTER FOR THE SPACE SHUTTLE
   NAMPHY, HENRI (AHN-REE' NAHM-FEE'), GENERAL, PRESIDENT OF NATIONAL COUNCIL OF GOVERNMENT IN HAITI
   NIDAL, ABU (AH-BOO' NEE-DAHL'), LEADER OF LIBYAN-BACKED P-L-O SPLINTER GROUP
   OAHU (OH-AH'-HOO), ISLAND IN HAWAII
   OBANDO Y BRAVO, MIGUEL (MEE-GEHL' OH-BAHN'-DOH EE BRAH'-VOH) ROMAN CATHOLIC CARDINAL IN NICARAGUA
   OCHOA, JORGE (HOHR'-HEH OH-CHOH'-AH), REPUTED COLOMBIAN COCAINE TRAFFICKER
   RABIN, YITZHAK (YIHTS'-HAHK RAH-BEEN'), ISRAELI DEFENSE MINISTER
   SHAMIR, YITZHAK (YIHTS'-HAHK SHAH-MEER'), ISRAELI PRIME MINISTER
   SHEVARDNADZE (SHYEH-VAHR-NAHD-SHEH), EDUARD, SOVIET FOREIGN MINISTER
   SOYUZ (SAH'-YOOZ) RUSSIAN SPACESHIP SERIES
   SRI LANKA (SREE LAHNK'-UH), FORMERLY CEYLON
   TAMIL (TAM'-IHL), MILITANT SEPARATISTS IN SRI LANKA
   TRANSKEI (TRAHNZ-KIGH'), SOUTH AFRICAN TERRITORY UNILATERALLY MADE INDEPENDENT IN 1976
   WAIHEE (WIGH-HAY'-AY), JOHN, DEMOCRATIC POLITICIAN IN HAWAII
   WALDHEIM, KURT, (KOORT VAHLD'-HIGHM), AUSTRIAN PRESIDENT; FORMER U-N SECRETARY GENERAL

B

example, it is easier to read "456 million" than it is "456,000,000." When you get into large figures, it is better to use an alphanumeric system. Imagine the difficulty of trying to announce the national deficit in pure numbers.

10. *Correcting.* Copy that is covered with cross-outs and penciled corrections is an ambush waiting to happen. All corrections should be made neatly and with absolute clarity. It is better to retype a story than to mark it up with corrections. Copy read on the air should never be laden with edits. Clean copy is imperative to good on-air presentation.

SUGGESTED FURTHER READING

Bittner, John R., and Bittner, Denise A. *Radio Journalism.* Englewood Cliffs, N.J.: Prentice-Hall, 1977.

Bliss, Edward J., and Patterson, John M. *Writing News for Broadcast,* 2nd ed. New York: Columbia University Press, 1978.

Cohen, Akiba A. *The Television News Interview.* Newbury Park, Calif.: Sage Publications, 1987.

Fang, Irving. *Radio News/Television News,* 2nd ed. St. Paul, Minn.: Rada Press, 1985.

Garvey, Daniel E. *Newswriting for the Electronic Media.* Belmont, Calif.: Wadsworth Publishing, 1982.

Gilbert, Bob. *Perry's Broadcast News Handbook.* Knoxville, Tenn.: Perry Publishing, 1982.

Hood, James R., and Kalbfeld, Brad, eds. The *Associated Press Handbook.* New York: Associated Press, 1982.

White, Ted. *Broadcast Newswriting.* New York: Macmillan, 1984.

Wulfemeyer, K. Tim. *Broadcast Newswriting.* Ames, Iowa: Iowa State University Press, 1983.

APPENDIX: UPI WIRE SERVICE NEWS COPY (COURTESY UPI)

```
NNNH.N01


Z1641NNNH.
         R H WORLD-HEADLINES 0226

   -O-
   THE NATION'S DEBT-RIDDEN FARMERS WERE HANDED A DEFEAT TODAY BY THE
SUPREME COURT. THE HIGH COURT RULED UNANIMOUSLY THAT A FARMER'S
EXPERIENCE AND LABOR CANNOT BE CONSIDERED CAPITAL IN CHAPTER 11
BANKRUPTCY PROCEEDINGS.
   -O-
   THE ARIZONA SENATE COURT OF IMPEACHMENT REFUSED TO GRANT IMMUNITY
TO A TOP FUND-RAISER AND FORMER POLITICAL APPOINTEE OF INDICTED GOVERNOR
EVAN MECHAM. ATTORNEY GENERAL BOB CORBIN SAYS GIVING IMMUNITY TO LEE
WATKINS IN EXCHANGE FOR TESTIMONY AGAINST MECHAM COULD JEOPARDIZE
CRIMINAL INVESTIGATIONS.
   -O-
   IN HARLEM, NEW YORK, A KIDNAPPING SUSPECT IS IN POLICE CUSTODY. HE
SURRENDERED SIX HOURS AFTER BARRICADING HIMSELF IN A HOSPITAL
SUB-BASEMENT. THE SUSPECT- WHO WAS HANDCUFFED TO A HOSPITAL BED-  BROKE
FREE, OVERPOWERED A POLICEMAN AND TOOK TWO HOSTAGES BUT LATER FREED
THEM.
   -O-
   BRITAIN ADMITS THAT THREE UNARMED I-R-A GUERRILLAS SHOT DEAD BY
MILITARY PERSONNEL YESTERDAY IN THE BRITISH CROWN COLONY OF GIBRALTAR
HAD NOT PLANTED A CAR BOMB. FOREIGN SECRETARY SIR GEOFFREY HOWE STUNNED
THE HOUSE OF COMMONS WITH THE ANNOUNCEMENT TODAY.


-----------
UPI 03-07-88 12:14 PES
```

Z1451NNNH.

      R H WORLD-HEADLINES 0213

-0-

A KIDNAPPING SUSPECT WHO BARRICADED HIMSELF IN THE SUB-BASEMENT OF A HARLEM, NEW YORK, HOSPITAL HAS SURRENDERED AFTER SIX HOURS OF NEGOTIATIONS. EARLIER TODAY, HE BROKE LOOSE FROM A HOSPITAL BED, OVERPOWERED A POLICEMAN AND TOOK TWO HOSTAGES.

-0-

ISRAELI SOLDIERS KILLED THREE ARAB GUERRILLAS WHO HIJACKED A BUSLOAD OF ISRAELI CIVILIANS ON A DESERT HIGHWAY 45 MILES SOUTH OF JERUSALEM. THE TERRORISTS KILLED ONE MAN BEFORE SOLDIERS AND POLICE STORMED THE BUS. TWO PASSENGERS WERE KILLED AND EIGHT OTHERS WOUNDED IN THE ASSAULT.

-0-

PAT ROBERTSON HAS AGREED TO PAY COURT COSTS IN HIS 35-MILLION-DOLLAR LIBEL SUIT AGAINST FORMER CALIFORNIA REPRESENTATIVE PETE MCCLOSKEY. THE DECISION ENDS THE VERBAL SKIRMISH OVER ROBERTSON'S MARINE CORPS RECORD DURING THE KOREAN WAR.

-0-

DISGRACED TELEVISION EVANGELIST JIMMY SWAGGART HAS PROMISED HIS FOLLOWERS HE WILL TELL THEM THE WHOLE STORY ``SOMEDAY WHEN THE TIME IS RIGHT.'' SWAGGART SAYS FOR EIGHT MONTHS PRIOR TO HIS CONFESSION OF MORAL FAILURE HE KNEW HE WAS ``LOSING IT.''

UPI 03-07-88 11:19 AES

BENTLI..

Z1959BENTL
        R U MA-ROBBERY 0152

-7-
   (BOSTON)- BOSTON POLICE ARE LOOKING FOR TWO MEN IN CONNECTION WITH
AN ARMED ROBBERY THIS MORNING AT A SHAWMUT BANK IN SOUTH BOSTON.
   POLICE SPOKESMAN JON EISENTHAL SAYS THE ROBBERY OCCURRED ABOUT
11:49 THIS MORNING AT THE BANK AT 231 NORTHERN AVENUE. WITNESSES TOLD
POLICE ONE OF THE MEN WAS BLACK... ABOUT 25 YEARS OLD... 5-FOOT-6-INCHES
TALL... WEARING A BLACK AND WHITE CHECKERED TRENCH COAT... HIGH TOP
SNEAKERS AND BLUE JEANS. EISENTHAL SAYS THAT MAN APPARENTLY WAVED A
SILVER GUN DURING THE HOLDUP.
   THE SECOND MAN WAS WHITE... ABOUT 25... WEARING GLASSES.
   THE TWO REPORTEDLY FLED WITH AN UNDETERMINED AMOUNT OF CASH IN A
SKY BLUE SEDAN ON NORTHERN AVENUE TOWARD THE EXPRESSWAY.
   NO INJURIES WERE REPORTED IN THE INCIDENT.
-7-
   DSW

UPI 03-07-88 01:43 PES

BXNTLARN BONTLARN

Z1962BXNTL
        R U CT-WELLSFARGO-SUB 0148

   (HARTFORD, CONNECTICUT)- ONE OF TWO WELLS FARGO DEFENDANTS WHO HAVE
BEEN HELD FOR MORE THAN 30 MONTHS WAS RELEASED TODAY.
   JUAN SEGARRA PALMER HUGGED HIS WIFE AND CHILDREN IN FEDERAL COURT
IN HARTFORD (CONNECTICUT) AND LEFT THE BUILDING... FREE PENDING HIS
TRIAL AND THAT OF 15 OTHER ACCUSED IN THE SEVEN-MILLION DOLLAR ROBBERY.
   SEGARRA PALMER'S FAMILY PUT UP A ONE-POINT-FIVE MILLION DOLLAR BOND
AND STRICT CONDITIONS INCLUDE AN ORDER THAT SEGARRA PALMER LIVE IN
HARTFORD AND WEAR AN ELECTRONIC SURVEILLANCE BRACELETT.
   THE GOVERNMENT CLAIMS SEGARRA PALMER AND OTHER DEFENDANTS ARE
MEMBERS OF THE PUERTO RICAN SEPARATIST GROUP LOS MATCHETEROS, WHICH THEY
SAY IS LINKED TO TERRORISM.
   ANOTHER KEY DEFENDANT, FILIBERTO OJEDA RIOS, HAD HIS LATEST BOND
APPEAL DENIED LAST MONTH AND WILL REMAIN IN PRISON IN HARTFORD.

UPI 03-07-88 01:43 PES

6 THE ON-CAMERA AND BOOTH VOICE

TELEVISION VOICE PERFORMANCE

The television voice performer works in an environment that is at once similar and quite different from that of the radio voice performer. Indeed, both work with audio equipment (microphones, tape recorders), wire service teletype machines, mobile apparatus, and a variety of other electronic devices, but the video medium thickens the stew, so to speak. The video voice performer must also deal with lighting, cameras, and crews while broadcasting.

Whereas the radio newscaster usually sits alone before a microphone in a small news booth, while a deejay or producer monitors audio levels in the on-air studio, the television newscaster works from a large, brightly lit studio—a sort of arena—equipped with several beaming cameras (three or four). Nearby a floor director and numerous other production people (camera operators, boom handlers, prop and cue card personnel) look on intently, as do other crew members (director, producer, video and audio equipment operators) from within a designated control area.

Typically, the medium market radio newscaster airs copy assisted by only one other person, who is not always within eyeshot. In contrast, the medium market television anchor is the object of attention for eight or more production staff members, who constitute a kind of miniature live audience.

APPEARANCE

Obviously, a radio audience does not judge a newscaster or announcer by the way he or she looks during a broadcast, but the opposite is true in television. Viewers respond emotionally and critically to the appearance of television communicators.

The television performer must select clothing carefully, not only to create the most positive image but to avoid conflicting with the inherent technical nature of the medium. For example, on-camera people must not wear colors (usually blue) similar to the chromakey matting used by stations for the purpose of inserting pictures into a portion of a

FIGURE 6.1A and B Although radio and television voice performers work in different settings, their goal is the same—to communicate with clarity and intelligence. Courtesy WMJX-FM and WJAR-TV.

A

FIGURE 6.1
Continued

B

live shot. An on-camera person dressed in chroma-key tones would be covered by a second image of the picture being keyed.

Clothing with checks and stripes causes a shimmering and pulsating effect, because television cameras are not able to absorb such patterns. White and black clothing create technical problems as well. On-camera performers are encouraged to wear soft colors, such as pastels, and to avoid colors that are too extreme or similar to their skin tones.

The proper use of makeup significantly en-

FIGURE 6.2
Weather person at chroma-key board.
Courtesy WJAR-TV.

hances appearance, too. Men with heavy beards can look freshly shaven with the application of the appropriate shade of pancake makeup. Makeup is used for practical purposes (to conceal blemishes, to reduce glare or shine) rather than to dramatically alter the appearance of a newscaster or program host.

The old adage that the camera does not lie is true to a great extent, although the intense lighting used in television does tend to highlight qualities many performers choose to deemphasize, and that is where makeup comes into service.

ADDRESSING THE CAMERA

Although television newscasters possess a script, they often read copy from a screen known as a teleprompter located near the lens area of the cameras used during broadcast. Learning to read smoothly while giving the appearance of directly addressing the home viewer takes skill and practice. When teleprompters are employed, on-camera performers use hand-held scripts for reference or as backup should the prompter malfunction. "You keep your place with the actual copy. It acts as a road map should you lose your bearings," says WRGB-TV's Borden.

Newscasters sometimes use scripts as props, believing that viewers feel reassured by the presence of hard copy. "It almost says 'Look, the reporter has prepared and worked hard gathering and writing the news.' It's a credibility factor, to some," says Borden.

Cue cards are used in television, although not to the extent that they were prior to the advent of teleprompters. Whereas electronic prompters can contain all the copy aired during a program or newscast, cue cards present space constraints, so they are used in situations requiring less script.

As the term suggests, cue cards are used to remind or prompt a performer to do something. Introductions, spot lead-ins, facts, and other short announcements are commonly written (in large, clear print) on cue cards. A member of the floor crew holds the cue cards adjacent to the live camera, allowing talent to maintain eye contact. "Again, the objective is to give viewers the impression that you are looking at them, not off to the side of the camera," says WPRI-TV's Graves.

Voicing (reading) over film or chromakeyed material during live broadcasts also tests the performer's ability to effectively di-

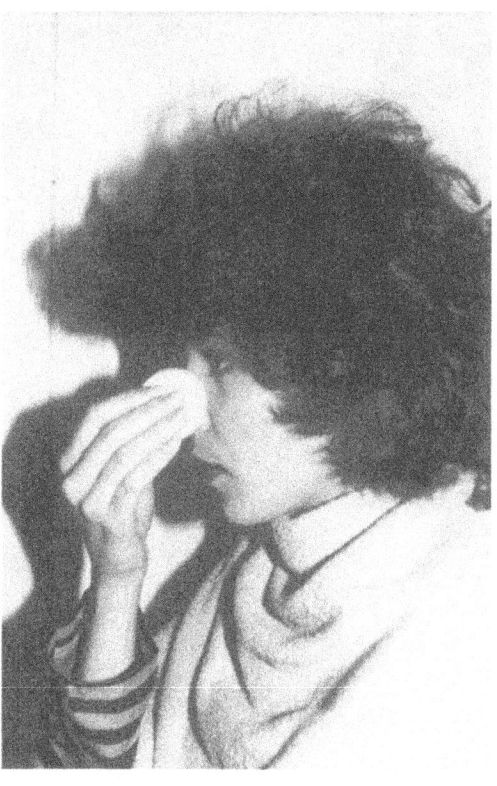

FIGURE 6.3
An on-camera performer prepares for a broadcast by applying makeup.

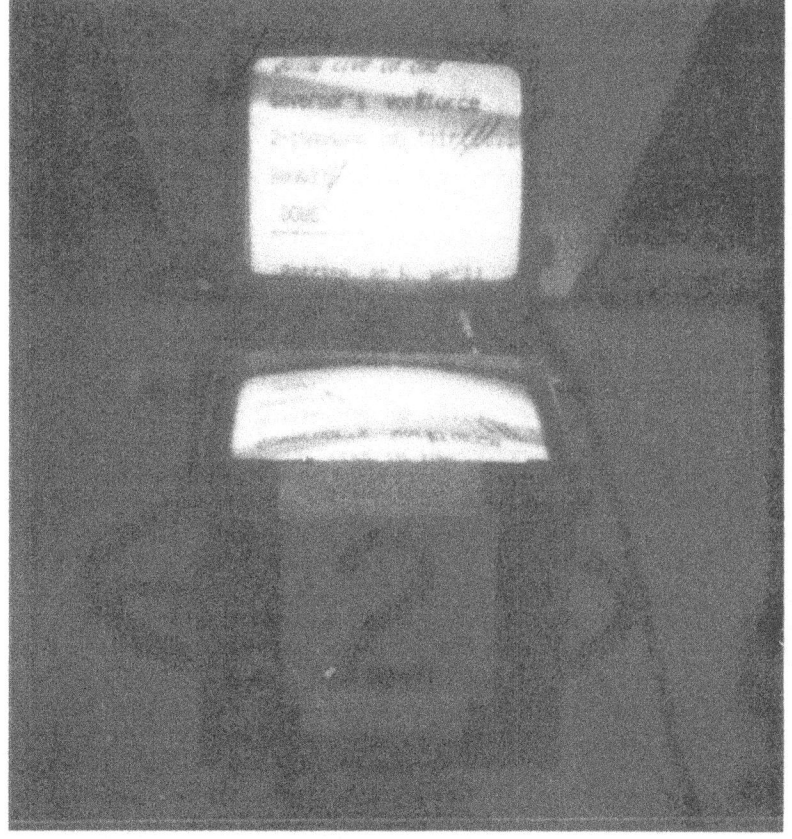

FIGURE 6.4
A television teleprompter.

FIGURE 6.5
A television cue card.

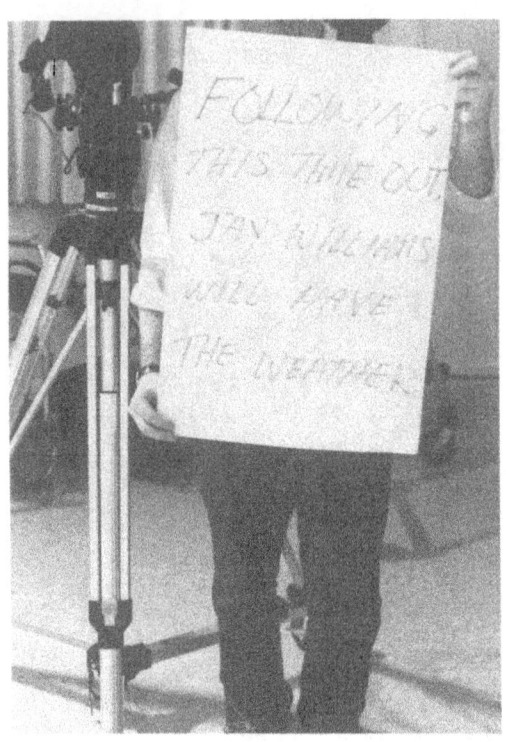

rect his message to the home viewer. Television employs numerous visual devices, and the on-camera performer must be able to integrate these into his or her presentation without appearing distracted.

Since several cameras are used in most productions, including news broadcasts, air talent must possess the ability to move naturally as the director calls for different camera shots. The red tallylight astride the camera is illuminated when the camera is "hot." On-camera people must address the live ("program") camera, or they are facing away from the home audience. During a broadcast, several camera shots are made for the sake of variety, pacing, and drama. The on-camera performer is expected to follow the lighted tally from camera to camera without drawing attention to his or her movements. An abrupt shift, instead of a smooth transition, looks awkward and clumsy and is unsettling to the viewer.

On-camera performers must often use props (hand-held material, visual aids, etc.) during broadcasts. This requires a steady hand, an appreciation for lighting, and an understanding of the camera's role. "Abrupt or jerky moves destroy a shot, as does glare from the lights if, say, a book with a glossy cover is held at a wrong angle. Displaying an object in the direction of the wrong camera doesn't help the cause, either. You shouldn't be afraid to handle props naturally, though. Hold them like you would something at home, but just be aware of the idiosyncratic nature of the medium. Cameras and lights impose special considerations," says Borden.

To reiterate a point made earlier about on-camera movement, any kind of unnatural or abrupt motion should be avoided. This is not to say performers should sit or stand statue-like while delivering copy. "You move too fast, say, jump up from a seated position, and the camera loses you. Avoid the 'pendulum' effect, too. Don't rock back and forth while standing. You'll give your viewers motion sickness. Stand still, and when you're supposed to move, do so slowly and naturally," says KSTP-TV's Larry Price.

MICROPHONE USE

Audio is an essential component of the television production. Each performer is "placed" on a microphone. The most frequently used microphone in the video medium is the lavalier ("lav"), a small clip-on mic sometimes referred to as a *lapel*. The wires of the lavalier are concealed in the clothing of the on-camera person so that the viewer is unaware of the microphone's existence.

Highly directional "boom" microphones, which hang from movable cranes, are used when performers need to be free of encumbering wires. For example, a boom mic may be used when a talk show host must move from a sitting down position to another point on the set during an actual broadcast or taping.

Desk-top microphones are employed but not as extensively as lavaliers and booms. A common application of desk mics would be during a panel discussion in which several individuals are seated at a conference table. Directional desk-top microphones are placed before each panelist. Some directors use desk mics for dramatic purposes, believing that they add a look of importance to the setting. Other directors or producers, perhaps even the majority, prefer desk mics for purely practical reasons, contending they are the best

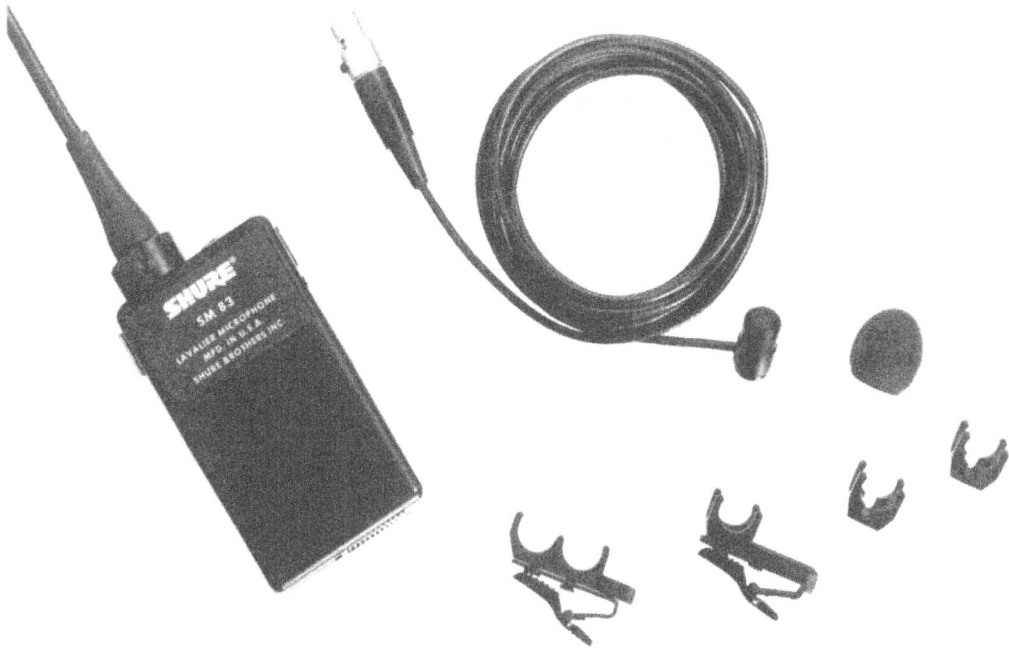

FIGURE 6.6
Lavalier microphone used by on-camera performers. Courtesy Shure.

type of microphone for this situation. (Chapter 9 examines microphones in more detail.)

Prior to broadcast or taping, microphone levels are established for each performer. In order to get the correct level, the crew person handling audio has each performer speak into his or her microphone. "Levels are not established by blowing or tapping into the mic. Nor are they achieved by counting. To get a true level, a natural read has to take place. The audio person takes a couple of levels for each person 'miked.' Levels are established at the position from which the performer actually delivers copy," observes WJAR-TV's Cugini.

Once mic levels are set, performers should not move, since doing so will create audio problems. "Just as talent must be cognizant of the camera's limitations, so must they be conscious of the microphone's. To set levels without factoring in movements is to invite problems. Speaking 'off' mic affects sound quality, as well as loudness," says WRGB-TV's Borden.

When using microphones outside the studio setting other factors must be considered. Typically, the on-camera person, especially reporter, works with one microphone, which usually is hand-held to accommodate other voices, such as interviewees (witnesses, officials, newsmakers) who are at the scene. In this case, the broadcaster must move the microphone between himself and his subject. If the microphone is not directed to the person speaking, audio will be insufficient.

Since on-scene taping or live broadcasting are seldom in an optimum setting in terms of sound, the reporter must make adjustments to ensure an intelligible transmission. Extraneous noise, such as that emanating from a crowd or passing vehicles, can seriously interfere with voice reports. It is up to the on-camera performer to work in as sound-stable an environment as possible.

A final point concerning microphone usage: The performer's proximity to a microphone will affect sound quality. Thus it is important to keep in mind the following:

1. Do not announce too close to the microphone. "Swallowing" the mic causes distortion, such as popping, thumping, and gusting.

2. Do not announce too far from, or out of the range of, the microphone. This affects levels and invites the absorption of surrounding noise.

3. Do not talk away from the microphone. Speaking off-mic reduces sound quality and creates the impression that the speaker is in a different location.

For the best results, announce about a hand's length away from the microphone itself.

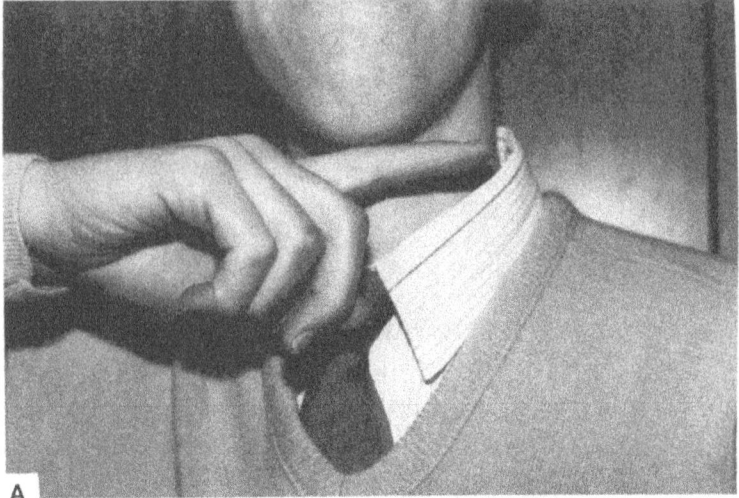
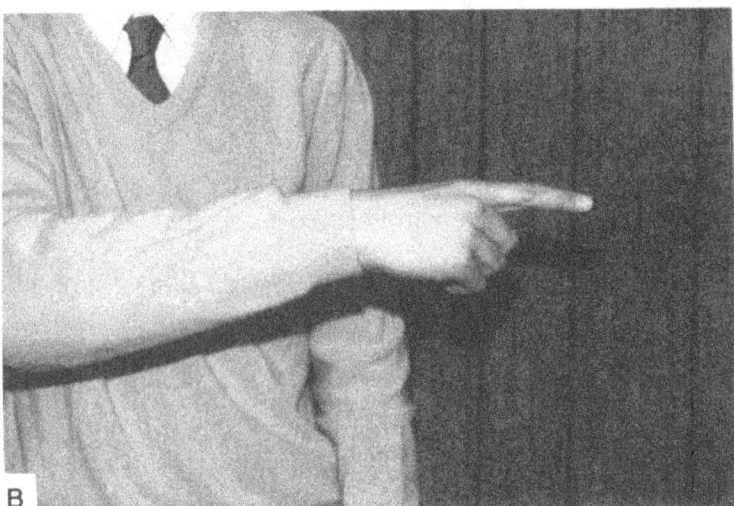
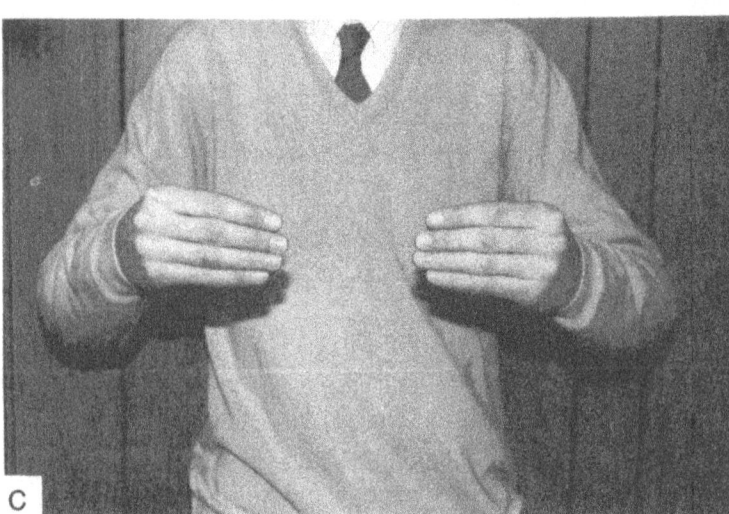

HAND SIGNALS

On-camera performers must be familiar with various cues or hand signals used by floor directors. It is very important that a performer confer with the floor director to make certain that the meanings of signals are clear.

Hand signals give direction. That is, a *pointed finger* means "you're on," a *sweeping arm and pointed finger* indicates the "live" camera, and so forth. Certain hand signals pertain to timing. For instance, *two fingers up* cue the talent that two minutes remain, and *one finger up* indicates that one minute is left. A *clenched fist* indicates a half minute, and *crossed arms* usually cue on-camera performers that fifteen seconds remain.

There are a variety of hand signals that on-camera performers must know. Again, verify hand signals with the floor director prior to any presentation. Misunderstanding cues during a broadcast can have unfortunate effects.

ON-CAMERA VOICE CRITERIA

One of the most popular and enduring television voice performers is Dick Clark, who credits sincerity and believability as the qualities that have brought him success. "The broadcast voice performance qualities most sought after by major market and network television broadcasters are sincerity and believability—two things that I have strived to communicate during my career. In the old days when radio announcers used to listen to their voices with a cupped hand held over an ear, they were listening for deep tone and resonance. The most sought after qualities in those days were authority and command. The male voice needed maturity and depth. These days, whether it's a male or female voice, the only quality that works is believability. One does not have to possess a super-mature, super-resonant voice to succeed. I believe it's a far more reasonable and realistic approach and should offer a great deal of hope for those not blessed with the old-fashioned characteristics," says Clark.

The qualities cited by Dick Clark rank high on the list of many television program directors. "Sincerity, that is, 'genuine' sincerity, is a winning quality. Feigned sincerity

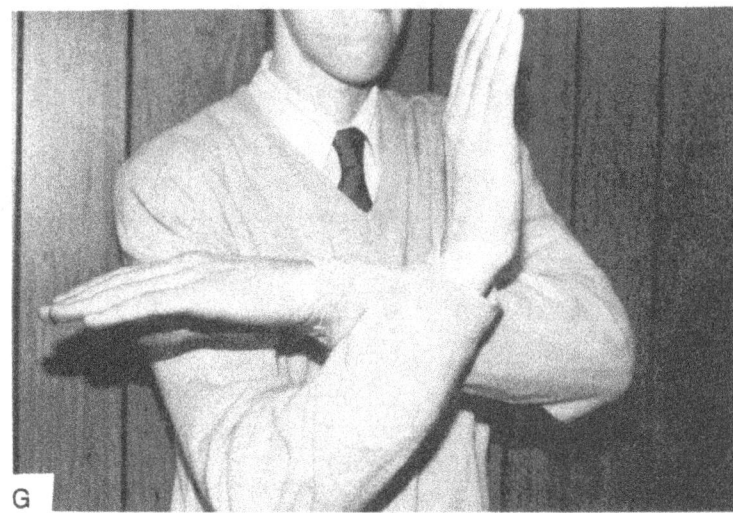

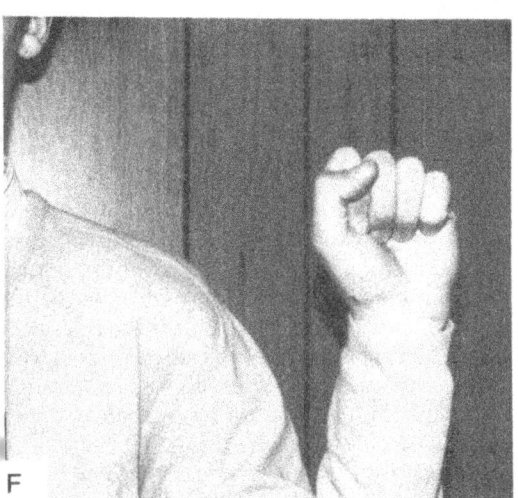

is pretty easy to see through. Honesty creates credibility. Phoniness has a negative impact on viewers," notes Ronald Bartlett, Program Director, WLTZ-TV, Columbus, Georgia.

Brian Roberts, Program Director, WAGT-TV, in neighboring Augusta, Georgia, also seeks talent capable of communicating in an unpretentious, natural style. "It is essential that on-camera people sound agreeable, pleasant, warm, and down to earth. One-on-one sincerity holds viewers."

Echoing the sentiments of Dick Clark, Ernie Bjorkman, Program Director, KWGN-TV, Denver, Colorado, places a naturally pleasant sounding voice above one that is bassy. "A voice that is acceptable, meaning pleasant to the ear, doesn't necessarily have to be deep or low. I've heard many anchors with thunderously deep voices who did not come across as effectively as those with voices in the higher range who conveyed a frank, down-to-earth sensibility."

The conversational style has been in fashion since the 1970s and continues as the reigning style today, says Ken Sneeden, Station Manager, WINK-TV, Fort Myers, Florida. "I believe on-camera performers must perfect a conversational delivery style. Announcers (anchors) need to be natural in their presentation, but at the same time they have to project a *disciplined* voice. I would contrast disciplined with *hyped*, too. Many young or otherwise inexperienced reporters/anchors/announcers try to deepen or hype their voices in some way in order to project an authoritative image. Mostly, they are un-

FIGURE 6.7A–G Widely used hand signals (A) Cut or stop action. (B) Directed to live camera. (C) Slow down or stretch. (D) Two minutes. (E) One minute. (F) Thirty seconds. (G) Fifteen seconds. Individual stations often devise their own additional hand signals.

FIGURE 6.8
Dick Clark's career as a broadcast voice performer spans four decades.

successful and end up sounding phoney or artificial. A disciplined speech pattern with a natural, conversational style is the best approach. When I talk *discipline* I'm referring to enunciation, articulation, inflection, emphasis, and diction."

Numerous television program directors do place a premium on the "heavy" voice, despite the general trend of the past two decades to deemphasize deepness, says Walt Baker, Vice President of Programming, KHJ-TV, Hollywood, California. "A nice, rich, resonant voice retains its appeal to me, and I think most p.d.'s. Sure, you don't hire someone just because he has a 'heavy' voice. But a deep voice never counted against anyone in an audition."

Norbert J. Gassensmith, Vice President and Program Director, WSBT-TV, South Bend, Indiana, adds, "A good resonant voice will win out over the one that isn't if the job candidates possessing the voices have comparable announcing skills and credentials. Broadcasting has always been keen on the 'good' voice."

WAGT-TV's Roberts concurs with both Baker and Gassensmith. "I want someone with a clear, resonant voice. Television is a sound medium as well as visual. Radio prefers voices with timbre because they enhance the signal. Well, television is not indifferent to voices that pack depth, and not just male voices, but female voices, too."

Vocal versatility is a quality television programmers admire. "Many aspiring on-camera performers can speak; few can present themselves in the various roles required. A newscast, for example, generally contains stories ranging from the tragic and solemn to the ridiculous and comical. This requires a well-trained voice, a voice than can communicate all the fine shades of emotion and meaning embodied in a story," notes WLTZ-TV's Bartlett.

Brian Holton, General Manager, KTSF-TV, San Francisco, California, carries Bartlett's observation a step further. "I believe TV voice performers do well if they possess an actor-like mentality. By this I mean anchors and emcees are most effective when they are able to project the emotional essence of a piece of copy, that is, without being histrionic. Look, a piece of copy about a highway tragedy should be delivered differently than a story about a planned sewer treatment plant. I'm not talking Shakespearian acting here. I'm talking 'full' expression to increase understanding and meaning."

Stephen Fuchs, Program Manager, KHAI-TV, Honolulu, Hawaii, has constructed an on-camera voice performance criteria checklist, which he refers to when reviewing audition tapes:

1. *Enunciation:* How clearly and intelligibly does the person speak? Are there any discernible speech problems?
2. *Vocal variety:* Does the person possess the ability to deliver copy with a diverse content?
3. *Directability:* Does the person exhibit a willingness to take direction? Is the person sensitive to the director's views and needs?
4. *Breathing:* Does the person have strong lung capacity? Is he breathy or short of wind? Is breathing natural?
5. *Personality:* Is warmth and sincerity present? Does the candidate have authority and credibility?
6. *Enthusiasm:* Is the person able to convey energy? Is delivery engaging?
7. *Memory:* Can the person work without a teleprompter? Is the candidate capable of memorizing copy?
8. *Intelligence:* Does the candidate fully grasp copy content? Was the presentation perceptive and astute?
9. *Sobriety:* Is the person completely aware of the serious nature of the position?
10. *Simpatico:* Does the person look like he belongs before the camera? Is there some magic taking place?

"These aren't in any specific order, but they're all equally important. There are other ingredients which must exist, too. A list like this really serves as an outline," notes Fuchs.

As discussed earlier in this chapter, appearance is weighed heavily. To possess all the right vocal skills is crucial but not enough in television. The television voice performer has to look good as well as sound good. "It's a fact, perhaps unfortunate for some, that the TV performer must be somewhat attractive. At the very least, not unpleasant to look at. I have seen radio announcers come to the microphone with a three-day facial growth, looking like they had combed their hair with an egg beater. They sound just fine even though they look forsaken. Obviously, the television announcer should be well groomed," says WSBT-TV's Gassensmith.

KHAI-TV's Fuchs says appearance is a primary factor in hiring. "You can read naked in radio. You don't have to shave or shower to sound beautiful. Obviously, physical appearance requirements are different in television. It is not enough to sound like Jennings or Rather, you have to look like them, too. The TV camera heaps more expectations on the performer. To a certain extent, makeup and lighting can primp a face. The casting director is the bottom-line person. If several candidates can read adequately, the person making the choice goes for the best on-camera look."

In television, good looks can compensate for weaknesses in other areas. "Like it or not, appearance is the central attribute in this medium, so it follows that the more physically attractive you are, the more appealing you will be to the people who hire. In fact, a weak voice can be offset by strong physical characteristics. If you look pleasing to the audience, your 'non-radio' voice will be accepted," believes KWGN-TV's Bjorkman.

Finding the job candidate who combines photogenic features with strong vocal qualities is the challenge, says WAGT-TV's Roberts. "As a broadcast medium incorporating both picture and sound, you search for someone who is impressive in both those areas—good looks and nice voice. All too often you encounter one without the other. You strike pay dirt when you find both."

WLTZ-TV's Bartlett believes that aspiring television broadcasters can transcend certain deficiencies by making the most of the talents and attributes they possess. "You don't have to look like Robert Redford or Christie Brinkley or sound like Walter Cronkite to succeed, but you do have to draw on your strengths. The visual nature of this medium requires that you control all available personal resources to heighten performance impact. Improve gestures and expressions, dress to strengthen image, and master the studio and equipment to maximize what you have at your disposal. Remember, the right attitude can be transforming, too."

PREPPING FOR ON-CAMERA

Strides in video technology on the domestic level have provided the aspiring on-camera voice performer with an excellent tool—the compact home video camera. "The domestic camcorder is an excellent device for practicing. If you don't own one, you can usually rent or borrow one. Sit in front of the video camera and deliver copy; then review yourself on-screen, and invite others to assess your performance, too," suggests KHAI-TV's Fuchs.

WLTZ-TV's Bartlett also believes that the use of home video equipment is valuable in the preparation process. "It is great that would-be television performers can work in front of a camera without great inconvenience. No doubt, on-camera practice is the most beneficial. Most people can get their hands on domestic video equipment. For those who cannot, I suggest working in front of a mirror as well as before small groups of people for immediate feedback. Video taping is the best approach, however."

Regardless of the devices employed, the sheer act of daily practice will improve and sharpen skills, contends WICS-TV's Spears. "Sure, video taping is a great help, but don't avoid practicing because you don't have access to equipment. Read aloud at every available opportunity. Tape your copy to a mirror and read while watching yourself. Improvise! If you have access to a video tape camera/recorder, practice that way. The best way to overcome the fear and speech problems created by inexperience is to see and hear yourself. We really are our own best critics."

Rehearsal is fundamental to solid on-camera execution, says KTSF-TV's Holton. "Rehearse before every taping, even at home before your own video camera. Get in the habit of rehearsing your copy and manner of presentation. That is the first practice step. Don't tape cold. You wouldn't be doing that in a professional situation, at least not routinely. Feeling comfortable comes from knowing your subject matter and how you are going to get it across to the viewer. Although television sometimes doesn't lend itself to rehearsals, it is important that some kind of rehearsing be done. Establish the rehearsal habit before entering the actual television studio. At home, do a rehearsal, then go for a 'take.'"

Since a good deal of copy will be read off electronic prompters and cue cards, becoming acclimated to these devices is a necessary part of the preparation process. "Try to simulate prompter reading by setting up some sort of makeshift apparatus. You must learn to read using the teleprompter. Videotape a long run of printed material, and deliver it out loud on playback. Work something up. Having two VCRs at your disposal would allow you to read from one while taping on the other, but you'll have to make adjustments to suit your own situation. Make note of your gestures. Did you move unnaturally or smile in a way that looked pretentious or forced while reading from your prompter? Was it apparent you were reading from it? Practice and then practice some more," advises WSBT-TV's Gassensmith.

Observing professionals is very helpful to the aspiring television performer, says KHAI-TV's Fuchs. "Tune in the media and try to understand why you like or dislike certain individuals you see and hear. Don't attempt to impersonate others. Emulate their excellences, but be cognizant of your own emerging style and qualities. Don't suppress the good in yourself by mirroring another performer's qualities. Ask yourself why the person you admire is good in your estimation and why the person you dislike is not. Try to be objective; it's not easy. Perhaps the performer you dislike is super in the opinion of most people. Watch and listen. To use an analogy, a good writer is first a good reader."

Several industry people have already stressed the importance of understanding the message before announcing it. WAGT-TV's Roberts considers this a crucial part of the practice and preparation process. "Read the copy and ponder its meaning. What are the words attempting to relate? What is the purpose for their being on the page? Think about what you get from the copy, and draw it out during your presentation. Don't just rattle off a series of words. Express their meaning. Know their meaning. This doesn't happen overnight. You've got to practice."

On a final note, WINK-TV's Sneeden recommends that on-camera performers, and those hoping to be, employ a relaxation technique as a prelude to performance. "Even though television generally doesn't lend itself to calm reflection before showtime, it is basically something performers should find time for. Relaxed vocal chords—a relaxed mind and body—will go a long way toward a good presentation. A few minutes outside the studio and a few deep breaths help achieve a composed and poised state. What I'm saying is, take a few minutes to collect your energies. Line up your inner resources. Calm the sea before setting sail. Meditate to accomplish focus and concentration." (Relaxation is further discussed in Chapter 8.)

BOOTH CRITERIA

Television stations also hire announcers for off-camera voicing duties. These individuals are called booth announcers because they deliver live copy from small audio studios usually large enough to accommodate only one person.

In the 1980s, the live booth voice has been supplanted by the prerecorded voice at many stations. Unionized stations are the most likely to retain the services of on-duty booth announcers, whereas other stations typically assign announcements to staff announcers for taping. In the latter case, voice-over announcers record commercial tags, p.s.a.'s, promos, and other material appearing on the station's daily program log. When booth announcers are employed, copy is delivered live, although lengthy pieces, such as thirty- and sixty-second commercials, are usually prerecorded to avoid on-air mistakes.

Booth announcers are called upon to do some on-camera work at many stations. "Booth people must be capable of fulfilling on-camera assignments in emergencies and when other needs arise. You need that kind of flexibility or versatility in a booth performer. Booth people also fill in for vacationing camera talent and very often are assigned regularly scheduled short pieces, such as news updates, during the day," says Jerry Williams, Program Director, WCTV-TV, Tallahassee, Florida.

Among the entries on the criteria checklist for booth or voice-over performers is the ability to assume the appropriate tone and attitude required by the wide variety of copy presented, says Nick W. Pfeifauf, vice president, WESH-TV, Daytona, Florida. "A voice that can adapt to the message, regardless of its nature—melancholy, humorous, hyped—is most valued in this area. There is no need to have merely a pleasing voice. Rough sounding voices are quite often effective in, for example, tire commercials. Females with 'husky'-sounding voices are effective in perfume or other intimate product commercials. To carry my point a step further, you have to be able to sound reassuring, peaceful, and somewhat sympathetic in a spot for a funeral home, yet you must be able to sound educated for a computer commercial or excited by a big sales event. The need here is for adaptability."

Today, in almost every area of broadcast voice performance, the conversational style is valued. This is also true in booth work, notes WCTV-TV's Williams. "While a 'boother' must have the versatility of an actor, he should be able to communicate in a casual, one-on-one fashion. Talk 'talk,' as they say. Most of the material delivered requires the conversational presentation, rather than one that is theatrical or overpowering. Booth performers have to be sensitive to surrounding elements, that is, the programming wrapping an announcement. You don't want to blurt out a message in the middle of a tranquil program landscape. In other words, don't frenzy-up an announcement in the midst of a program on gardening. When all is said and done, the listener should have absorbed the message delivered, not have been distracted by the performer's quirky pitch. The message is important, not the person delivering it."

Timing is a crucial consideration in all aspects of on-air work. "Anyone delivering copy, especially live, must be able to adjust their pacing to fit the time allotted—for example, slowing down when you only have twenty seconds of copy for a thirty-second spot or speeding up when there's thirty-five seconds' worth of copy for a half-minute spot. The key is being able to do this without sounding like there is anything wrong. You also have to know how to 'hit the clock,' or meet the network. A sense of timing is a basic criterion for broadcast voice work," says Williams.

FIGURE 6.9
Wire service marine and regional forecasts. Courtesy UPI.

Seeking Employment

A significant percentage of booth and voice-over announcers come from radio backgrounds. "I had ten years in radio before making the switch to television. Many TV voice performers have experience in radio. I recall before applying for a TV position that I practiced long and hard on reading, even though I was an experienced radio announcer. I would not only read 'wire copy' out loud over and over again, changing in-

```
Z15440FZ6-
        R O FZUS6 KBOS 292000   0217

    COASTAL MARINE FORECAST   NATIONAL WEATHER SERVICE BOSTON MA    300
PM EST TUE MAR 29 1988
    FROM MERRIMACK RIVER MA TO WATCH HILL RI...OUT TO 25 NAUTICAL MILES

    SYNOPSIS...WEAK HIGH PRESSURE OVER NEW ENGLAND THROUGH  WEDNESDAY.
A COLD FRONT WILL PASS EAST FROM THE COAST WEDNESDAY   NIGHT.
    MERRIMACK RIVER MA TO PLYMOUTH MA...OUT TO 25 NAUTICAL MILES
CHATHAM MA TO WATCH HILL RI...OUT TO 25 NAUTICAL MILES   CAPE COD BAY
    WIND SOUTHEAST 10 TO 20 KNOTS OVERNIGHT AND WEDNESDAY.   WEDNESDAY
NIGHT WIND SOUTH 15 TO 20 KNOTS LIKELY SHIFTING NORTHWEST BY SUNRISE.
AVERAGE SEAS 2 TO 4 FEET THROUGH WEDNESDAY NIGHT.$$
    BOSTON HARBOR
    WIND SOUTHEAST 10 TO 15 KNOTS OVERNIGHT AND WEDNESDAY.   WEDNESDAY
NIGHT WIND SOUTH 15 TO 20 KNOTS LIKELY SHIFTING NORTHWEST BY SUNRISE.
WAVES LESS THAN 1 FOOT THROUGH WEDNESDAY NIGHT.$$
    BUZZARDS BAY
    WIND SOUTH 10 TO 15 KNOTS OVERNIGHT SHIFTING SOUTHWEST WEDNESDAY.
WEDNESDAY NIGHT WIND SOUTHWEST 15 TO 20 KNOTS LIKELY SHIFTING   NORTHWEST
BY SUNRISE. AVERAGE SEAS AROUND 2 FEET THROUGH WEDNESDAY   NIGHT.$$
    THF



OFP1-BOS


Z15860FP1-
        R O FPUS1 KBOS    292100  0083

    STATE FORECAST FOR SOUTHERN NEW ENGLAND NATIONAL WEATHER SERVICE
BOSTON MA 400 PM EST TUE MAR 29 1988
    PARTLY CLOUDY TONIGHT.   LOWS IN THE 30S.   INCREASING CLOUDINESS
WEDNESDAY.   HIGHS IN THE 50S NEAR THE SHORE AND IN THE 60S INLAND.
MOSTLY CLOUDY WITH A CHANCE OF SHOWERS WEDNESDAY NIGHT.   LOWS IN THE MID
30S TO MID 40S.   BECOMING MOSTLY SUNNY THURSDAY.   HIGHS 50 TO 55.
    RRF-CSH

---------
UPI 03-29-88 03:15 PES
```

flection as the copy mood shifted, but I would read the page backwards and even through the back of the page as I held it up to the light. It prepped me to read anything that was handed me. I became known as 'one take.' Competition for TV slots is formidable, so sharpen your skills before auditioning," suggests WESH-TV's Pfeifauf.

A solid education and professional coaching increase the odds of gaining a position. "Get a good education, especially in English. Get voice training from a professional, if possible. These give you some good entry-level credentials," WCTV-TV's Williams says.

Pfeifauf agrees with Williams, adding, "There's nothing better than the courses offered at many colleges and universities, providing announcing is coached properly. Also, many junior and community colleges utilize local broadcast talent as instructors to help train people in radio/TV announcing and newscasting. In my opinion, the best type of coaching comes from instructors who actually have hands-on experience in the electronic media. I have found, as have others in the business, that too many broadcast instructors have absolutely no actual experience in broadcast performance. It can certainly be immediately detected when we interview or audition a fresh-out-of-college grad only to find he or she has no concept of the real world of broadcasting."

Jobs in booth announcing are not plentiful. Therefore, proper training and preparation are essential when competing for a position.

WEATHERCASTING

Until the late 1960s and 1970s, weathercasting responsibilities often fell to staff or booth announcers. These individuals rarely had formal training in meteorology, but depended on information provided by the wire services and regional and national weather bureaus.

As weathercasting became more technologically sophisticated and a more important and integral part of news broadcasts, stations turned to qualified meteorologists, who brought with them greater knowledge and credibility.

Today, most television stations employ at least one full-time meteorologist, who often possesses the American Meteorological So-

FIGURE 6.10
Television station weather center. Courtesy WJAR-TV.

ciety's seal of approval—a fact commonly touted by stations to enhance their weather information image.

In order to prepare forecasts, meteorologists derive information from in-house computer data bases and printing machines that generate weather graphics, such as maps.

A typical television meteorologist arrives at a station midafternoon to prep weather forecasts, which he or she delivers during the evening (6:00 P.M. and 11:00 P.M.) news programs. At many larger stations, a meteorologist is assigned to cover early morning news broadcasts as well.

As any other type of broadcast voice performer, a station meteorologist is expected to possess solid on-camera delivery skills.

Radio stations rarely employ full-time meteorologists. Rather, they rely on forecasting firms that provide local feeds to stations for a fee.

SUGGESTED FURTHER READING

Barnouw, Eric. *Tube of Plenty: The Evolution of American Television*, revised edition. New York: Oxford University Press, 1982.

Dubek, Lee J. *Professional Broadcast Announcing*. Newton, Mass.: Allyn and Bacon, 1981.

Frank, Ronald E., and Greenberg, Marshall C. *The Public's Use of Television*. Beverly Hills, Calif.: Sage Publications, 1980.

Broughton, Irv. *The Art of Interviewing for Television, Radio, and Film*. Blue Ridge Summit, Pa.: Tab Books, 1981.

Millerson, Gerald. *Video Production Handbook*. Boston: Focal Press, 1987.

Rather, Dan. *The Camera Never Blinks: Adventures of a Television Journalist*. New York: William Morrow, 1977.

7
THE BROADCAST SPORTS VOICE

SPORTS ANNOUNCING

More people are exposed to sporting events over television and radio than at the sites where games actually take place. It is the broadcast sports voice performer who communicates to the home audience all the action and details of athletic events while they are underway and reports the results when they are over.

Aspiring sports announcers who possess only a casual interest in sports should consider another profession. Perhaps no other area of broadcast voice performance requires such a dedication and love for its subject matter. Sports announcers must first be fans before they can become reporters. "You must be a sports enthusiast to start with. Sports has got to be something that is an integral part of your life. Most of us have a sort of obsessive appreciation for sports. If you love something, it is easier to be good at it. Most sports announcers are players at heart," says Ron St. Pierre, Sports Reporter, WPRI-TV, Providence, Rhode Island.

The overwhelming majority of sports reporters boast backgrounds, either as youths or adults, in some type of amateur sports. A significant number of major market and network sports voices come from professional athletics, especially play-by-play color announcers and analysts. Almost always the successful sports reporter has a deep and abiding affection for the field of athletics. "Sportscasters aren't conceived in a vacuum. At eighteen you don't pick up the occupation from a guidance counselor's list of things to be. You know from an early age that you want to be involved in sports broadcasting. Generally speaking, I don't know a group of professionals who love what they do more than sportscasters," says Kurt Haider, Sports Director, KSRM/WHQ, Soldotna, Alaska.

SPORTS VOICE DUTIES

The primary areas of employment in sports voice performance are sportscasting or reporting, play-by-play, and analysis. Sportscasters primarily deliver game results, pertinent information about players, and data concerning upcoming athletic events. Play-by-play announcers narrate the action of sporting events for the benefit of the home audience, and analysts—sometimes referred to as color commentators—provide statistical data and biographical information on players as well as observations intended to embellish a broadcast.

The role of the station sportscaster is significantly affected by the size of the facility at which he or she is employed. A small-market station seldom employs a full-time sports person. Financial strictures preclude doing so. This results in a member or members of the on-air staff, either a deejay or newsperson, assuming sports reporting responsibilities. To illustrate this point, WXXX-AM in Center City, Maine, will serve as a fictional model. Center City is a town of nine thousand inhabitants, and WXXX is the only local radio station. WXXX broadcasts from 6:00 A.M. to 11:30 P.M. daily and employs one full-time newsperson who holds the title of news and sports director.

A representative day for this person may appear something like this: From 6:00 A.M. to noon, Monday through Friday, the preparation (gathering, selecting, and editing copy) and presentation of ten five-minute newscasts, each of which include a one-

FIGURE 7.1
Sports coverage is an important part of programming at many stations. Here WTIC recalls its coverage of sports events over the years. Courtesy WTIC AM/FM.

Covering the play by play.

Sports coverage became a bigger part of the action at WTIC in the 50's. Floyd Richards and Ed Anderson teamed up to cover local college football rivalries at Wesleyan, Trinity, Amherst, Williams, the Coast Guard Academy and others. Bob Steele continued to bring his special touch to boxing, interviews and other kinds of sports commentary.

In 1952, the Greater Hartford Jaycees sponsored their first professional golf tournament. The idea was to generate money for worthy local charities and draw national attention to the Hartford community. When the "Insurance City Open" began, WTIC radio was there. WTIC has covered and supported the event since its inception, with exclusive, on-the-course reporting.

WTIC added George Ehrlich to its sports staff in 1957. George was considered the best basketball play-by-play man in New England. Together with Floyd Richards, Ehrlich brought listeners all the action and excitement of UConn basketball and football. Also in 1957, the area's "Fenway Faithful" could follow the ups and downs of Ted Williams and the rest of the Boston Red Sox in regular WTIC broadcasts. Red Sox baseball has been an important part of WTIC's sports schedule ever since.

▲ *WTIC came to be known as "the sports station" in the 50's and 60's. Bob Steele continued with special sports features and interviews. Here, he prepares to do an interview with Brooklyn Dodger great and Hall of Famer, Jackie Robinson.*

▼ *WTIC was there for the first nicks at the "Insurance City Open", later renamed the "Greater Hartford Open". Since it began in 1952, for 35 years, WTIC has provided exclusive coverage. Shown here in 1952 are WTIC sportscaster Floyd Richards, the first winner, Ted Kroll (right), Edwin H. May, Jr., of the Greater Hartford Jaycees and 1952 Co-chairman of the event (center).*

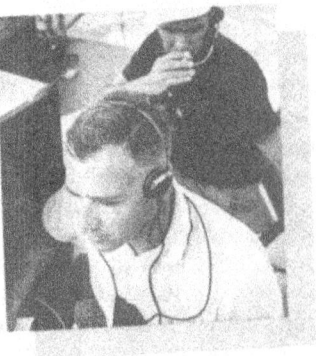

▲ *George Ehrlich was considered the best basketball play-by-play man in New England. He joined the WTIC sports staff in the 50's and later became WTIC Sports Director in the 60's. Here he is seen at the 19th green at Wethersfield Country Club while covering the Greater Hartford Open. Director/Producer Ted Bedrosian is on the second end.*

minute sports roundup. Following the noon news, the responsibility for hourly newscasts is assumed by deejays. During the afternoon, the news and sports director follows up local stories in order to provide actualities (tape reports) for on-air staff delivering news. In addition, this person prepares to cover local sports events, which usually take place during the early evening hours.

On a typical night the assignment may be to broadcast the play-by-play action for any of a number of Center City High School teams. This is a demanding task, not only due to the extended hours that the news and sports

FIGURE 7.2
Small market radio station play-by-play coverage. The sports reporter is responsible for setting up audio equipment as well as broadcasting the action. Courtesy WGAO-FM.

director must work, but because he or she must be prepared to broadcast the action with authority and credibility. This person must know about the sport that he or she is covering to be believable and should, at the very least, be able to properly pronounce local player's names. This requires doing some homework, even when time is at a premium.

When games are not scheduled for broadcast, the news and sports director bones up on local and national athletics by conducting interviews with sports figures, reviewing statistics, and reading newspapers and sports magazines.

Larger stations, especially those that emphasize sports, commonly employ personnel whose responsibilities fall exclusively in the area of sports coverage. For instance, if WXXX-AM were operating in Mega City, New Jersey, it might well employ two full-time sports reporters.

The duties of one reporter may appear as follows: Prepare and deliver four hourly five-minute sports roundups daily, between 6:00 A.M. and 10:00 A.M. Following these broadcasts, this person (who is likely to be given the title of sports director) tapes an interview with a sports personality for the noon news block. Before departing from the station for the day, he will write additional sports stories and tape actualities for later broadcasts. This individual may also be expected to cover afternoon and evening sporting events deemed important to the listening audience.

The station's other sports reporter may have the following duties: Prepare and deliver two, two-minute and three five-minute sportscasts between 2:00 P.M. and 7:00 P.M., serve as host of *Sports Talk* (a two-hour telephone conversation and interview show aired nightly between 7:00 P.M. and 9:00 P.M.), and record onto cartridge actualities from the show considered to be of interest to the morning audience.

Both sportscasters share weekend and holiday coverage responsibilities, and the morning sports person substitutes on *Sports Talk* when the need arises.

TELEVISION SPORTS VOICE RESPONSIBILITIES

While the duties of the television sports voice performer are somewhat different from his or her radio counterpart, there are parallels. For the sake of illustration, let us assume

WXXX is a television station located in Mid-size City, Michigan. Most television stations employ at least one full-time sports reporter. Again, this individual generally wears the mantle of sports director. Some major-market television stations employ between three and five sports voice performers. Returning to our illustration, because WXXX-TV is located in a medium-size market and does not have the resources of a large, metropolitan station, it is budgeted for one part-time and two full-time sports announcers.

The duties of these television sports voice performers may be configured as follows: One sports reporter covers the morning and midday newscasts, plus prepares a taped feature for broadcast on the evening report. The other full-time sports reporter delivers the sports news he has gathered and prepared on the 6:00 and 11:00 P.M. broadcasts. These television sports reporters alternate coverage of weekend athletic events when they are scheduled. The part-time sports reporter is responsible for weekend broadcasts and is on standby status during the week should a need exist.

The television sports reporter is responsible for producing sports footage for airing during broadcasts, which are typically scheduled as part of a station's news show. Quite often, in addition to his or her other duties, the television sports reporter is expected to produce a weekly sports feature that is aired either within or outside of regularly scheduled newscasts. Although somewhat less frequently today than in the past, established television sportscasters are invited by local professional teams to serve as play-by-play or color announcers.

Calling the Game

Team sports reporters, that is, individuals exclusively employed by professional or semiprofessional clubs, travel with their teams and broadcast from stadiums or arenas where games take place. Network sports reporters do not travel with teams, but rather fly to where the "game of the week" is to be played. Needless to say, in both instances the sports voice performer must be an expert on the team and on the sport he is covering. Professional team sports reporting is anything but a game.

SPORTS VOICE CRITERIA

The love of athletics is a prime motivator for broadcast sports voice performers. "To be honest, there are many sports announcers who'd much prefer suiting up and hitting the field with the players they report on," contends KSRM's Kurt Haider.

Despite the longing to be a part of the action on the field, sports reporters take very seriously their responsibilities behind the mic, chief among them vocal presentation. "In the old days you could hear some strange sounds calling the action. Today voices are clean and professional. Voice control, pitch, breathing, inflection, and such must be up to standards. Sure, there are some pretty unusual styles calling sports, for example, Cosell and, in Boston, Johnny Most for the

FIGURE 7.3
The sports report is an integral element of evening television news broadcasts. Here WJAR-TV's sports reporter prepares for broadcast. Courtesy WJAR-TV.

Celtics, but in general, good announcing basics are required. Don't place style over solid oratory. Style is great when it is *great*, but you must first be clearly understood and, of course, not aggravating to listen to," notes Steve Shortz, Sports Director, KXGO-FM, Arcata, California.

The natural, conversational style popular in other areas of announcing is also effective in sports broadcasting, says Paul Lepisto, Sports Director, KABY-TV, Aberdeen, South Dakota. "Personally, I feel that anyone interested in being a sportscaster should not try to 'announce,' per se. He or she should *talk* the game to viewers. What I'm saying is don't put on a sports 'voice.' A forced, contrived announcer-type delivery (not unknown in this business) is tedious to hear, and people don't want to be subjected to a person caught up in his or her own sound, but rather they want to be told in a direct, unpretentious way what is going on. There are a lot of imitators out there, too, especially in sports calling. Be natural. Be yourself."

Up for the Game

Interest, energy, and enthusiasm must always be present, says Marc Soares, Sports Director, KARZ-FM, Burney, California. "There is nothing worse than an indifferent or apathetic sports reporter. You must reflect the same excitement and appreciation for the action as the fans. I don't mean do the 'wave,' froth at the mouth, or scream until the transmitter explodes, but be upbeat and involved. Even in the wrap-up segment you shouldn't sound like you're reading the Dow Jones closing averages."

Ron Reina, Sports Director, KSDO-AM, San Diego, California, says that sounding like a fan increases audience acceptance. "You don't have to display bias to be enthusiastic. You can maintain a certain balance and perspective and exhibit a joy for the game. The audience wants this. A healthy respect for the sport needs to come through, whether it's baseball, football, basketball, or hockey. Furthermore, a voracious appetite for sports information has to exist. In other words, a sports voice professional doesn't just leave the game when it's over and forget about it. He continues to 'live' athletics by listening to and watching other sports broadcasts, reading about athletics, and talking to insiders."

A "Game" Voice

As in every other area of broadcast voice performance, voice quality is a factor. "A good voice is always a plus, but you don't have to have a real boomer to get a job, either. It takes a while to develop your voice, so the more you work on it the better it gets," says KSRM/WHQ's Haider.

A "good" voice does not strictly mean a "deep" voice, says Carl Thoreson, Sports Director, KPAY-AM, Chico, California. "A broadcast sports person must possess a good, strong voice. It doesn't necessarily need to be really deep or very resonant, even though those things are marketable, but it does need to be strong. Situations occur in tournament play where a sportscaster must call several games in a row, sometimes during the same day or evening. If a voice isn't strong, it won't hold up to that kind of pressure and strain. Of course, although a voice doesn't need to be deep or particularly resonant, it does have to be pleasant to the ear. It is very important that a sportscaster learn how to effectively use his voice in order to maximize his natural talents."

The Word Game

Word power—the ability to turn a phrase in a colorful, imaginative way—is necessary in sports announcing, contends KSDO's Reina. "In play-by-play you're really dealing with language in a variety of forms. To begin with, a sports announcer must have the ability to speak the English language. Ball game-ese or colloquialisms come later. Of course, a strong repertoire of relevant adjectives is our stock in trade. Sports involves so many descriptions, you must know how to use words."

KRAY's Thoreson agrees. "A good knowledge of vocabulary is necessary. Descriptive terms are integral to any game-calling, and not just sports terms, either. A wide understanding of the English language is required. Cosell is an extreme example of word prowess, or word flaunting, but having a deep well of words, quotes, terms, and phrases to draw from makes you a heck of a lot more interesting to listen to."

A Game Plan

Sports reporting requires an agile mind, a person who is able to think on his or her feet. "I think of all the attributes needed by the sports broadcaster, the ability to think spontaneously is most important. Things happen fast on the field. Anything can happen. The individual behind the microphone can't put the audience on hold while he collects his impressions. You've got to be there with the stats, insights, and observations on the spot. Presence of mind, knowing where you're at at all times, keeps you from losing control," says KARZ's Soares.

Providing an audience with comprehensive coverage requires a system, says Roger Crosley, Director of Sports Information and Communication, Massachusetts Institute of Technology. "An on-air sportscaster should keep some type of running note on any game covered. This is not unlike a print reporter's note about a game. This allows the sports voice performer to spot trends. Trying to speak and write simultaneously is not the easiest thing in the world to do, but in the long run it is very helpful. Each sports broadcaster should try to find an individual system for doing this. On another point, one of the most important things, and one of the things that is most neglected, is reporting the score of a contest at regular intervals. This is less important on television when graphics can convey information, but it is essential in radio. I can't tell you the number of times I've tuned into a game on radio and waited forever to hear the score or the inning. I've heard of some broadcasters who use a three-minute egg timer to remind themselves to give the score."

KSRM's Haider believes that organization keeps the sports reporter from potential disaster. "Organization helps a sports person immensely. Knowing where you're going next keeps you from finding yourself in an embarrassing place. Know your score sheets and know ahead of time what you're going to do in all possible situations. Anticipate. Keep your play-by-play organized. Make it easy for the listener to know where that ball or puck is. I always divide the court or ice into sections using the proper terms of the sport. Sports reporting goes beyond talking into the mic. This is especially true for play-by-play. Keep the game flowing. Herky-jerky broadcasting creates an atmosphere of uncertainty. Stay 'linear,' as they say."

Self-Assessment

Haider also believes that self-criticism is a way to avoid falling into counterproductive habits. "Good sportscasters, in my opinion, possess the ability to look into themselves, to assess their performance, objectively—to put themselves in the listener's seat. You have to be able to step outside of yourself and survey your actions. People who become so immersed in themselves that they can't see 'the forest for the trees' often perform poorly.

"While I'm on the subject of what makes a good sportscaster, let me add that 'fitting in' is important. If you work at a small station like I do, don't be afraid of being a little bit of a 'homer.' Get excited about your home team. Build them up. This is particularly good when the local high school or college team is playing. Parents love to hear you get excited, and so do other fans. Try to mention the kids sitting on the bench as often as you can if it fits in with what is happening on the field. If it's football, don't forget those linemen. I've even had the cheerleaders up to the booth to talk during halftime. It's a lot of fun, and it generates interest and good will.

"As long as I'm going down the list of what makes a good sportscaster, let me say that client awareness and sensitivity score big points. Treat the sponsors well. Mention them often, because they are the ones making your broadcast possible. One last point which ties in with one previously made, when you're working with high school athletes, keep criticism to a minimum. I always stress positive things with the kids. There are enough bad things in the news. Sports should be fun, and that should be reflected in your broadcasts."

PREPARING FOR A SPORTS VOICE JOB

Sports voice performance positions are obtained through careful planning and preparation. According to KXGO's Shortz, this means precollege involvement in both broadcasting and athletics. "By this I mean watching games on television and listening to them on radio at an early age. Listen to the folks in the business. Analyze what they are saying and how they are saying it."

Close observation of professional sports reporters is an invaluable experience for those aspiring to jobs in the field. "Believe me, nothing beats watching and listening. Expose yourself to all kinds of sports reporting and critique it. Pick out the pluses and minuses, and develop your own criteria for sports announcing. School yourself before you get formal schooling, and never stop observing," offers KSDO's Reina.

KARZ's Soares concurs with Reina and Shortz. "Watch all kinds of sports on ESPN and the major networks. Emulate the good qualities of the top sportscasters. In most cities sports are broadcast around the clock, especially with cable. Watching the pros at work is the best way to learn."

Participation in sports gives the would-be sports reporter an insider's appreciation. This translates into a greater understanding of the events unfolding on the field of play. "Participation in sports is invaluable preparation for mic duty. Get into all the sports you can. Have fun, but learn about each one. Although you may not be blessed as an athlete, I think it is important to be involved in sports, either as a player, student manager, or water boy. But you need to be involved in the games to really know how athletes act and how coaches think. The more inside information a sportscaster has on a sport, the better the broadcast," says KPAY's Thoreson.

Having actually played a sport gives a person an important edge when calling a game, contends KSRM's Haider. "I feel that even before you think about getting into the business you need to put time in on the field. Sure, not every successful sports reporter has participated in athletics, but most have. Having been a player, you bring that little something called insight to the broadcast. Beyond playing, you should attend a lot of games."

As in any other area of voice performance, practice cultivates skills. "If you have becoming a sportscaster in mind, you must practice. Get a cassette tape recorder, find an empty seat at a sporting event, and practice play-by-play. After the game, listen to the tape, and note what you like and what you don't like. The next time you record yourself, work on eliminating the negatives. For almost any sportscaster it takes several years to achieve the smoothness that is required for a top notch broadcast. So the earlier you start, the sooner you will get to where you hope to be," says Thoreson.

Haider gives similar advice. "Go to the games and bring that little dime store recorder with you. Pretend that you're on the air. Never mind the people around you who might give you weird looks. Do the game, then go home and listen. Critique yourself. Usually you'll know what you have to work on. Go to the local radio or cable station and ask for advice and help. Get involved with local sports broadcasts. Volunteer. You'll put in a lot of hours, but if you really love the work, it will be worth it in countless ways."

It is precisely what Haider and Thoreson are suggesting that turns an aspiring sportscaster into a practicing professional, says

A

B

FIGURE 7.4A and B Sports broadcasts have been a mainstay for radio since the 1920s. Courtesy WTIC and WJZ.

FIGURE 7.5.
Station sports promotional piece. Courtesy WJR-AM.

the field of athletics. Become a sports historian. Know what happened to a team twenty years ago. Background is wonderful material in a broadcast. Subscribe to the sports newspapers and magazines, and pore over the data. Computers are great. You can store facts and statistical data and call it up in an instant. The actual broadcast is the result of intense preparation."

Finally, the importance of formal training cannot be overlooked, says KSDO's Reina. "A well-rounded education makes for a stronger sports reporter. Practically all of your major sports broadcasters have college backgrounds. Take classes in a variety of subjects, including Phys. Ed. General knowledge is important. History, sociology, psychology, literature, law, and math courses are all valuable to the future sportscaster. Sometimes sports people get a little myopic. Maintain an open mind and interest in all things."

Many large colleges, and some smaller ones, offer specific sports courses, such as history of American sports, and sports psychology. These are certainly of value to the future sportscaster.

KARZ's Soares. "Call the games you see, whether in person or over the home receiver. Turn on a game with the sound down and do the announcing through to the conclusion. Record the game onto a VCR and your play-by-play onto a tape cassette. Rewind them after the game, and play them back. Critique yourself. Another pretty good way to practice is to read the sports page out loud all the time. Volunteer to announce local little league games and recreational softball games. Keep working at your delivery, and you'll become a pro."

KABY-TV's Lepisto reiterates a point made earlier in this chapter. "Before you can expect to get a job calling sports you have got to acquire a body of knowledge about players, teams, and regulations. Study the stats and the rule books. Delve into the personal stuff about players and coaches. It's the little background stuff that gives a broadcast that something extra. Be a student of the game."

There is no such thing as being "overprepared" for a broadcast, says KARZ's Soares. "While you are advancing toward your goal of becoming a sports reporter, bone up on

SPORTS VOICE DO'S AND DON'T'S

It is the consensus of sports reporters across the country that preparation is the number-one "do." "Do your homework! If you come into a game unprepared you will give a weak presentation. Make sure you have all the relevant information and know the coaches and players before the game begins. It means spending extra time, but extra time is what contributes to a quality broadcast," says Reina.

Researching local teams and leagues is a necessity, believes KXGO's Shortz. "To get things rolling right, I contact everybody. I get on all the mailing lists and let the clubs and groups know I'm here and that they have air time on my station. This gives me regular input, which is what I need to do the job right. I don't have to get my info second-hand from the newspaper—a last resort. Here are a few types of clubs to contact: kennel, equestrian, skeet/trap shooting, pool, tennis, gymnastics, and little league. Do keep the flow of information current and constant. Get to know everyone. Using first and last names of athletes during sports coverage makes a positive statement."

Prebroadcast preparation also includes equipment and personnel checks, says Haider. "Even before going to the broadcast site, do make sure you're familiar with what is going on back at the station. Know who you're working with, and make sure your equipment is performing properly. Another thing—always be courteous with everyone you come in contact with. Get to know the people you'll be working with at the broadcast site—grounds keepers, building officials, maintenance people."

Treating people with courtesy and kindness should always be a criterion, KABY-TV's Lepisto says. "Although this may never directly affect your broadcast, it may affect your working conditions and ability to gain access to areas. So be nice to the so-called little people: the attendants, janitors, ushers, security guards, and so on. They can do a lot of things to help you out, or they can make your life a living hell. Remember, treat them the way you wish to be treated, and you'll get along well. They can really be a big help when you need something."

Lepisto encourages sports broadcasters to treat each event with seriousness and enthusiasm. "Treat each game you cover as something important. It may not be the Super Bowl or World Series, but it's important to the audience or they wouldn't be tuned in. Never get blasé or sound apathetic. Remember, enthusiasm is contagious."

While prepping for broadcast ranks foremost on the "do" list, inflated egos rates prominently on the "don't" roster, contends KPAY's Thoreson. "Don't let your position go to your head. You may think you're the second coming of Mel Allen and believe you know it all, but don't convey that to people. Egomaniacs turn us all off. Don't be a smug 'Mr. Star Sports Reporter.' Regardless of how good you think you are, you can always improve. Be humble. Remember, there are dozens of men and women waiting in the wings who are equally capable. Don't make the mistake of thinking you are perfection personified."

People on "head trips" are difficult and unpleasant to work with. "A sports announcer who thinks he's above it all is a turnoff to the audience as well as his colleagues. Never think that you are bigger than the event you're covering. The listeners aren't tuned because of you. They want to find out what's going on in the game. Check your ego at the gate," advises Lepisto.

KSDO's Reina cautions future sports reporters against taking themselves too seriously. "Sports reporting is a serious and noble profession, but don't become so filled with yourself that you become obnoxious. Look, giving the results of a football game, calling the play-by-play of a basketball game, or interviewing Dwight Gooden does not change the course of events in Washington, Beirut, or Del Rio, Texas. In my opinion, prima donnas are not fully self-actualized human beings."

M.I.T.'s Crosley shares Reina's opinion. "Remember to keep things in perspective. The events you are covering, whether it's the Super Bowl or a high school junior varsity basketball game, are just games. While some contests may have more impact than others, they are still simply part of what David Letterman calls the 'candy store of life.' As former Dallas Cowboys running back Duane Thomas once said when asked about the importance of the Super Bowl, 'If this is the ultimate game, why do they play it again next year?' The sportscaster has got to keep a grip on things, and this means his ego, too. Sorry, but the people tune in for the game, not the on-mic performer."

Losing sight of reality in the face of some public acknowledgement is the first step toward losing touch with fans, athletes, and co-workers. "Keep both feet firmly on the ground. Don't forget who you are and why you're doing what you're doing. Don't be a know-it-all or denigrate others. For example, don't criticize the official too much. If you feel he has made a bad call, say so, then move on. Don't harp on it. I never mention officials' names during the game of after. Don't focus attention on yourself, either. Keep on the action. Remember, you're there to call the game, not to win converts to your fan club," says KSRM's Haider.

Haider points out a propensity to exaggerate among some sports reporters. "Be honest. Call the game as it happens. Don't overdo. State what you see in excited terms, but avoid hyperbole. Keep things simple when you're on the air. Use vocabulary and terms that clarify, not confuse. It's good to be colorful, but don't obscure the picture in doing so."

Exaggeration can lead to misinformation—anathema for any sports voice performer—says KXGO's Shortz. "Don't use unverified information or any you have doubts about. Get the straight data before going on-mic. Be careful that in the heat of your own play-by-play you don't go overboard and make erroneous statements. Some sports reporters forget that they are 'reporters' and create fiction out of facts. That is not a good thing, to put it mildly."

Haider and Reina advise their reporters to remove clichés and trite expressions from their repertoire. "Develop a vocabulary that is fresh and at the same time accessible, and don't recycle old expressions or rely on clichés," says Reina. Haider contends, "You don't have to make off-the-wall comments to be interesting to the listener, but inane and worn-out clichés reveal a lack of imagination."

Haider and Crosley round out the roster of "do's" and "don't's" by reminding aspiring sports announcers to remain conscious of the special nature of their chosen medium. "In radio you never use numbers in your play-by-play. What I mean is, the numbers on the player's jerseys. Those numbers don't mean much to listeners. In radio you've got to create the scene through language. On the other hand, in television you really have to know when to let the picture do the talking," says Haider.

"Here are a few more things to add to your performance checklist," notes Crosley. "1. If you're working television sports, be careful not to be redundant with the graphics you use. The sportscaster must remember that most of his or her audience can read. It is acceptable to call attention to a graphic, but to simply read it insults the audience's intelligence; 2. Identify!! This is especially key in radio. By this I mean identification of formations and positions, as well as players. There are times when, for some reason or another, you are unable to see numbers and identify players by name. You can buy yourself some time by using the position of the player until you can make a positive ID. In some sports, especially football, it is important to have a 'spotter' accompany you to a game. This person feeds the air talent the names of players; and 3. When doing a television broadcast you have to keep one eye on the monitor and one eye on the field. Your job is to report on what both you and your audience sees. If something takes place off camera that is of importance to the game, you must report on it as if you were doing radio (that is, without benefit of pictures). This is another instance when a spotter can help you."

SUGGESTED FURTHER READING

Barber, Red. *The Broadcasters*. New York: Dial Press, 1970.

Coleman, Ken. *So You Want to be a Sportscaster*. New York: Hawthorn Books, 1973.

Harwell, Ernie. *Tuned to Baseball*. Notre Dame: Diamond Communications, 1985.

Spence, Jim. *Up Close and Personal*. New York: Atheneum Publishers, 1988.

VanderZwaag, Harold J., and Sheehan, Thomas J. *Introduction to Sports Studies*. Dubuque, Iowa: William C. Brown Company Publishers, 1978.

8 THE BROADCAST VOICE WORKSHOP

The voice box is an instrument. Properly played, it has endearing and enduring qualities.
Ed McMahon

You will recall the above quote from Chapter 2. It is the objective of these pages to examine how the voice may be enhanced for the purpose of broadcast performance. Indeed, as Mr. McMahon states, the voice box is an "instrument," and it is up to the voice performer to derive the most out of his or her instrument for the satisfaction of the audience.

VOICE QUALITY

Not all instruments are created equal. That is to say, not all people are born with a Stradivarius-caliber voice. However, most people can cultivate their voices to a level that is pleasing and appealing to listeners. Even an individual with a high-pitched, even shrill, voice can acquire certain skills that will make it more sonorous and resonant.

It cannot be disputed that a naturally rich and lushly textured voice is a tremendous asset to any aspiring on-air broadcast performer. Television and radio have been, and continue to be, partial to fuller, mature voices, regardless of their owner's gender. However, the lack of so-called big pipes can be overcome to a considerable degree, and it should be stated at the onset that a deep voice alone does not an announcer make.

Take a survey. Not all of the top broadcast voice performers possess "golden" voices. What they do possess, however, is the ability to communicate in a clear, concise, and personable style. They are, in the truest sense of the word, communicators.

There are numerous ways to improve voice quality, that is, to strengthen a weak or thin voice. For example, correct breathing helps enormously. Allow the lungs to be replenished with oxygen at pauses. Do so in a gentle, rhythmic, and even manner. Do not gasp or force air into the lungs, but breathe in naturally and plentifully. The lack of oxygen when speaking accentuates voice quality deficits.

Become more aware (not self-conscious) of breathing—inhaling and exhaling. Determine the lung's capacity. The voice box, like a trumpet, is activated by the surge of air passing through it. Needless to say, the high notes of a trumpet cannot be reached without sufficient wind emanating from the player. The same can be said of the voice performance and the announcer. Shallow or uneven breathing affects voice quality. Air fuels and enriches the voice.

Poor breathing may be linked to bad posture. Check posture while sitting in front of a microphone. Do not slouch or slump over or sit as taut as a military academy plebe. In these configurations the lungs and diaphragm are twisted and contorted, thus inhibiting the flow of oxygen. It is impossible to inhale deeply and fully when the torso is bent over. Sitting too rigidly or erectly tightens the diaphragm and tenses the muscles. Again, this inhibits free and natural breathing.

Bad posture also communicates in a negative way to the viewing audience. As stated in an earlier chapter, a performer who is slumped over or leaning to one side appears lazy or indifferent, regardless of whether this is true. Conversely, the on-camera performer who sits arrow-like conveys rigidity and an uptight feeling.

A relaxed voice sounds best, too. A nervous or agitated voice loses its depth, range, and texture. The voice has considerable range, but tension diminishes it. Performers must learn to relax before air time. There are several exercises useful in "loosening up." Tightness in the neck or shoulders can be relieved by slowly rotating the upper body, including the head, for a minute or two. Casually flexing the shoulder muscles also helps, as does letting the jaw hang open loosely and shaking the arms. Breathing should be deep during this exercise. Some people find it helpful to keep their eyes shut while engaged in this routine.

The voice box itself involves some delicate internal muscles not necessarily affected by rotations, flexing, and shaking, notes speech expert Patricia Culbert. "I'd suggest humming and sighing before going on. Simple, but effective. These allow the loosening-up to work internally on the voice as well."

Broadcasters have been known to meditate, using various methods, to achieve a state of relaxation prior to air time, and many have devised their own techniques for unwinding before the on-air light flashes. For instance, a short walk in the fresh air may help. Of course, this is not feasible if the station is located on the upper floors of a high rise building. Plain old stretching exercises aid in relaxation. Long-time New England radio voice performer Allen Ford finds singing in an operatic fashion before going on-mic calms him, while New Jersey announcer Gunther Purdue regains composure by standing on his head in the newsroom minutes before broadcast. The point being made here is to devise a system to help deflate the balloon of tension that draws away from performance.

Be careful of pacing, also. Acceleration affects voice quality. Generally, the faster a deejay speaks, the higher his or her voice sounds. Create the environment most conducive to maximum voice quality. Rapid-fire delivery does little to enhance the natural qualities of a voice.

ARTICULATION

I want that glib and oily art
To speak and purpose not; since what I well intend,
I'll do't before I speak.
                        Shakespeare—King Lear

Voice quality does not hinge exclusively on the maximum utilization of the voice box. How a performer says something is as important as the plait, trellis, and weave of the voice itself. Proper articulation and enunciation add substance to the voice. *Webster's Dictionary* defines a person who is articulate as one who expresses himself or herself easily and clearly. Few people can achieve this state with clenched teeth, rigid jaw, or closed lips. It calls for movement and animation.

To begin with, a voice performer should take notice of how the mouth is utilized while speaking. Words are formed in the mouth and must be given enough room to take flight. Few words are understood when they are uttered. When not effectively constructed by the tongue, lips, and jaw, words lose their import. Several excellent speech texts devote considerable print to the correct articulation of word components, such as consonants, vowels, and diphthongs. For a thorough study of speech sounds and patterns, I suggest you consult one of the Suggested Further Readings listed at the chapter's conclusion.

To improve articulation and enunciation—practice!! Emote. Be expressive, even deliberately dramatic, when vocalizing prior to actual taping or broadcast. Self observation is most revealing. Aspiring voice performers gain considerable insight into articulation problems by watching themselves speak. Unclear speech, unless caused by a physical impediment, generally stems from deficient use or misapplication of the mouth and jaw muscles. Slurred or mumbled words are roadblocks to audience comprehension, and thus anathema to the broadcast voice performer. Simply put, program directors do not hire inarticulate announcers. "Learn to fully utilize what nature has provided you," advises Ed McMahon.

INFLECTION

Out of the air a voice without a face
Proved by statistics that some cause was just
In tones as dry and level as the place.
                        W.H. Auden—The Shield of Achilles

A broadcast voice performer improves his or her "listenability" by varying tone and pitch. Moving the voice's pitch from low to high or vice versa creates color and conveys emotion. Notice, for example, what happens when a play-by-play sports reporter calls a great play. His voice is transformed and the audience becomes transfixed. Excitement charges the voice. Variety gets our attention. By altering the tone of his voice, the sports reporter captures and conveys the drama unfolding on the court to the listener. A monotone delivery—what writer Tom Wolfe refers to as the "pale beige tone"—deprives the audience of the full range of human experience.

To overcome a monotone delivery, voice performers are encouraged to tape record material (anything from a commercial or news story to a passage from *Hamlet* or a Neil Simon play) and assess it on playback. Repetitious or unvaried inflection can be overcome through awareness and work.

A word of caution to anyone intent on eliminating tonal deficits: do not overcompensate. A delivery with exaggerated inflection sounds affected and pretentious. Nobody wants news delivered in a "To be, or not to be" style.

MIC FRIGHT

Let me assert my firm belief that the only thing we have to fear is fear itself.
  Franklin D. Roosevelt

President Roosevelt made this memorable and often quoted statement during his first inaugural address in 1933, as the nation writhed from the pain and ignominy of financial collapse. His words were meant to remind his audience that fear is self manufactured and inevitably self defeating if left unchecked.

Many things can inspire fear within us. Roosevelt was telling his listeners that only they could neutralize and vanquish their apprehensions. This is equally applicable to the broadcast voice performer experiencing mic fright.

Fear of performing is not an unusual phenomenon, especially for newcomers. With experience comes the confidence to overcome mic anxiety. There are, however, a number of things that the inexperienced broadcast voice performer can do to lessen the unpleasant effects created by mic fright.

To begin with, a broadcaster who is well prepared automatically feels more confident and secure. Lack of proper preparation has negative consequences and does not instill a sense of stability and control. The result is frequently a fear of failure.

By focusing on the preparation of material needed for broadcast, an announcer feels less tentative about performing. Concentrating on the content of the broadcast rather than on the actual performance can help quell the pre-on-air jitters. This is not to suggest one ignore the on-mic presentation; however, a disproportionate concern for performing can inspire anxiety.

Earlier in this chapter the benefits of learning to relax prior to going on the air were discussed. Nervousness is a by-product of fear. Dealing with the "tremors" can mitigate their source. In other words, if a performer knows how to treat the symptoms of fear, then fear becomes less affecting.

One way to deal with fear is to understand it. Taking from the famed French existential philosopher Jean Paul Sartre the dictum that "man creates himself" and applying it to fear (given that fear is subjective and evolves from within), a performer can assume a degree of control. By putting fear in perspective, by understanding that an individual is ultimately responsible for what he or she feels, the spectre of fear can be held at bay, if not completely vanquished.

ACCENTS

Yea, but we found him bald too, eyes like lead, Accents uncertain.
  Robert Browning—*A Grammarian's Funeral*

Most program directors seek announcers who are free of regional and ethnic accents. Strange though it may seem, although Bostonians are known to drop "r's" from their words (such as "cah" for car and "yahd" for yard), broadcast voice performers in that city are expected to pronounce all their letters. This also is true of southern accents—okay for the average guy on the street, but taboo on the air. "Y'all" does not cut it over the microphone. Southern announcers, like their cohorts anywhere, are expected to speak in a clear, generic fashion without discernible regional tint or coloration.

To increase the likelihood of securing an on-air position, the job candidate must endeavor to rid himself or herself of what *Webster's Dictionary* describes as any "distinguishing regional or national manner of

FIGURE 8.1
Copy as marked for delivery: o, watch pronunciation; _____, emphasis; --, pause; and ∩, accent (pronounce r's). Marking copy in such a manner can highlight important aspects of the delivery.

WJR AM RADIO 76
Stands for Detroit

2100 FISHER BUILDING
DETROIT, MI 48202

L-3933

CLIENT: ORECK XL VACUUM
LENGTH: :60
EFF: _____

:10 —

WORLD FAMOUS <u>AMAZINGLY</u> LIGHT 8-POUND ORECK° VACUUMS ARE NOW USED THROUGHOUT THE U.S.A. IN OVER 50-THOUSAND HOTELS AND MOTELS. AND THE ORECK VACUUM HAS BEEN RATED AS "BEST BUY" BY A <u>LEADING</u> CONSUMER PUBLICATION. ISN'T IT ABOUT TIME YOU RETIRE YOUR OLD HEAVY TIRED DINOSAUR OF A VACUUM AND SWITCH TO THE EASIEST TO USE VACUUM MADE...THE ORECK XL. ORECK OFFERS THE <u>LIGHTEST</u>, MOST <u>POWERFUL</u>, MOST <u>DEPENDABLE</u> VACUUM THAT CAN BE PRODUCED....NOW AVAILABLE AT YOUR LOCAL INDEPENDENT VACUUM DEALERS THROUGHOUT SOUTHEAST MICHIGAN.

:30 —

ORECK VACUUMS ARE ON <u>SALE</u> NOW AT: POINTE VACUUM IN GROSSE POINTE° WOODS....OR DEARBORN VACUUM ON FORD ROAD, 3/4 MILE EAST OF TELEGRAPH IN DEARBORN....OR RON'S VAC SHOP IN NORTH LANSING, LOCATED AT THE CORNER OF NORTH WASHINGTON AND GRAND RIVER.....OR VISIT VACUUM CLEANER CENTER IN ANN ARBOR, ON PACKARD BETWEEN STATE AND STADIUM AT WELLS. FOR FURTHER INFORMATION OR THE ORECK DEALER NEAREST YOU, CALL <u>TOLL FREE</u>, 1-800--4-2-2--V-A-C-S. THAT'S 1-800--4-2-2--8-2-2-7. REMEMBER, NOTHING GETS BY AN <u>ORECK</u>.

:60 —

---

pronouncing" or "speech peculiar to a region." In other words, the aspiring broadcast voice performer must purge from his or her delivery any remnants of an accent.

A couple of suggestions:

1. Underline words that fall prey to an accent—the Bostonian "r," whereas the letter is often dropped from where it belongs and added to where it does not belong ("I wrote my idear down while sitting in my yahd.").

2. Tape copy and play it back. Listen carefully and mark in red the accent trouble spots. Rerecord, correcting the places where an accent becomes manifest.

It is not always easy for announcers to detect their own accents. Therefore, it is a good idea to seek an objective ear. Try to recruit someone who does not have an accent. Remember, accents are only accents to people without accents. Listen to other voice performers. Time and again throughout this text industry figures have recommended tuning in seasoned professionals as a reference and source of guidance and inspiration. Be encouraged by the fact that many on-air performers were faced with similar obstacles and challenges, and keep working toward an accent-free delivery.

PRONUNCIATION

You have only, when before your glass, to keep pronouncing to yourself nimini-pimini—the lips cannot fail of taking their plie.
General Burgon—*The Heiress*

Inaccurate pronunciation of words reduces intelligibility, and if a broadcast voice performer is unintelligible he serves no one.

Pronunciation problems can stem from several factors. Poor articulation of word parts (syllables, vowels, consonants) affects pronunciation. A lazy mouth (resulting in the slurring of words) cuts down on clear pronunciation. Effective articulation enhances pronunciation. It is advisable to carefully review the section on articulation if pronunciation problems are the result of poor or faulty articulation.

Perhaps the most common pronunciation problems stem from ignorance, that is, a lack of familiarity with a word or name. On-air people have a responsibility to broadcast with accuracy and must take every step possible to ensure that they are doing so. This means checking pronunciation when encountering strange and unfamiliar words. Guessing is dangerous. There is no excuse for not consulting a dictionary or another person concerning correct pronunciation.

Names of people and places pose the biggest challenge. The author recalls an incident at the beginning of his announcing career during which he was operating the studio controls for a remote sports broadcast (little league game) at a small New England station. The station's young play-by-play announcer made the cardinal error of failing to check the pronunciation of player's names prior to game time. The station was located in a very ethnically diverse area that boasted a large population of Polish, German, and Italian residents. The unprepared sportscaster proceeded to butcher the pronunciation of practically every team member's name.

Meanwhile, your author was inundated with telephoned complaints (even threats) lodged by incensed relatives and friends of the players. The protest was so vociferous that the station appointed another announcer to call the action at future games. For a considerable time the defrocked sportscaster was persona non grata at the station and around the town. The moral is clear: check pronunciation before engaging mouth and microphone.

PHONETICS

Take care of the sense, and the sounds will take care of themselves.
Lewis Carroll—*Alice's Adventures in Wonderland*

Phonetics is a common-sense method to help announcers pronounce words correctly. Phonetic spelling involves writing words the way they sound. The news wire services offer phonetic translations of difficult words, primarily names. For example: Sri Lanka (Shree Lan-ka); Tel Aviv (Tel Ah-Veev); and Montreux (Mon-truh). The wire services offer a daily phonetic vocabulary consisting of hard-to-pronounce words appearing frequently in stories. At many stations it is standard practice to post this list where it is easily referred to (see Figure 5.15 in Chapter 5).

Less likely to appear on wire service phonetic (pronunciation) lists are common usage words, which may present their own problems to voice performers unfamiliar with them. Words like *assuage, dais, beige, aperture, pneumonia, aplomb, apostrophe, docile, elegiac, encephalogram, flaccid, gauze, kudos, laud, levee, physique,* and hundreds more can create problems for the uninitiated.

Phoneticizing words that are troublesome prevents repeated mispronunciation. All good dictionaries break words into syllables and provide symbols indicating where the accents and stresses are to be placed.

Obviously, the pronunciation of foreign words can be made less problematical through phonetic spelling. Of course, a voice performer must first ascertain the proper pronunciation of a foreign word before phoneticizing it. There are plenty of foreign language dictionaries and vocabulary guides that can be of tremendous assistance. For example, Cassell's foreign language dictionaries (published by Macmillian Publishing Company, New York) contain comprehensive pronunciation keys and are available in bookstores and libraries. Linguist Eugene Jackson has also written several foreign language guides that provide useful pronunciation information. (Jackson's books are published by Doubleday and Company.) Broadcast newsrooms frequently have these reference books on hand.

AD-LIBBING

We've got to rehearse our ad-libs, Ed.
　　　　　　　　　　Johnny Carson—*Tonight Show*

. . . the liveliest effusions of wit and humor are conveyed to the world in the best chosen language.
　　　　　　　　　　Jane Austen—*Northanger Abbey*

The term *ad-libbing* is described as unrehearsed, spontaneous speech, but knowledge of the subject extemporized is the cornerstone of effective ad-libbing. Nothing operates in a vacuum. A good ad-lib is good because it comes from somewhere, is relevant, and has poignancy and meaning.

There are innumerable situations that require a broadcast voice performer to possess ad-lib skills. Play-by-play sports announcers, deejays, news reporters, and talk show hosts, among others, must be able to improvise conversation.

Insight and knowledge of a subject gives the voice performer somewhere to prospect for unscripted comments. Effective ad-libbing cannot be accomplished without a thorough appreciation of a situation. The voice performer who gets caught without anything to say is out of touch with his or her subject and surroundings. On the other hand, a voice performer who does his or her research has a deep well from which to derive pertinent observations.

Staying in focus with the events of the moment gives the voice performer a springboard from which to launch insights and comments. In other words, listen and watch closely, and stay in touch and in tune with the unfolding drama taking place.

The ability to think quickly and to be able to adapt to a situation are especially valuable to the broadcast voice performer. The author recalls another incident from his early days in the business when, as an account executive for a Miami radio station, he was called upon to make intermittent, on-the-scene broadcasts from a boat show held in the Miami Beach Convention Center. The station, short of staff, recalled the author's previous on-mic experience. In a pinch they summoned him to the remote (field broadcast) location and said, "Do it." Not knowing the first thing about boats or boating, nor having a script from which to derive information, the one-time announcer had the presence of mind to focus on the reactions and expertise of those attending the show. It all worked out well enough, because the pinch-hitting reporter was able to draw from those attending the show their understanding and appreciation of the marine craft on display. To ad-lib with authority and ease, a voice performer must have an agile mind.

Like everything else, practice can enhance the ability to ad-lib. Following are a few suggestions that may help increase ad-lib skills.

1. On a tape recorder, without a script, of course, speak randomly on selected subjects or objects. For instance, look out a window and describe, as comprehensively as possible, what is going on. When objects (cars, people, animals) enter the scene, make them a part of the impromptu commentary.

2. As the tape rolls, attempt to structure the narrative. Establish a sense of continuity. Don't leap from one unrelated object to another. Try to tie things together. Perhaps start the discourse from the nearest object and move outward to the most distant. There are many different approaches to blocking or framing a scene or event. Continuity enhances audience understanding. The traditional three-part narrative structure (open, middle, and conclusion) found in most forms of writing can be imposed on the spontaneous monologue.

3. Don't stop when the narrative falters. Sustain the ad-libbed description. Keep going. Remember, the on-air voice performer cannot stop and start fresh during a live broadcast. Learn to recover from a stumble. Regroup quickly and forge ahead.

	THE ANNOUNCER'S WORK										
NAME:	CBS RADIO ANNOUNCER AUDITION ANALYSIS										
ADDRESS:					TELEPHONE:				CLASSIFICATION:		
SAMPLE	RATING				COMMENTS	ELEMENTS	RATING				COMMENTS
	E	G	F	P			E	G	F	P	
Ad Lib.						Voice					
News						Delivery					
Music Serious						Enunciation					
Music Dance						Pronunciation					
Music Misc.						Phrasing					
Spl. Annct.						Tempo					
Speaker						Pace					
Com'l						Variety					
Com'l						Color					
Lead-In						Personality					
						Imagination					
						Style					
						Overall					
General:											
Interview:											
Date:					Heard By:	Audition #:					F1516 10/54

FIGURE 8.2
CBS Radio announcer audition analysis checklist used in the 1950s. Courtesy CBS.

Roget's Thesaurus uses the word *rehearse* as a synonym for practice. Therefore, you can rehearse your ad-libs.

INTERPRETATION

Egad, I think the interpreter is the hardest to be understood of the two.
Richard Brinsley Sheridan—*The Critic*

Let your voice reflect the life of your copy.
Mike Morin—WCGY-FM

Throughout this text, industry professionals have stressed the importance of accurate interpretation of copy. It seems appropriate to conclude this chapter by reiterating some of their concerns.

Time and again the experts have emphasized the necessity of fully knowing and understanding the message before attempting a delivery. Cold readings seldom capture the essence of a commercial or news story.

Misinterpretation often arises from a lack of familiarity with copy. In other words, the voice performer does not "deep" read a piece of copy before hitting the mic switch. A cursory reading is dangerous, even for old pros.

It is the obligation and responsibility of the copy performer to bring to the audience what the writer intended. This means reviewing written material and digesting its design and structure before attempting to communicate it over the airwaves.

Inexperienced voice performers frequently make the mistake of focusing exclusively on their "sound," not aware that how they sound is directly tied to the way they interpret copy. They read without "realizing." Put another way, they deliver copy ignorant of its meaning. The result is unconscious communication (though the word *communication* hardly fits), which rarely leaves a positive impression on the receiver.

A broadcast voice performer must work from the "center" out when interpreting a written message. Surface reading leaves meaning untouched. Involvement is necessary for effective delivery.

The author recalls his own announcing professor advising his students to wrap themselves in the words and sentences of the copy until their meaning completely dressed them, adding that there was nothing worse than a half-naked announcer.

SUGGESTED FURTHER READING

Crannell, Kenneth C. *Voice and Articulation.* Belmont, Calif.: Wadsworth Publishing, 1987.

Eisenson, Jon. *Voice and Diction.* New York: Macmillan Publishing Company, 1985.

Fairbanks, Grant. *Voice Articulation Drillbook,* 2nd ed. New York: Harper, 1960.

Fisher, Hilda B. *Improving Voice and Articulation,* 2nd ed. Boston: Houghton-Mifflin Company, 1975.

Kenyon, John S., and Knott, Thomas A. *A Pronouncing Dictionary of American English.* Springfield, Mass.: Merriam Company, Publishers, 1953.

Linklater, Kristin. *Freeing the Natural Voice.* New York: Drama Book Publishers, 1976.

McKay, Ian R. A. *Introducing Practical Phonetics.* Boston: Little, Brown and Company, 1978.

Morris, William, and Morris, Mary. *Harper Dictionary of Contemporary Usage.* New York: Harper, 1985.

Partridge, Eric. *A Dictionary of Slang and Unconventional English.* New York: Macmillan Publishing Company, Inc., 1974.

Speech Foundation of America. *Self-Therapy for Stutterers.* Memphis: SFA, 1984.

9 BROADCAST STUDIOS AND EQUIPMENT

TOOLS OF THE TRADE

Equipment is an integral part of the broadcast voice performer's world. While program directors look for excellent vocal qualities in the announcers they hire, they also expect announcers to be completely adept at operating the equipment that will surround them in a studio. Voice skills alone are not enough for the on-air deejay who must (to use the vernacular) run a "tight board." The broadcast news person must be equally at ease and in control when using the variety of equipment necessary for assembly and preparation of stories. Play-by-play sportscasters, television anchors, talk show hosts, and other like personnel are by no means exempt from possessing knowledge of the use and application of studio and field equipment. The simple fact is that to be a broadcast voice performer is to be an audio and video equipment operator.

Many broadcast voice performers find themselves in production situations where they are expected to operate equipment with great proficiency and artistic sensibility. For example, a deejay mixes commercials, p.s.a.s, and promos (incorporating bed music, voice, and sound effects), while a news person places taped actualities into the context of important news stories, and a play-by-play sports announcer assembles a video recap of the high points of a game.

Broadcasting is an art and science, and voice performers must, out of necessity, wear the hats of both the artist and technologist. The art and science of broadcasting are not mutually exclusive. There is, indeed, a science to the art of voice performance and an art to the science of broadcast technology. Where would the announcer be without the microphone, for instance? Thus it is an integral aspect of the broadcast voice performer's job to deal skillfully and effectively with the technology, that is, the equipment, that constitutes the medium.

THE RADIO STUDIO

The number of studios a station has depends on its size—income and market rating. Obviously, the more prosperous a station, the more it is able to invest in its physical plant. The bigger and more successful stations often possess elaborate studio facilities. Regardless of size, all radio stations must have an

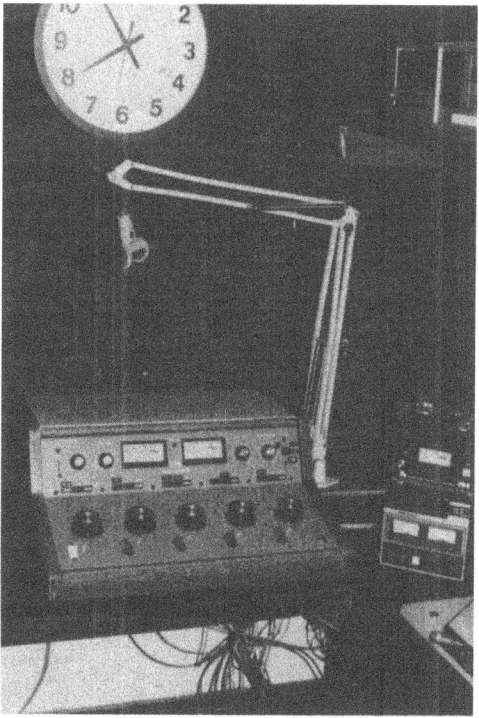

FIGURE 9.1
Radio station news booth. Studio includes audio mixer (left) and cart machines (right).

on-air studio (control room), and most, if not the majority, have an off-air studio (production room). Those that do not have the latter use their on-air room for both broadcast and production purposes. Large, metro market stations typically have two or more fully equipped, off-air production studios.

Nearly all radio stations have a news booth. These small rooms, sometimes barely large enough to sit in, may be stocked with various pieces of audio equipment or only a microphone.

Studio design is fairly standardized. Equipment is generally arranged in a U-shape for the sake of accessibility—equipment wraps around or surrounds the production person. The equipment found in radio studios includes audio consoles, turntables, tape machines (reel-to-reel, cartridge, and cassette), microphones and, in many, compact disc players.

Audio Consoles

The audio console (known as the "board") is the central nervous system of the radio studio. It is the piece of equipment through which all audio is processed. Consoles come in all shapes and sizes and are available from a variety of manufacturers in monaural, stereo, and multitrack.

All boards, elaborate or simple, contain *inputs*, which allow the audio signal to access the console, *outputs*, from which the audio

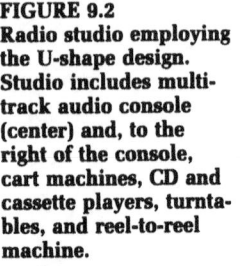

FIGURE 9.2
Radio studio employing the U-shape design. Studio includes multitrack audio console (center) and, to the right of the console, cart machines, CD and cassette players, turntables, and reel-to-reel machine.

signal is distributed to other locations, *VU meters*, which display levels of volume, *pots* (faders), which control the audio level, *monitor gains*, which adjust in-studio volume, *master gains*, which handle general output levels, and *cue mode*, which permits an operator to hear audio from selected sources prior to its distribution to other elements without affecting the program audio output.

Prior to the late 1960s, most console manufacturers marketed rotary pot units rather than those featuring slide faders. Today, the latter design is most prominent. Rotary pot boards are still popular, however, primarily because they are less expensive. "The majority of deejays prefer fader consoles because they find them easier to operate and more responsive," says Peter Drew, Production Director, WTIC-AM, Hartford, Connecticut.

Reel-to-Reel Machines

The reel-to-reel tape recording machine plays a central role in the production of most prerecorded programming material, such as commercials, p.s.a.s, promos, and features. In an earlier text (*The Radio Station*, Focal Press, 1986), the author refers to the reel-to-reel machine as the "production studio

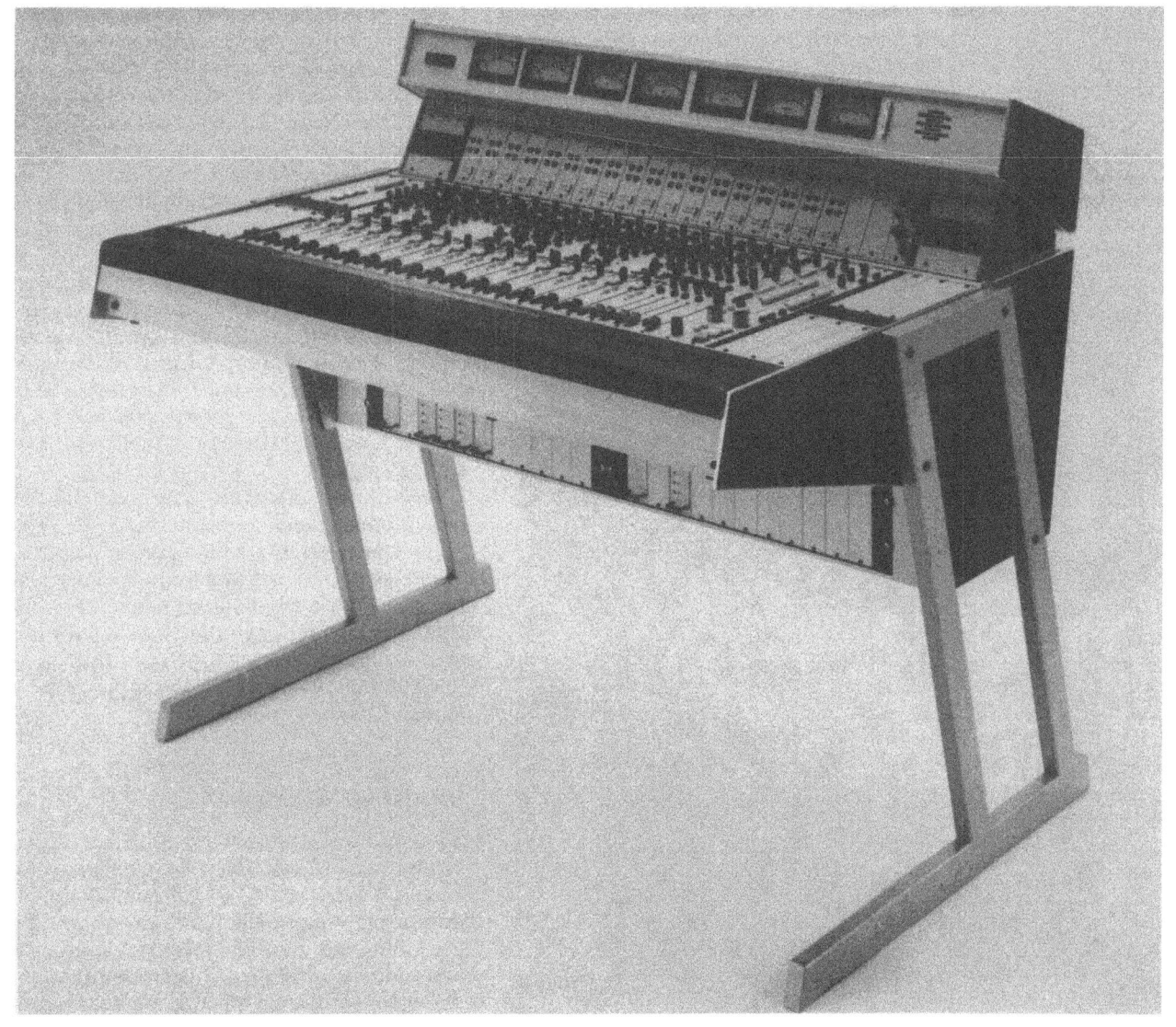

FIGURE 9.3
Stereo and multitrack fader audio consoles. Courtesy Auditronics.

FIGURE 9.4
Rotary pot audio console. Courtesy Broadcast Electronics.

FIGURE 9.5
Reel-to-reel recorder. Courtesy Fostex.

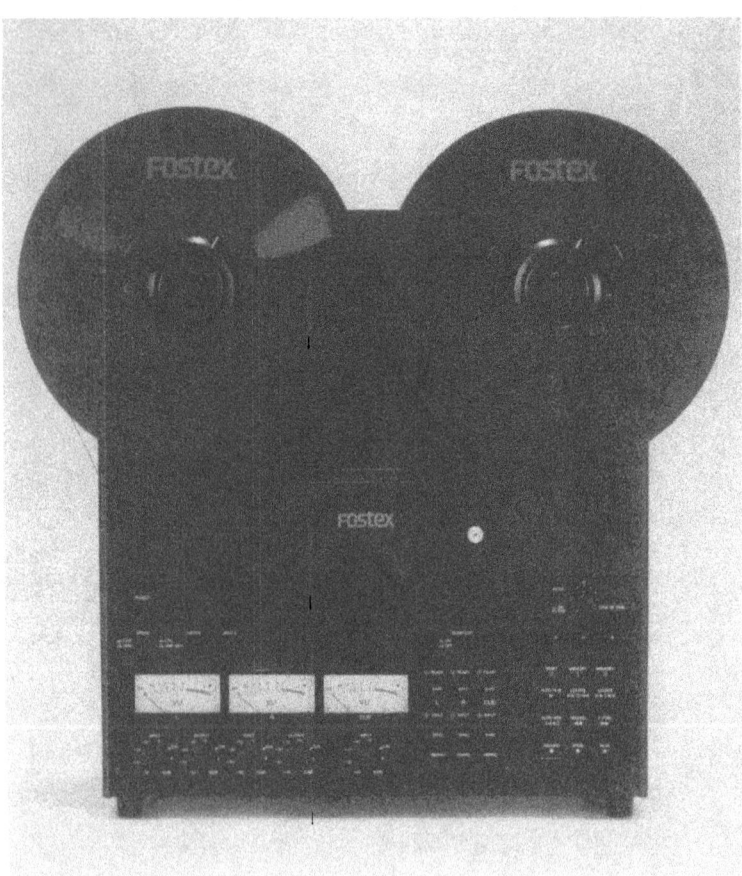

workhorse," and for good reason. All tape editing is done on this piece of studio equipment because its design allows for accessing tape heads where marking for splicing purposes takes place. Reel-to-reel machines feature three magnetic heads configured thus: *erase*, *record*, and *playback*. The editor marks magnetic tape with a grease pencil at the playback head. Because of their design configurations, other tape machines make this act virtually impossible.

Reel-to-reel machines allow for recording in various speeds, most commonly 3¾, 7½, and 15 inches per second (IPS). The vast majority of reel-to-reel recorders offer two speeds rather than three. Although some offer 3¾ or 15 IPS speeds, 7½ IPS is universally available. Because of this fact, most recording or dubbing intended for outside distribution is done at this middle speed. While a station may have the ability to run 3¾ or 15 IPS, it may not be able to do so at both speeds. Therefore, 7½ IPS has become the industry standard. "Keep this in mind when sending out reel-to-reel audition tapes. A station can always spin it at 7½, but it may not be able to do so at another speed," observes Joe Krause, Program Director, WCSX-FM, Detroit, Michigan.

Reel-to-reel machines are available in mono, stereo, and multitrack formats. The latter makes adding sound tracks possible. This gives producers greater range and flexibility in the mix of sound elements. Multitrack reel-to-reel recorders come in four-, eight-, sixteen-, twenty-four-, and thirty-six-track models. The four-tracker is in wide use at many larger stations.

Cartridge Machines

Most audio studios are equipped with two or more "cart" machines. The majority of a station's prerecorded material is aired over this piece of equipment. Cart machines are used for recording and playback purposes and employ plastic cartridges (reminiscent of the old eight-track cartridges), which contain magnetic tape spliced into a continuous loop. A subaudible cue tone is impressed on the tape when a cart machine is activated in the record mode. This allows the cartridge to recue once the audio has played. Cartridges may contain a few seconds or several minutes of tape. Like other recording machines, cart record units are available in mono and stereo. Some machines feature fast forward (to cue point) capability, while all lack erase heads. Magnetic tape erasers (also known as demagnetizers, degauzers, and bulkers) are another standard piece of studio equipment.

Cassette Recorders

Cassette machines have risen to popularity since the late 1960s. The small tape cassette used by the machine can contain up to two hours of playing time. One-eighth-inch wide magnetic tape is driven at a speed of 1⅞ inches per second.

Cassette recorders are widely used for airchecking on-air personnel and for the broadcast of lengthy features (public service programs and concerts) and news actualities. At a good number of stations, music also is aired over cassette machines. However, the recent rise in the popularity of the compact disc (CD) player has reduced this role to a large degree. The introduction of digital audio tape (DAT) players may restore the cassette-type deck as a primary source for airing music. Of course, conventional cassette players will not be able to accommodate digital audio tape.

Turntables

No studio is complete without turntables, although many stations have reduced the actual number of turntables in their on-air studio as a consequence of their reliance on carted music and the new audio technologies (CD and DAT). However, there are invariably two or more turntables in production studios, since a preponderance of bed music and sound effects exist in vinyl form.

Broadcast turntables are designed for fast start and cueing purposes, which lets the producer set up elements (music, sounds) to be integrated into a mixdown.

Most broadcast quality turntables feature two speeds, 45 and 33⅓ rpm, but some also offer 78 rpm.

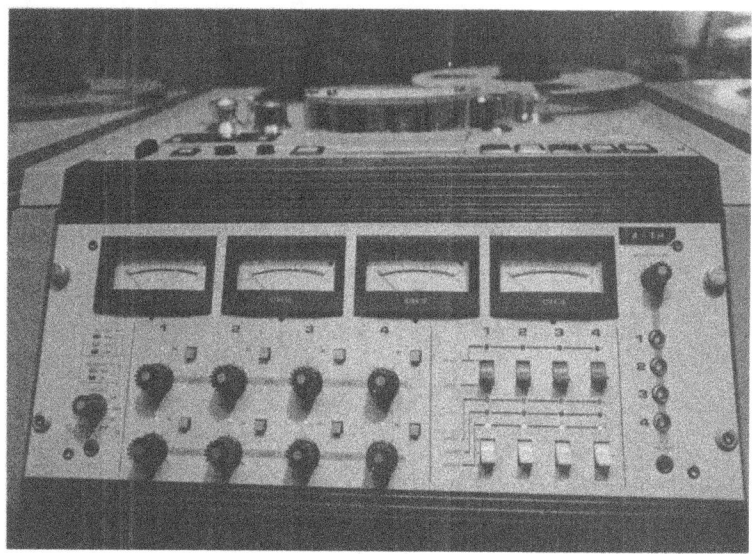

Compact Discs

CDs, as they are called, are one of the most recent innovations in sound reproduction technology to be embraced by broadcasters. Introduced in the early 1980s, a sizable per-

FIGURE 9.6
Four-track, reel-to-reel tape recorder.

FIGURE 9.7
Triple-deck cartridge machine. Courtesy Broadcast Electronics.

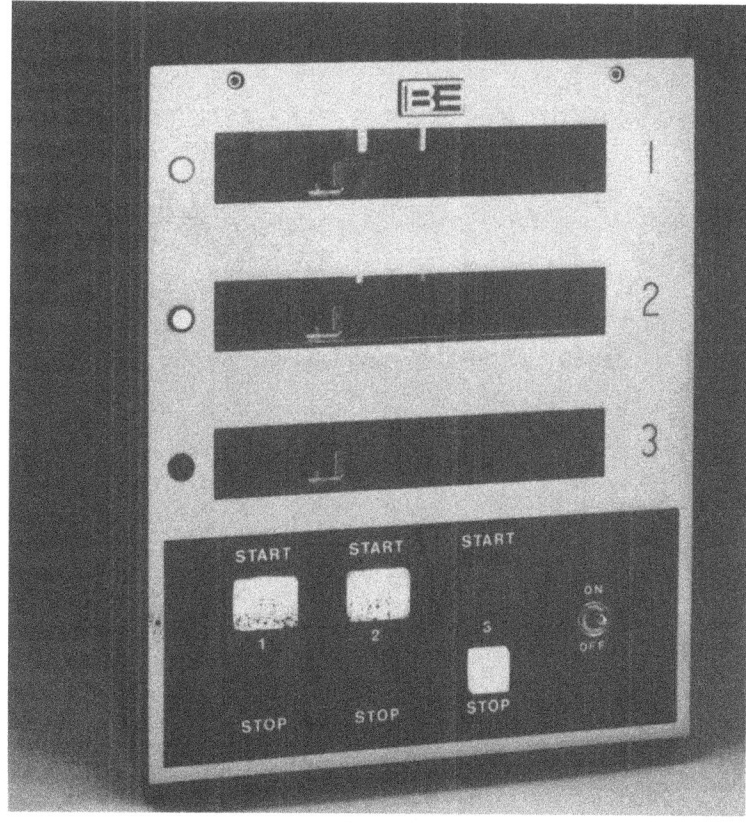

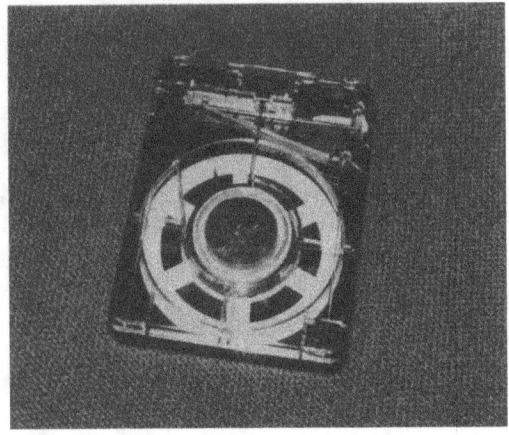

FIGURE 9.8
Continuous loop tape cartridge.

centage of stations have converted their libraries to compact disc. However, the majority of stations making the conversion are doing so gradually. Cost is the chief factor that prevents many stations from making a complete or abrupt switch. Lack of product has also been a factor, but the recording companies are now placing nearly all of their inventory on compact disc.

What makes CD technology so appealing to broadcasters is its superior sound fidelity, durability, and size.

The hissing, clicking, and scratching sounds often apparent on vinyl recordings are all but nonexistent on CDs, which use a laser beam rather than a stylus to decode (transcribe) a disc's surface. Since the laser beam is all that touches the disc, the chance of damage is minimal. Furthermore, compact discs are coated to further ensure superior fidelity.

The size of compact discs makes them easy to store and far less space consuming than LPs. "You need a third the space for a music library with CDs than you do with standard albums. What's more, they don't damage like vinyls," notes WCSX's Krause.

The fact that CD equipment and discs are costly and that they do not offer recording capability has kept the new technology out of smaller stations. The development of digital audio tape has caused some stations to hold off adopting CD technology until word is out as to which of the two performs the best.

Audio Tape

As of this writing, the new breed of audio tape already mentioned (DAT) is nearing its market debut. It will compete with the compact disc on both the retail and industry levels. Which technology will end up the victor is difficult to predict. In all likelihood both will find receptive markets and thus coexist and prosper. However, the standard magnetic tape in use by broadcasters since the 1950s is not likely to fade from the scene, at least not in the immediate future.

Magnetic audio tape comprises a polyester (sometimes acetate) sheet, which is chemically coated on the nonrecording surface for the sake of preservation and durability. Audio tape comes in varying degrees of thickness: 0.5, 1.0, and 1.5 millimeters. Usually, the thicker the tape, the more durable and less likely it is to snap or stretch under pressure. On the other hand, the thinner a tape, the more that can be contained on a reel. For example, a seven-inch reel of 0.5 millimeter tape holds 2,400 feet, whereas the same size reel containing 1.5 millimeters holds 1,200 feet. The industry shows a preference for thicker recording tape because it holds up better and lasts longer.

The width of audio tape also varies. The most typical width to be found in the production studio is ¼-inch. However, multi-

FIGURE 9.9
Tape demagnetizer.
Courtesy Fidelipac.

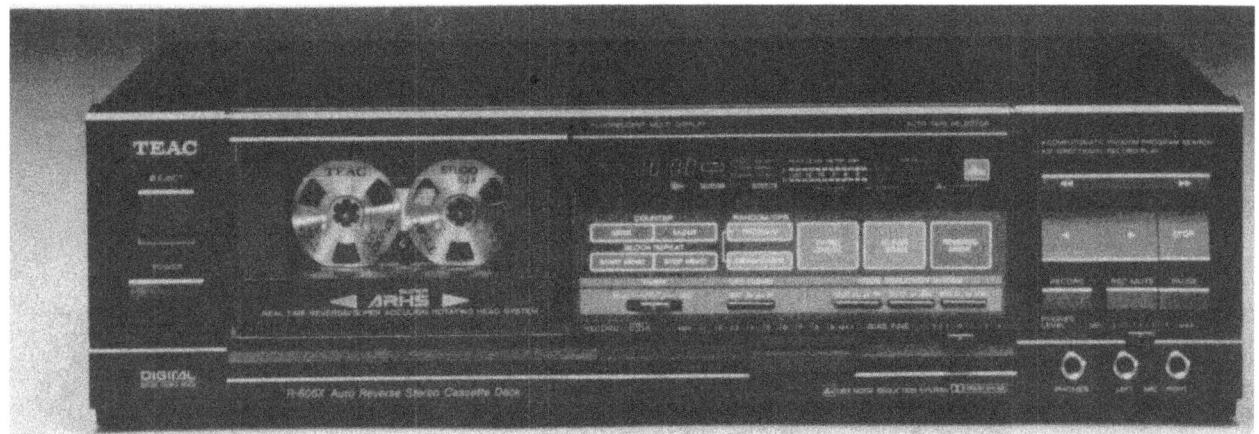

FIGURE 9.10
Cassette recorder.
Courtesy TEAC.

track recorders require more tape surface; thus the size of the tape used can be as wide as two inches, depending on the number of tracks employed.

Tape Head Cleaning

Since the recording surface of magnetic tape is treated with oxide particles, a residue is deposited on tape heads when the tape moves. Dust and dirt also build up on tape heads. It is therefore necessary to clean tape heads regularly. Letting residue accumulate

FIGURE 9.11
Cassette cartridge.

FIGURE 9.12
Broadcast turntable.
Courtesy Broadcast Electronics.

FIGURE 9.13
Broadcast quality compact disc player. Courtesy TEAC.

FIGURE 9.14
Compact disc recordings.

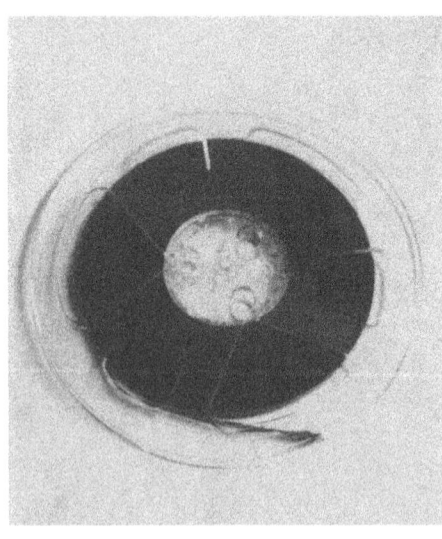

FIGURE 9.15
Seven-inch reel of magnetic tape. The tape is ¼-inch wide.

on the heads affects sound reproduction quality. Stations use isopropyl alcohol applied to cotton swabs to remove dirt from tape recorder heads.

Microphones

There are a wide variety of microphones especially suited for particular needs. To simplify things, consider all microphones as fitting into one of the following categories: omnidirectional, bidirectional, or unidirectional. The prefix before the word *directional* reveals a microphone's area of pickup. An omnidirectional microphone is receptive to sound occurring in multiple directions, usually a 360-degree area. This feature makes this type of microphone useful in round-table discussions when only one mic is available. A bidirectional microphone, as the prefix suggests, draws sound from two directions, and a unidirectional mic picks up sound from a single direction.

Microphones convert sound into electrical energy and possess either high or low impedance characteristics. Low impedance microphones, such as the ribbon, condenser, and moving coil, generally provide better sound quality and are preferred by many broadcasters.

Proper positioning and handling of microphones is important. Broadcast voice performers must become familiar with microphone features. Speaking out of the path of a microphone (off-mic) yields low levels and a hollow (boxy) sound, whereas speaking too close to a microphone (swallowing) may create distortion, such as popping and gusting.

Moving to and fro while speaking causes levels to seesaw (higher close to mic and lower away from mic) and an alternatingly hollow or off-mic effect. In addition, the rustling of paper and the tapping or drumming of fingers near an open microphone can prove very distracting to the listener.

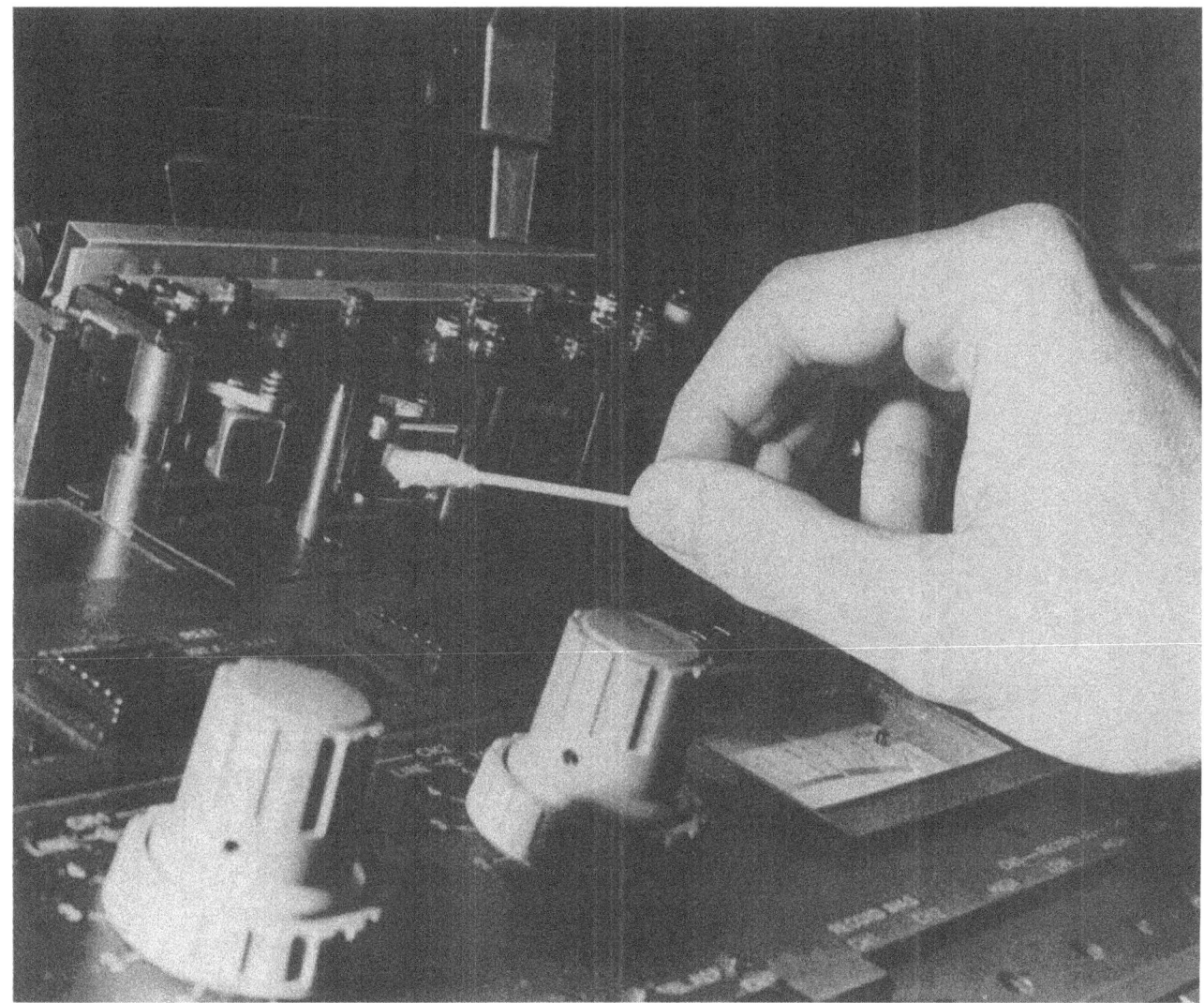

FIGURE 9.16
Frequent head cleaning prevents sound degeneration.

THE TELEVISION STUDIO

Television stations contain camera studios and control booths, as well as editing (postproduction) suites. Like radio, the size of a station (market rating) affects the physical plant itself. A metro-market television station may have two or three staging areas or camera studios and two or more control centers, whereas the small-market television station typically has only one camera studio and control booth.

The Camera Studio

The camera studio is an amalgam of equipment. Studio cameras on pedestals, monitors, prompters, dozens of lights hanging from grids, and microphones compose the bulk of the equipment found in the camera studio.

Cameras. Nonportable cameras mounted on pedestals or tripods are used in the station studio, whereas the portable camera (camcorder/portocam) is taken on location. The portable or field camera is usually shoulder-mounted and lightweight for that reason. Over the years, the portable video camera has become less cumbersome to handle and its picture quality has been considerably enhanced.

Television cameras comprise several features. The operator must fully understand all of them, as the director may call for a variety of different shots.

FIGURE 9.17A–C Several different types of microphones common to broadcasters. (A) A unidirectional mic. (B) A bidirectional mic. (C) An omnidirectional mic. Courtesy Fostex.

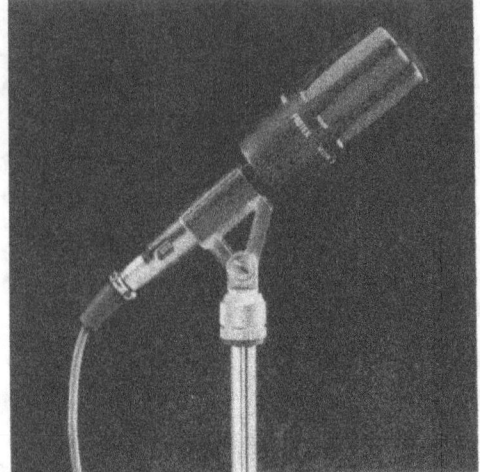

A

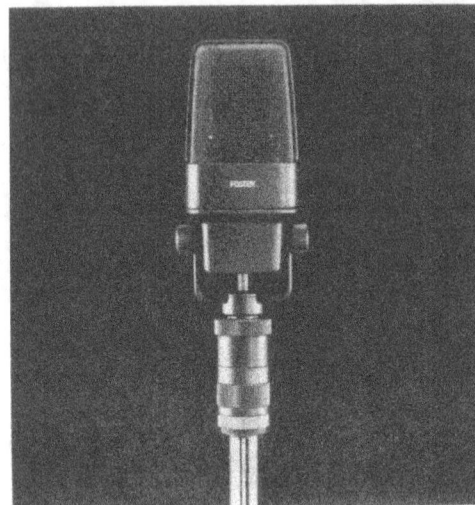

B

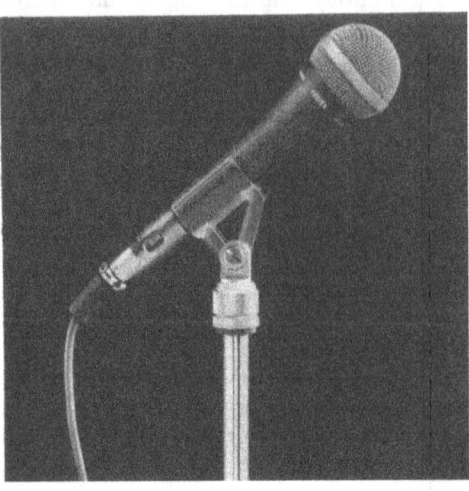

C

A representative studio will have between two and four cameras, and larger stations frequently possess crane mounts, which provide for elevated camera shots.

Tally lights (usually red) are a component of studio cameras. These let performers know which camera is live (hot).

Lights. Becoming acclimated to the intense brightness and heat generated by high-powered studio lighting is a challenge confronting the on-camera voice performer.

A standard television station studio often has between fifty and 100 lights, each of which radiates from 500 to 2000 watts. Of course, all of these lights are not activated simultaneously, but a single performer may have anywhere from six to a dozen lights (ten to fifteen thousand watts) directed on him or her.

Stations frequently use quartz lamps and defusers to mitigate the heat that these lights generate.

Back, fill, and key lights (usually set up in a three-point configuration) hang from row after row of grids secured to lofty studio ceilings. The lighting supervisor (light board operator) and director arrange illumination for a production. Performers may be asked to sit through this process and must remember not to move out of the established lighting parameters to prevent unevenness and shadows.

Video Control Booth

The control booth is the central artery of the television station. From this room the director orchestrates the production, either live or taped. The control room is an imposing array of sophisticated equipment, which, to the uninitiated, often resembles NASA's launch control center.

While a small video control booth may contain only a couple dozen pieces of equipment, a large station often has a near inestimable amount of the most advanced state-of-the-art video hardware.

At the very least, a television voice performer should possess a familiarity with the fundamental items that compose a video control room.

Switcher. As mentioned in an earlier section of this chapter, the audio console (board) is the centerpiece of the radio studio. The switcher

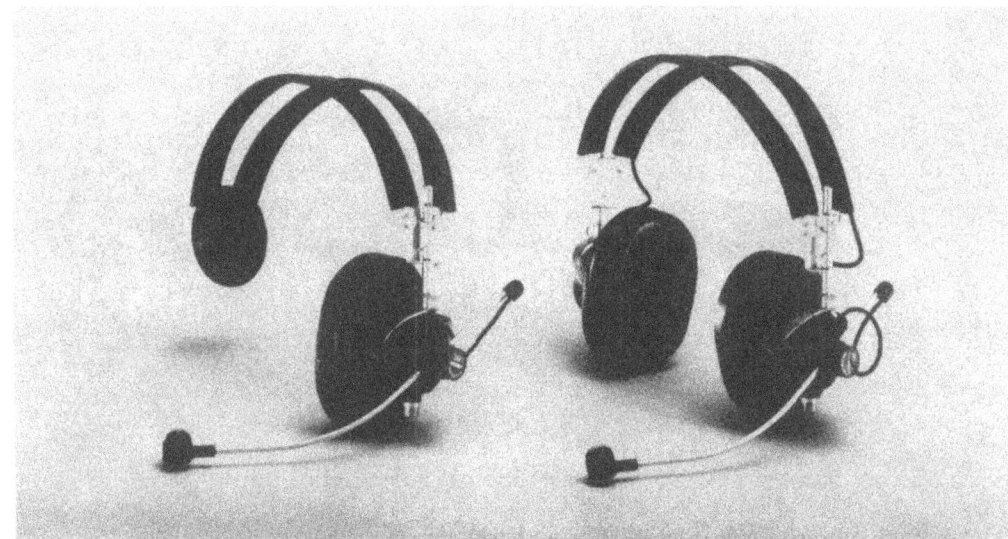

FIGURE 9.18
Headphone mics often used by on-scene news and sports reporters. Courtesy Shure.

holds a similar status in the video control booth in that it inputs and outputs signals, namely from cameras. The switcher primarily makes the changes between cameras. It is a live camera editing device that controls what is fed to various monitor points (preview, programming).

The technical director (TD) usually operates the switcher, sometimes called the special effects generator (SEG), since it frequently incorporates effects options in addition to basic features such as fade, dissolve, and wipe.

A switcher contains buttons arranged in horizontal rows called *buses*. These are for the purpose of preview, program, and effects mix. Bus inputs are tied to individual studio cameras, as well as videotape players, film chain camera (telecine), and so on.

Switchers come in all sizes and makes, and prices (depending on complexity) start at a few thousand and range to over several hundred thousand dollars.

Video Recorders. Video tape recording machines represent an essential part of the control and editing room inventory. Two types of recorders may be found in most television stations: video cassette recorders (VCRs) and open reel video tape recorders (VTRs).

The latter machine is reminiscent of the audio reel-to-reel recorder in that it is designed to handle reels of videotape. In fact, videotape recorders physically resemble audio reel machines and actually operate in a somewhat similar fashion: tape runs across record, playback, and audio heads. Video tape recorders (VTRs) most typically accommodate two-inch video tape on large reels.

Video cassette recorders, on the other hand, are analogous to audio cassette recorders in that they utilize cartridges of magnetic tape. The most prevalent video cassette tape widths are

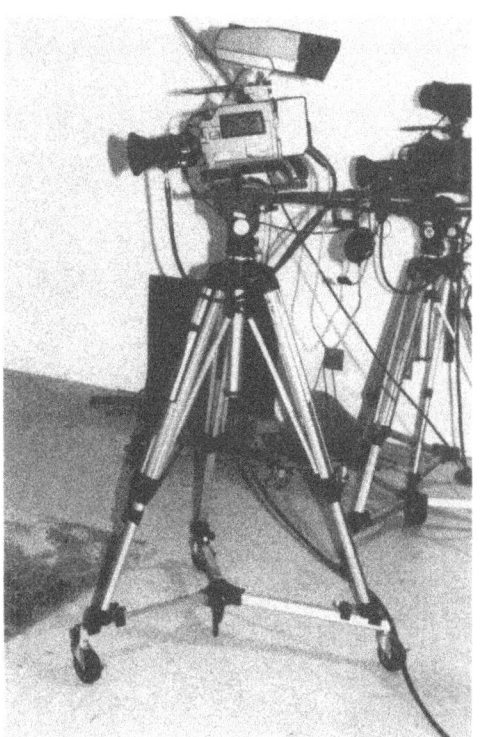

FIGURE 9.19
In-studio camera on tripod.

FIGURE 9.20
Field camera designed for shoulder mounting. Courtesy NEC.

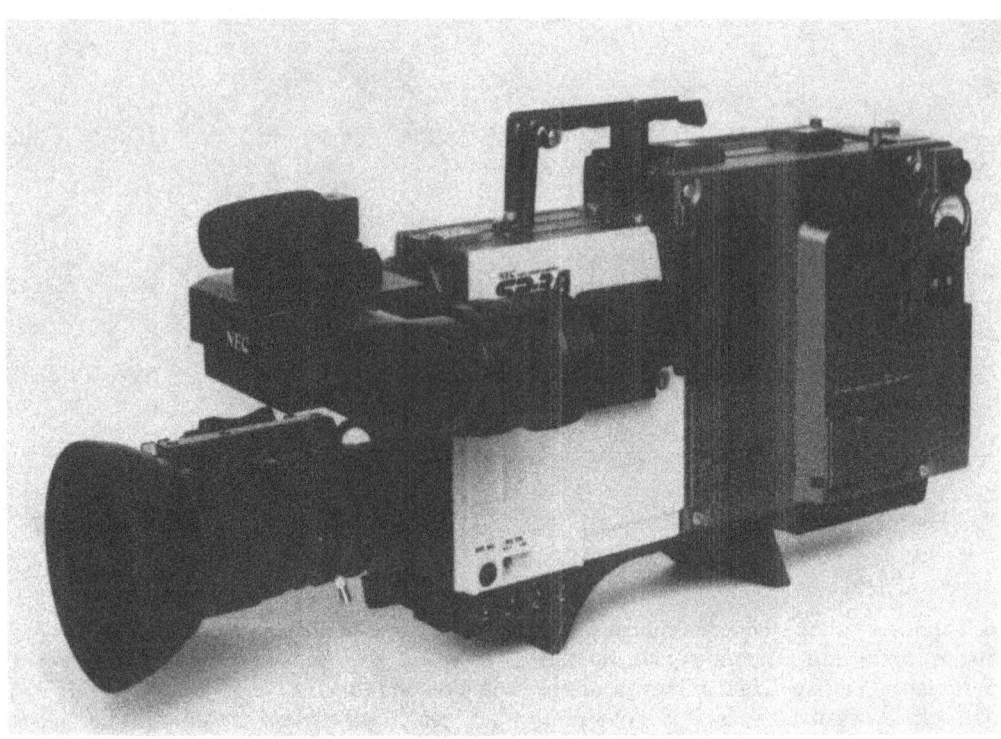

FIGURE 9.21
Television studio lights attached to grids.

BROADCAST STUDIOS AND EQUIPMENT 145

FIGURE 9.22
Small station control booth. The booth includes monitors, switchers (lower left), character generator (right front), and stacked VCRs (far right).

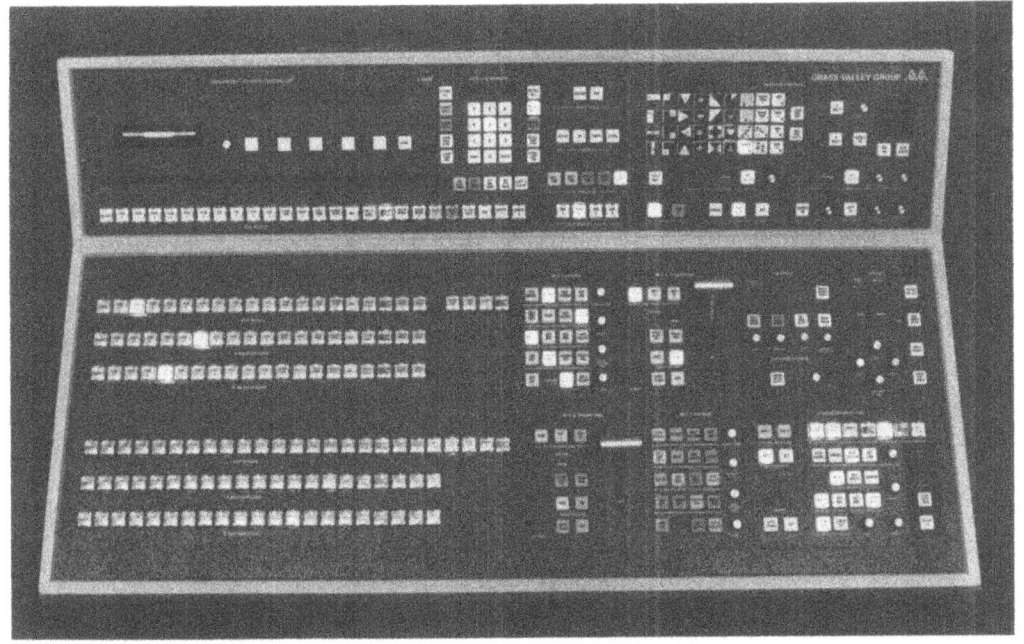

FIGURE 9.23
Video switcher. Courtesy Grass Valley Group.

FIGURE 9.24
A rack containing ½- and ¾-inch VCRs.

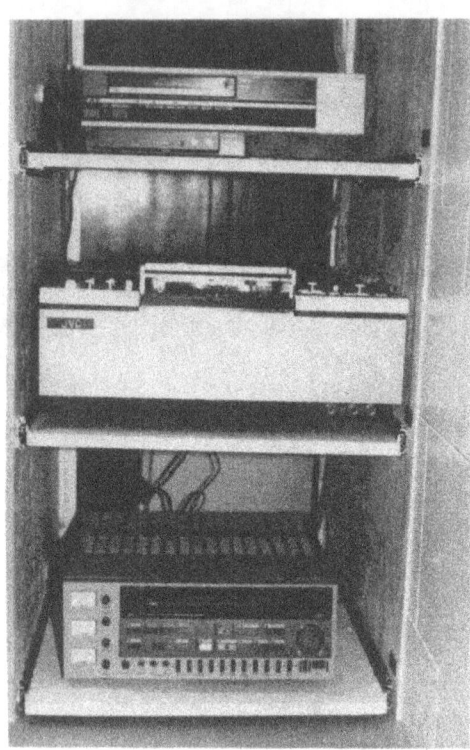

¾- and ½-inch. The latter width has gained prominence in the 1980s.

The smaller eight-millimeter video cassettes, ½-inch Beta and (Super) VHS, and video discs may eventually supplant the open reel video tape recorders. However, the large professional VTRs are still an important piece of production equipment at commercial television stations.

Audio Mixer. Comparisons have been made between various types of audio and video equipment, and another may be made. The video studio audio mixer is a close relative to the radio studio audio console (board). However, unlike the radio board, the video studio mixer is used primarily to input microphones. Of course, other audio sources are frequently wired into the mixer, such as turntables and cart and cassette machines. The audio mixer usually does not input as many pieces of audio equipment as does the radio studio console, which may be linked to a dozen or more components.

The audio mixer and radio board share design characteristics. Both possess potentiometers (pots or fader bars), input switches, monitor gain controls, VU meters, and so forth.

Audio mixers can be large and elaborate, possessing multiple faders (eighteen or more)

FIGURE 9.25
Video studio audio mixer. Courtesy Tascam.

and a variety of features, and they can be quite basic, with as few as four or five faders.

Monitors. The control booth is a videophile's dream come true, since it commonly houses between a half dozen and several dozen video screens, called *monitors.*

Among other things, monitors permit the director and production staff to set up camera shots, cue video for roll, prep effects, and observe programming as it is being broadcast or taped.

Individual monitors are dedicated to specific studio cameras (CAM 1, CAM 2, CAM 3 . . .) and preview and program lines, as well as test equipment (wave form, vectorscope, etc.) and remote links.

Monitors come in all sizes. Often the preview and program monitors are larger than the camera and test monitors for the sake of viewing and differentiation.

Character Generator. A character generator (CG) is an electronic device resembling a keyboard that creates (generates) letters for video production. Opening and closing titles and captions are examples. Many CGs offer effects features like crawl, roll (scroll), and memory to store pages of letters or copy.

Character generators are manufactured with the basics necessary to produce airable program material and with elaborate characteristics afforded only by the larger and more prosperous stations.

Microphones. Television is an audio medium as well as a visual one. Frequently, more microphones are used during a video production than a typical radio presentation because more voice performers may be involved.

All types of microphones are used in video. For example, hand-held (remote/field) mics are used by news people on location. Unidirectional mics with extraneous noise reduction features are popular in this situation. Hand-held microphones are used to interview in-studio audiences. Recall Johnny Carson playing "stump the band" with members of the *Tonight Show* audience. Carson uses a hand-held, highly directional "shotgun" microphone designed to eliminate surrounding (ambient) audience sounds.

Desktop microphones are typically employed in panel discussion situations and during interviews when participants are seated across from each other. A word of advice when using this mic setup: do not tap or bump the desk, as this sound may be amplified.

FIGURE 9.26
Control booth monitors in a small-market station.

FIGURE 9.27
Character generator with limited bells and whistles.

Perhaps the most widely used microphone in television is the lavalier. As discussed in Chapter 6, lavs are extremely popular for several reasons but are used primarily because they are small and unobtrusive and can be clipped to clothing or hung around a performer's neck. Lavalier mics are connected to a cord that can be concealed by clothing. This permits performers to move more freely without the fear of speaking off-mic.

FIGURE 9.28
Broadcaster using hand-held microphone.

There are drawbacks to lavalier microphones. Because of their proximity to the performer's throat and mouth, they can pick up heavy breathing sounds. Lavs are also apt to rub against clothing as the performer moves. This creates extraneous noise.

A microphone placed at the end of a counterbalanced, projectable pole and mounted atop a pedestal or tripod is called a *boom mic*. Highly directional shotgun microphones are most often placed on a boom. These microphones are moved about the set to accommodate the action.

For true mobility, however, nothing surpasses the newest innovation in microphone technology—the wireless or cordless mic. Wireless mics have become popular on network and syndicated talk shows (*Oprah, Donahue*) and game shows because they maximize a performer's ability to move about. Smaller stations sometimes find the cost of wireless mics exorbitant. However, the benefits of wireless microphones usually outweigh the cost considerations, even at lower budget operations, and thus they are becoming a standard piece of audio equipment.

Edit Suite

The editing suite, also known as postproduction, is usually separate from the video

FIGURE 9.29
Surface-mount microphones are one type of mic used for desktop setup. Courtesy Shure.

control room. Because of space strictures, some video control studios house editing equipment.

Edit suites can be quite lavish in terms of the sophisticated, state-of-the-art equipment they contain, such as computers and special graphics and effects machinery. They also can be very rudimentary, possessing only no-frills, single source editing units. Again, station size impacts the scope and range of editing facilities. For instance, rarely will a small market television station own a computerized multiple source time-code editing unit. Such items are simply too expensive for most stations outside metro markets. It is not uncommon for a piece of high-tech editing equipment to run in the five- and six-figure range.

A typical postproduction room possesses tape decks (VCRs and VTRs). Their size will

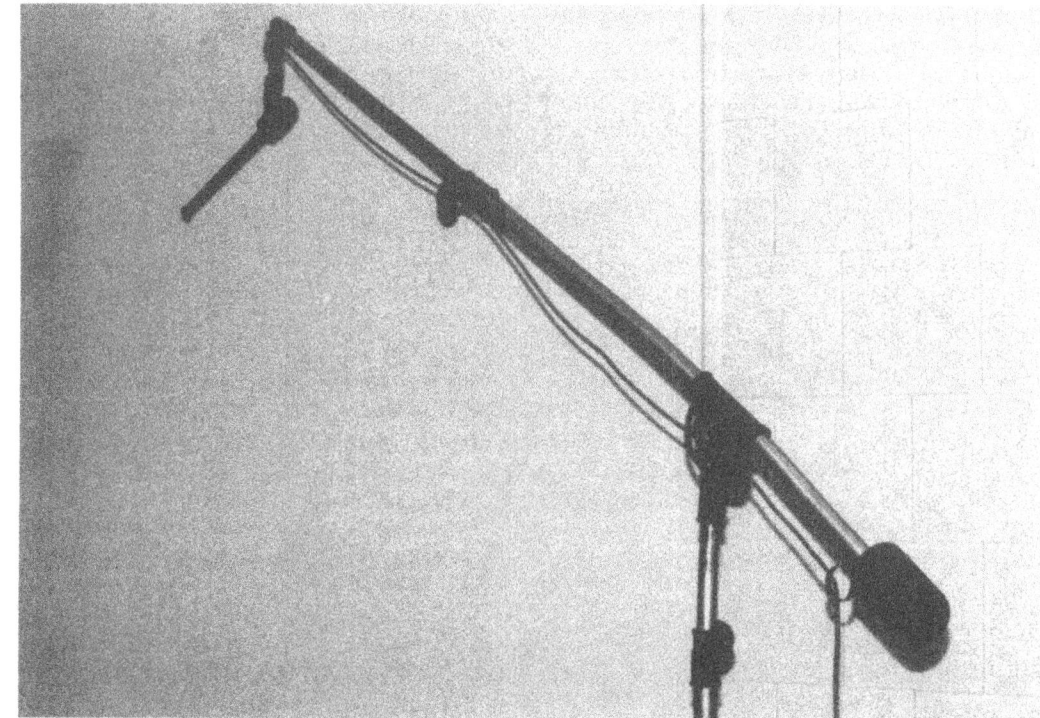

FIGURE 9.30
Boom microphone.

150 BROADCAST VOICE PERFORMANCE

FIGURE 9.31
Small format edit suite. The edit suite contains audio mixer (left front), ¾-inch VCR (left top), audio cassette unit mounted on top of a ½-inch VCR (center), monitors, and single-source edit unit (right front).

vary depending on the video tape format used by the station. Small format machines (VCRs) accommodate ¾- and ½-inch video tape, whereas one- and two-inch open reel machines (VTRs) are available for editing purposes as well. The latter recorders are in greater use at larger production outlets.

An edit suite must contain an edit control unit (ECU) for rough cutting or preliminary editing. Tape assembling and inserting is done on this piece of equipment. The edit control unit is an electronic device that allows its operator to dub and edit video from a *source* VCR to a *record* VCR. Like the audio console and the video switcher, the edit control unit is the central tool in the postproduction process.

In addition, the edit suit is equipped with a character generator, possibly an SEG (switcher/special effects generator), audio

FIGURE 9.32
A single-source editing unit. Courtesy JVC.

mixer (for sound sweetening), other audio accoutrements (cart/cassette/reel recording machines), and video monitors.

SUGGESTED FURTHER READING

Alten, Stanley R. *Audio in Media*, 2nd ed. Belmont, Calif.: Wadsworth Publishing, 1986.

Mezey, Phiz. *Multi-Image Design and Production*. Boston: Focal Press, 1988.

Millerson, Gerald. *Video Production Handbook*. Boston: Focal Press, 1987.

INDEX

Accents, 48, 90–91, 127–129
Acid Rock format, 40–41, 60
Adams, Mason, 31
Adaptability, of booth voice, 111
Ad-libbing, 61, 71, 83–84, 130–131
Adult Contemporary (AC) format, 43, 44–49
  announcing criteria for, 46–49
  full-service, 46
Advertising. *See* Commercial(s); Commercialism
Affectation, 54
Age. *See* Demographics
Airchecking, 48–49
Album-Oriented Rock (AOR) format, 59–64
  announcing criteria for, 61–64
Allen, Mel, 31
Allman Brothers, 54
All Things Considered, 64
Amos 'n' Andy, 27
AM stations
  combination licenses and, 38, 57
  Federal Radio Commission standards and, 25
  freeze on construction of, 38
  job prospects in, 15
  Oldies format, 68
  response to popularity of FM stations, 41
Anderson, Ida Lou, 29
Announcements, cluster, 64
Announcers, 2
  booth and voice-over, 111–113
  fitting the format and, 43
  news, 81–85
  prominence of, 43, 44–49
  specialized, 2
  sports, 115–124
  staff, 44
  women as, 2–4
Announcing criteria
  for Adult Contemporary format, 46–49
  for Album-Oriented Rock format, 61–64
  for Classical format, 64–66
  for Contemporary Hit Radio format, 51–54
  for Country format, 55–57
  for Vintage format, 68–70
Apathy, 49

Appearance
  auditioning and, 15
  for television, 91, 101–103, 109–110
Arlin, Harold W., 22
Armstrong, Edwin, 21
Articulation, 126, 129
Associated Press, 73
Attitude, 51, 57, 71, 119
  auditioning and, 14
Atwood, David E., 51, 53
Audience. *See also* Demographics
  of Album-Oriented Rock stations, 61
  of AM versus FM radio, 41
  cable television and, 41
  of Contemporary Hit Radio stations, 61
  radio programs focussing on segment of, 35–36
Audio consoles, 134–135
Audio mixer, in television station, 146–147
Audio tape, 138–139
Auditioning, 14–15
Authoritative presence, for newscasters, 82
Automation, 45–46. *See also* Computers
Avery, Gaylord, 31

Baker, Walt, 108
Barnouw, Erik, 25
Barrett, Jim, 47, 48, 49
Bartlett, Ronald, 107, 109, 110
Baty, Jack, 82, 83, 86
Baxter, Ted, 89
Beautiful Music (BM) format, 36–37, 38, 57
Believability, 81, 85–86, 106
Bell Laboratory, 34
Benny, Jack, 34
Berle, Milton, 34
Berry, Chuck, 36
Bidirectional microphone, 140
Big Band format, 67
Bird, Richard, 82, 84, 86, 90
Bjorkman, Ernie, 107, 109
Bliss, Ed, 28, 31, 75
Block, Martin, 35
"Board," 134
Bolke, Mark, 51
"Boom" microphones, 104, 148

154 INDEX

Booth criteria, 111–113
Borden, Daryl, 85, 89, 94, 103, 104
Bowie, David, 61
Breathing, voice quality and, 125
Brewer, Theresa, 36
Brinkley, David, 75
Broadcast job services, 14
Brokaw, Tom, 70, 83
Brokenshire, Norman, 24
Brooks, Monica, 81, 84, 86
Buckley, J. Carroll, 46, 48, 49
Burroughs, Eric, 31
Buses, in video control booth, 143
Byard, Jim, 68

Cable News Network (CNN), 78
Cable television, 15
   entry level jobs in, 13
   news on, 78
   shrinkage of network share and, 41
Caesar, Sid, 34
Camel News Caravan, 75
Camera studio, 141–142
Campbell, Glenn, 54
Cantor, Eddie, 34
Carlin, Phillip, 24
Carpillio, John, 82, 83
Carson, Johnny, 147–148
Carter, Boake, 27, 73
Carter, Raymond, 27
Cartridge machines, 136–137
Cash, Johnny, 54
Cassette recorders, 137
Castengera, Michael, 82, 84, 87, 93
Castle, Charles C., 58
CBS. *See* Columbia Broadcasting System
Character generator, 147
Clarity, of newscasters, 83
Clark, Dick, 106
Classical format, 37, 38, 64–66
   announcing criteria for, 64–66
Classic Hits format, 66, 67–68
Clichés, 49, 52–53, 90, 124
Clooney, Rosemary, 36
Close, Upton, 27
Clothing, for television, 101–102
Cluster announcements, 64
CNN. *See* Cable News Network
Coaching, 113
College stations, 13
Collier, Dan, 10
Colligan, Glenn, 68, 69, 70
Collingwood, Charles, 75
Colloquialisms, 49, 90
Columbia Broadcasting System (CBS), 25, 28, 75

Combination licenses, separation of, 38, 57
Commercial(s)
   live, size of radio station and, 9
   television, early, 34
Commercialism
   beginnings of, 22–24
   compensation and, 24–25
Communication skills, 65, 71
Como, Perry, 36
Compact discs, 137–138
Compensation, 15
   commercialism and, 24–25
Complacency, 70
Computers
   job opportunities and, 15, 18
   newscasting and, 78–79, 81
Concentration, 48
Condescension, in newscasting, 90
Confidence, 15, 81–82
Conlin, Ken, 83, 87
Connectedness, 55
Conrad, Frank, 22
Conscientiousness, 55
Constantine, Dennis, 61, 64
Contemporary Country format, 54
Contemporary Hit Radio (CHR), 49–54, 61
   announcing criteria for, 51–54
Control booth, video, 142–143, 146–148
Control room, radio, 134
Conversational style, 82, 107, 111
Cooke, Alistair, 31
Copy
   consistency of, for newscasting, 87
   format of, 95–97
Cordless mic, 148
Corroboration, importance of, 49, 93–94
Cortese, Joe, 11
Corwin, Norman, 31
Cosell, Howard, 118, 119
Coughing, 57
Country format, 37, 54–57
   announcing criteria for, 55–57
Courtesy, in sports announcing, 123
Cowan, Thomas H., 24
Credibility, 81, 85–86, 106
Cronkite, Walter, 31, 39, 75, 83
Crosley, Roger, 120, 123
Crutches, 49, 52–53
Cue cards, 103, 110
Cue mode, 135
Cue sheet, for newscasting, 87
Cugini, Betty-Jo, 91, 105
Culbert, Patricia, 126

Daley, John, 28
Davis, Elmer, 27

DECtalk, 18
Deejay(s)
  early, 35
  job jumping periods for, 14
  LPs and 45s and, 35
  in major market, 8–10
  Progressive, 40
  in small market, 5–8
  Top 40, 36
Deejaying, newscasting versus, 84
Dees, Rick, 43
De Forest, Lee, 21
Demographics
  for Adult Contemporary format, 45
  for Album-Oriented Rock format, 61
  for Country format, 54–55
  for Easy Listening format, 57–58
  for Vintage format, 68
Desktop microphones, 104–105, 147–148
Determination, 51–52
Dialects, 48
Diaz, Jose, 61, 63, 64
Documentary, 75–76
Domino, Fats, 36
Dorsey, Tommy, 36
Douglas, Paul, 30
Douglas Edwards with the News, 75
Drake, Bill, 49
Drew, Peter, 135
Drive-time, 6–7
Drugs, coverage of, 40
Dumit, Edward S., 3

Easy Hits format, 44–49
Easy Listening (EL) format, 57–59
  announcing criteria for, 58–59
Edit control unit (ECU), 150
Editorial comments, in newscasting, 89
Edit suite, in television studio, 148–151
Education, 11–12
  for booth and voice-over announcers, 113
  for Classical format, 65
  for newscasters, 89
  for sports announcers, 122
Edwards, Douglas, 75, 83
Edwards, Webley, 75
Ego, overactive, 49, 123
Electronic news gathering (ENG), 79
Electronic prompters, 110
Empathy, 52, 71
Equipment, 133
  need for knowledge of, 61–62
  in radio studio, 133–140
  in television studio, 141–151
Errors, handling on the air, 89–90

Everett, O.C., 51, 52, 54
Exaggeration, in sports announcing, 123–124
Experience, 12–14
Eye contact, 91–92, 103

Facial expression, 92
Fang, Irving, 27, 94
Farkas, Art, 61, 64
Federal Communications Commission (FCC)
  separation of combination licenses by, 38, 57
  stereophonic sound approved by, 38
Federal Radio Commission (FRC), 25
Fessenden, Reginald, 21
"Five W's" rule, 93
Fleming, Ambrose, 21
Flippancy, 53
FM stations, 13
  Classical format, 38, 64–66
  combination licenses and, 38, 57
  Easy Listening format, 57
  evolution of, 37–38
  growth in popularity of, 41
  Oldies format, 68
  women employed by, 4
Ford, Allen, 126
Ford, Mary, 36
Formality, for Easy Listening format, 58
Format, 43. *See also specific formats*
  announcer prominence and, 43, 44–49
  of news, 76–77
  for news copy, 95–97
Formula radio, 36
45 rpm singles, impact on radio, 35
Freed, Alan, 36
Friendliness, 55, 68
Friendly, Fred, 75
Fruen, Bob, 55, 56, 57
Fuchs, Stephen, 109, 110
Furness, Betty, 3, 34

Gabel, Martin, 31
Gallup, Frank, 31
Gassensmith, Norbert J., 108, 109, 110
Gibbons, Floyd, 27
Gishard, R. "Bob," 81, 91
Godfrey, Arthur, 70
Going "directional," 8
Gold format, 66
Grammar, 49
Grauer, Ben, 31
Graves, David, 79, 89, 103
Great Depression, impact on radio, 27–28

156   INDEX

Haider, Kurt, 118, 119, 120, 121, 123, 124
Haley, Bill, 36
Halper, Donna, 15, 54, 71
Ham, Al, 67
Hand-held microphones, 147–148
Hand signals, for television, 106
Hare, Dennis, 58
Harvest of Shame, 75
Harvey, Paul, 29, 70, 87
Headline Hunter, The, 27
Heatter, Gabriel, 3, 27
Heltzer, Marilyn, 65
Hendrix, Jimi, 41
Henneke, Ben Graf, 3
Hill, Edwin C., 73
Hodges, Steven M., 82, 84, 86, 87, 89, 93
Holton, Brian, 109, 110
Hoover, Herbert, 23
Hope, Bob, 34
Hot Adult format, 44–49
"Hot Country" format, 54
Hottelet, Richard C., 28
Houseman, John, 28
Humor, in newscasting, 89
Huntley, Chet, 39, 75
Hurt, William, 89
Husing, Ted, 24, 25

Imus, Don, 43
Inflection, 83, 126–127
Insincerity, 57
Intelligence, 70, 82
International News Service, 73
Interning, 13
Interpretation, 131–132
Interviewing, by newscasters, 84–85

Jackson, Eugene, 130
Jackson, Jeanne D., 82, 83, 84, 85, 86, 87, 89, 90, 95
James, Harry, 36
Jameson, House, 31
Jarvis, Al, 35
Jewett, Larry, 81
Jobs
    auditioning for, 14–15
    compensation and, 15, 24–25
    computer technology and, 15, 18
    education and, 11–12, 65, 89, 113, 122
    experience and, 12–14
    future prospects for, 15
    part-time, 13
    sources of, 14
Joseph, Mike, 49

Kaltenborn, H.V., 3, 27, 73
KDKA, 22, 73

Kennedy, Bob, 39
Kennedy, Robert F., assassination of, 40
Keyes, Donald C., 82, 83, 86, 89, 90
King, Martin Luther, Jr., 40
Kirby, Doc, 48, 49
Koch, Howard, 28
KOWH-AM, 36
Krause, Joe, 136, 138

Landry, Mike, 70
Language, for newscasting, 93
Language skills. *See* Verbal skills
Lavalier ("lav") microphone, 104, 148
Laziness, 65–66
Lazy mouth, 129
Leary, Timothy, 40
Lepisto, Paul, 119, 122, 123
Lewis, Fulton, 27
Lights, for television, 142
Listening, as preparation for newscasting, 86–87
"Lite Country" format, 54
Lite rock format, 44–49
"Live-assists," 44
Long-playing albums (LPs), impact on radio, 35
Low-power television (LPTV) stations, 15
Lujack, Larry, 43
Lynyrd Skynyrd, 54

McCarthy, Joe, 75–76
MacDonald, J. Fred, 34
McLendon, Gordon, 36, 49, 57
McMahon, Ed, 30, 31
McNamee, Graham, 24
Make Believe Ballroom, 35
Makeup, for television, 102–103
Male voice, preference for, 2–4
Marble, Harry, 31
Marconi, Guglielmo, 1, 21
Martin, Charlie, 70
Master gains, 135
"Match flow," 58
Maynard, Dave, 43
Mentor, 65
Meredith, Burgess, 28
Meteorologists, 113–114
Mic fright, 127
Microphones
    for radio, 140
    for television, 104–105, 147–148
Middle of the Road (MOR) format, 37, 71
Middle of the Road Country format, 54
Military, early use of radio by, 21–22, 73
Mills Brothers, 36
Misinformation, 49
Mitchell, Mianne S., 71

Monitor(s), in television station, 147
Monitor gains, 135
Monotone, overcoming, 127
Monroe, Vaughn, 36
MOR. *See* Middle of the Road format
Morrow, Bruce ("Cousin Brucie"), 36
Morse Code, 21
Moss, Arnold, 31
Most, Johnny, 118
Movements, on television, 91, 104
Murray the K, 36
Murrow, Edward R., 27, 28, 29, 75–76
Music, Knowledge of, 61, 64, 68

Narrowcasting, 43
National Association of Broadcasters (NAB), 25
National Broadcasting Company (NBC), 25, 73
Nelson, Chris, 14
Networks
  early television newscasting by, 75
  formation of, 25
  growth of broadcasting spurred by, 25–27
  radio, newscasting and, 28, 73
  television, shrinking share of, 41
Network sports reporters, 118
News and Talk format, 71
News booth, 134
Newscasters
  criteria for, 81–84
  interviewing by, 84–85
Newscasting
  Classical format and, 64
  on Contemporary Hit Radio, 51
  deejaying versus, 84
  early, on radio, 73–74
  formatting and, 76–77
  local news and, 77
  modern, 78
  radio, 26–29
  television, 75–77
  television versus radio, 91–94
  wire services and, 74, 92, 97–99
  World War II and, 28–29, 74–75
News copy, 92–94
  format of, 95–97
  from wire service, 97–99
News format, 37
Nostalgia format, 66, 67, 68

Off-air skills, 61–62
Off-air studio, 134
Oldies format, 66, 67, 68
Omnidirectional microphone, 140

On-air studio, 134
"Op-assists," 44
Overpreparation, for newscasting, 87, 89

Pace. *See* Timing
Parton, Dolly, 54
Patience, in newscasting, 90
Paul, Les, 36
Pearson, Drew, 27
"Pencil" editing, for newscasting, 90
Perfectionism, cautions against, 55–56
Perseverance, in newscasting, 90
Personalities, 43–44, 64, 68
Perspective, in newscasting, 89
Pfeifauf, Nick W., 111, 113
Phillips, Charles, 51
Phonetics, 129–130
Pingree, Marni, 71
Planning, for newscasting, 90
Poise, in audition, 14–15
Police, 61
Poole, Bob, 35
Porter, Bill, 85
Posture
  television newscasting and, 91
  voice quality and, 126
Pots, 135
Practice, 48
  for interviewing, 85
  for newscasting, 81, 86, 90
  for on-camera, 110
  for sports announcing, 121
Preparation, 48, 54, 58
  for interviewing, 85
  for newscasting, 81, 85–87, 89, 90
  for on-camera, 110–111
  overpreparation and, 87, 89
  for sports announcing, 123
Prereading, for newscasting, 86
Presence, of newscasters, 82
Press-radio Bureau, 73
Price, Larry W., 81, 85, 89, 90, 93, 95, 104
Production room, 134
Program hosts, 44
Programming
  specialized, on radio, 35–36
  syndicated, 57
Program syndicators, 57
Progressive format, 40–41. *See also* Album-Oriented Rock format
Projection, of newscasters, 83
Prompters, 103, 110
Pronunciation, 55, 129
Psychedelic format, 40, 60
Public Radio stations, 64
Purdue, Gunther, 126

Radio Act of 1927, 25
Radio and Television News Directors' Association (RTNDA), 78
Radio Corporation of America (RCA)
  early radios produced by, 22
  NBC formed by, 25
Radio stations
  Acid Rock format, 40–41, 60
  Adult Contemporary format, 43, 44–49
  Album-Oriented Rock format, 59–64
  AM, 15, 25, 38, 41, 57, 68
  announcing styles and, 43
  Beautiful Music format, 36–37, 38, 57
  beginnings of, 22
  Big Band format, 67
  Classical format, 37, 38, 64–66
  Classic Hits format, 64, 67–68
  college, 13
  combination licenses and, 38, 57
  Contemporary Country format, 54
  Contemporary Hit format, 49–54, 61
  Country format, 37, 54–57
  Easy Hits format, 44–49
  Easy Listening format, 57–59
  entry level positions at, 13
  FM, 4, 13, 37–38, 41, 64–66, 68
  formula, 36
  Hot Adult format, 44–49
  "Hot Country" format, 54
  impact of Great Depression on, 27–28
  impact of LPs and 45s on, 35
  impact of television on, 29–30
  "Lite Country" format, 54
  Lite Rock format, 44–49
  Middle of the Road Country format, 54
  Middle of the Road format on, 37, 71
  News and Talk format on, 71
  newscasting and, 26–27, 73–75, 91–94
  News format, 37
  Nostalgia format, 67, 68
  Oldies format, 66, 67, 68
  Progressive format, 40–41
  Psychedelic format, 40, 60
  Public Radio, 64
  reaction to television, 34–35
  Religious format on, 70–71
  Soft Rock format, 44–49
  specialized programming and, 35–36
  Talk format, 37
  Top 40 format, 36, 37
  Traditional Country format, 54
  value demonstrated during power failure, 39
  Vintage format on, 66–70
  weathercasting and, 114
  World War II and, 28–29, 74–75

Radio studio, 133–140
  audio consoles of, 134–135
  audio tape in, 138–139
  cartridge machines in, 136–137
  cassette recorders in, 137
  compact discs in, 137–138
  microphones in, 140
  reel-to-reel machines in, 135–136
  tape head cleaning and, 139–140
  turntables in, 137
Randall, Vischer, 22, 24
RCA. See Radio Corporation of America
Reading
  as preparation for newscasting, 85–86, 87
  surface, 131
Reel-to-reel recording machines, 135–136
Reina, Ron, 119, 121, 122, 123, 124
Reiplinger, J. E., 83, 84
Relaxation, prior to performance, 111
Religious format, 70–71
Rewriting, 93
Reynolds, Gary, 11
Rhythm, 49. See also Timing
  inner, for newscasting, 87
Richards, Dave, 12
Richards, Jay, 58
Rip and read, 87
Roberts, Brian, 107, 108, 109, 111
"Rock 'n' roll," 36
Rodgers, Kenny, 54
Ronstadt, Linda, 67
Roosevelt, Franklin D., 27–28, 127
Ross, Dave, 55
RTNDA. See Radio and Television News Directors' Association

St. Pierre, Ron, 115
Salaries, 15
  commercialism and, 24–25
Sarnoff, David, 21, 22, 73
Sartre, Jean Paul, 127
Satellites, newscasting and, 78–79, 81
Script, hand-held, 103
See It Now, 75, 76
Segue, 51
Self-assurance, 51
Self-criticism, 48–49, 120
Sevareid, Eric, 28, 75
Shirer, William, 28, 31
Shortz, Steve, 119, 120, 122
Signal interference, 25
Simulcasting, 57
Sinatra, Frank, 36
Sincerity, 106–107
Skegdell, Robert, 31

Sklar, Rick, 49
Slang, 49, 90
Sloppiness, 64
Smith, Howard K., 28, 75
Smith, Jim, 70
Smith, Judy, 79
Smith, Kate, 34
Sneeden, Ken, 107, 111
Soares, Marc, 119, 120, 121, 122
Soft Rock format, 44–49
Spears, 110
Special effects generator (SEG), 143
Specialization, in radio announcing, 43
Sponsors, sports announcing and, 120
Sponsorship, 23–24
Sports announcing, 115–124
   do's and don't's for, 122–124
   duties in, 115–117
   preparing for job in, 120–122
   for television, 117–118
   voice criteria for, 118–120
Spot sets, 57
Staff announcers, 44
Stedman, W.C., 55
Steel, Stan, 46, 48, 49
Stereophonic broadcasting, 38, 57, 64
Stern, Howard, 43
Steward, Bill, 36, 49
Storz, Todd, 36, 49
Stowe, Jim, 68, 69
Sullivan, Ed, 34
Surface reading, 131
Swayze, John Cameron, 75
Sweep method, 61
Switcher, in video control booth, 142–143
Syndication, 57

Talbot, 84, 86, 89
Talk format, 37
Talking Heads, 61
Tallylight, 104
Tape head cleaning, 139–140
Taping, as preparation for newscasting, 86
Team sports reporters, 118
Teare, Paul, 64, 65
Teleprompter, 103
Television, 101–111
   addressing the camera and, 103–104
   appearance and, 91, 101–103, 109–110
   early, 29–30, 34
   hand signals and, 106
   microphone use and, 104–105
   prepping for on-camera and, 110–111
   radio's reaction to, 34–35
   sports voice responsibilities for, 117–118
   voice criteria for, 106–110
   women in, 3, 4
Television stations
   cable, 13, 15, 41, 78
   documentaries and, 75–76
   early commercials on, 34
   growth of, 33–34
   impact of cable television on, 41
   impact on radio, 29–30
   increase in, 15, 41
   jobs with, 13–14, 15
   local, 13
   low power, 15
   newscasting by, 75–77
   newscasting by, radio versus, 91–94
   UHF, 15
   weathercasting and, 113–114
Television studio, 141–151
   camera studio in, 141–142
   edit suite in, 148–151
   video control booth in, 142–143, 146–148
Thomas, Duane, 123
Thomas, Lowell, 27, 73
Thompson, Dorothy, 27
Thoresen, Carl, 119, 121, 123
Throat clearing, 57
Timing, 49, 58–59
   for booth voice performance, 111–112
Titanic, radio broadcasting and, 21, 73
Top 40 radio, 36, 37
Trade journals, as job source, 14
Traditional Country format, 54
Transistors, impact of, 34
Transradio Press Service, 73
Trout, Robert, 28, 75
Tucker, Marshall, 54
Turntables, 137

UHF stations, 15
Unidirectional microphone, 140
United Press International, 73

Verbal skills, 48, 51, 58, 65, 68
   accents and, 48, 90–91, 127–129
   articulation and, 126, 129
   clichés and, 49, 52–53, 90, 124
   dialects and, 48
   grammar and, 49
   inflection and, 83, 126–127
   of newscasters, 81
   phonetics and, 129–130
   pronunciation and, 55, 129
   for sports announcing, 119
   vocabulary and, 69, 81, 119

Verbosity, 63–64, 65, 71
Video control booth, 142–143, 146–148
Video recorders, 143, 146
Vietnam war, coverage of, 40
Vintage format, 66–70
   announcing criteria for, 68–70
Vocabulary, 69, 81, 119
Vocal system, control of, 57
Voice
   deep, 108
   disciplined, 107–108
   male, preference for, 2–4
   manipulation of, 49, 89
   relaxed, 82, 126
Voice criteria
   for sports, 118–120
   for television, 106–110
"Voice of America," 22
Voice quality
   for Adult Contemporary format, 48
   for Classical format, 65
   for Contemporary Hit Radio format, 51
   for Easy Listening format, 58
   improving, 125–126
   for News and Talk format, 71
   for newscasters, 82–83
   for Religious format, 70
   for sports announcing, 119
   styles in, 30–31
Voice synthesizer technology, 18
Voicing over, 103–104
Volunteering, 13
VU meters, 135

Wages, 15
   commercialism and, 24–25
"Wallpapering," 49
Warmth, 55, 68

War of the Worlds, 28
WBZ-AM, 39
WEAF, 22, 24
Weathercasting, 113–114
WEEI-AM, 79
Welles, Orson, 3, 28
White, Paul, 28
Williams, Jay, 48, 53
Williams, Jerry, 111, 112
Winchell, Walter, 29
Wireless, 73
Wireless mic, 148
Wire services, 74, 92, 97–99
WJZ, 24
WLLH, 30
WNYC, 24
Wolfe, Tom, 127
Women, exclusion from broadcasting, 2–4
Women's movement, 4
WOR, 40
Wordiness, 63–64, 65, 71
"Word whiskers," 49
World War I, radio during, 21–22, 73
World War II
   growth of radio spurred by, 28–29
   radio newscasting and, 74–75
   women in announcing and, 3
WQXR-AM, 64
Wray, Don, 55, 57
Writing skills, 68–69
Writing style, for electronic versus print news, 92–93
WWL, 35
Wynne, Ed, 34

Yarbor, Bill, 81, 84, 87, 89, 90
Your Hit Parade, 35

For Product Safety Concerns and Information please contact our EU representative GPSR@taylorandfrancis.com
Taylor & Francis Verlag GmbH, Kaufingerstraße 24, 80331 München, Germany

www.ingramcontent.com/pod-product-compliance
Lightning Source LLC
Chambersburg PA
CBHW080737300426
44114CB00019B/2618